Parliament in Elizabethan England

QUEEN ELIZABETH IN PARLIAMENT

A. L.ᵈ Chancellor B. Marquiſes, Earles &ᶜ C. Barons D. Biſhops E. Iudges F. Maſters of Chancery G. Clerks H. Speaker of y̆ Com̄on
I. Black Rod K. Sergeant at Armes L. Members of the Com̄ons houſe M. S.ʳ Francis Walſingham Secretary of State

Parliament in Elizabethan England

John Hooker's *Order and Usage*

Vernon F. Snow

New Haven and London, Yale University Press

1977

Designed by John O. C. McCrillis
and set in Baskerville type.
Printed in the United States of America by
The Haddon Craftsmen, Inc., Scranton, Pennsylvania.

Published in Great Britain, Europe, Africa, and
Asia by Yale University Press, Ltd., London.
Distributed in Latin America by Kaiman & Polon,
Inc., New York City; in Australia and New
Zealand by Book & Film Services, Artarmon,
N.S.W., Australia; and in Japan by Harper & Row,
Publishers, Tokyo Office.

The frontispiece is reproduced from
the 1693 edition of Sir Simonds D'Ewes's
A Compleat Journal in the George Arendts
Research Library, Syracuse University.

Library of Congress Cataloging in Publication Data

Snow, Vernon F 1924–
     Parliament in Elizabethan England.

     Includes index.
     1. Great Britain. Parliament—History. 2. Great
Britain—Politics and Government—1558–1603.
3. Hooker, John, 1526?–1601. I. Hooker, John,
1526?–1601. The order and usage of the keeping of
a Parliament in England. II. Title.
JN525.S64   328.41'09   77-23301
ISBN 0-300-02093-7

To William L. Sachse

Mentor and Friend

Contents

Preface

In 1572 the chamberlain of Exeter, John Hooker alias Vowell, brought out two versions of a political tractate entitled *The Order and usage of the keeping of a Parlement in England*. Each version included (1) a dedicatory epistle, (2) an English translation of the *Modus Tenendi Parliamentorum*, and (3) a contemporary description of parliament—its composition, personnel, and modus operandi. Fifteen years later, exercising his editorial prerogative, Hooker inserted his descriptive analysis of parliament (3, above) in the second edition of Holinshed's *Chronicles* along with a short narrative account of his experiences in the Irish parliament of 1569. Taken together, these publications provide posterity with an intelligent, insider's picture of parliament in mid-Elizabethan England.

Although several prominent Elizabethans appreciated the value of Hooker's publications, the author has not yet received the credit and attention he justly deserves. He was the first scholar to publicize the *Modus;* he was the first MP to publish a treatise on parliament; he was the first Englishman to champion the cause of the House of Commons through the medium of the printed word. Throughout his writings Hooker relegated to parliament considerable authority—more than other contemporaries—claiming specifically that each house possessed its own customs and procedures. The lower house, in particular, had jurisdiction over duly elected members who did not meet certain qualifications and over those members whose behavior violated the specific orders and unwritten code of conduct. Commons could deny admission to outlaws and excommunicants, for example, and it could sanction and punish those who violated the *lex parliamenti*. Upholding the collective will of the members, Hooker contended that a majority in the House of Commons could overrule the Speaker. While less explicit and detailed, he allowed the House of Lords similar authority and jurisdiction. Though Hooker may well have overstated his case for the jurisdictional independence of each house, especially in reference to freedom of speech and freedom from arrest, his opinions were well received by numerous MPs and by common law proponents like William Lambarde and Sir Edward Coke. More important, his views on the origin, structure, composition, and jurisdiction of parliament triggered a prolonged debate involving the Elizabethan antiquaries, Archbishop Laud, William Prynne, Richard Overton, and several others—a controversy which did not abate until after the Revolution of 1688.

Yet, despite the impact of Hooker's publications, the original edition has never been reprinted in its entirety. The most useful portion of the first edition, namely the third part, entitled "The Order and Usage how to Keep a Parlement in England," was incorporated in the second edition of Holinshed's *Chronicles* by Hooker himself. Two centuries later, in 1792, Viscount Mountmorres included this same section in the introduction to his *History of the Principal Transactions of the Irish Parliament.* It also reappeared in the 1808 reissue of Holinshed's *Chronicles,* edited by Sir Henry Ellis. The second segment of Hooker's tract, namely his English translation of the *Modus,* has also appeared in print. In 1751 the editor of *Somers' Tracts* inserted that section in the second volume of the collection. Sir Walter Scott, following suit, included it in his second (1809) edition of *Somers' Tracts.* However, the introductory comments to those editions, while noting the original publication date as 1572, erroneously stated that the *Modus* appeared in Holinshed's *Chronicles.* Both were replete with minor variations, probably introduced by the editors or compositors. None of the above republications have included Hooker's dedicatory epistles and his appended list of members summoned to parliament.

This edition reproduces the first edition of Hooker's 1572 tractate in its entirety. Although the first edition appeared in two versions—one dedicated to Exeter officials, the other to

Sir William Fitzwilliam, the lord deputy of Ireland—the principal text followed herein is based on the Exeter version. It was
written first; it served as the basis for the Holinshed republication; and it was more readily available to Englishmen in
printed and transcript from. Since large segments of the two
versions are identical or only slightly variant, complete rendi-
tions of both versions would involve unnecessary duplication
and expense. However, all textual variations are fully discussed in the critical introduction and either incorporated in
the appendixes or pinpointed in the footnotes. The original
organization, syntax, orthography, and punctuation have been
retained; only the typography and page format have been
modernized.

In my researches on Hooker's *Order and Usage* I have con-
tracted many debts of gratitude. I am indebted to the staffs of
numerous libraries and archives for assistance: the Beinecke
Library of Yale University; the Bodleian Library, particularly
Mr. R. J. Roberts; the British Library, especially Mr. T. C.
Skeat; the Cheshire Record Office; the College of Arms, in
particular Sir Anthony Richard Wagner and Mr. F. S. Andrus;
the Exeter Cathedral Library; the Exeter City Library, especially Mr. N. S. E. Pugsley; the Exeter College (Oxford) Li-
brary; the Exeter Record Office, particularly Ms. Margery M.
Rowe; the Folger Shakespeare Library; the House of Lords
Record Office, in particular Mr. Maurice F. Bond and Mr.
H. S. Cobb; the Huntington Library and Art Gallery, especial-
ly Ms. Jean Preston; the Kent Archives Office, particularly
Mr. Felix Hull; the Lambeth Palace Library, particularly Mr.
E. G. W. Bill; the Lincoln's Inn Library, especially Mr. Rode-
rick Walker; the Northamptonshire Record Office, particularly
Mr. P. J. King; the Queen's College (Oxford) Library, espe-
cially Ms. Helen Powell; the Royal Commission on Historical
Manuscripts; Syracuse University Library, especially Dr.
Metod Milac; and Trinity College (Dublin) Library, particu-
larly Mr. William O'Sullivan.

I am most grateful to the following individuals for helpful

information and special courtesies: Professor David B. Quinn, University of Liverpool; Professor Gerald Sims, Trinity College, Dublin; Professor Wesley M. Stevens, University of Winnipeg; Professor Elizabeth Foster, Bryn Mawr College; Professor John Taylor, University of Leeds; Professor Cedric Ward, Union College; Dr. Ron Finucane, University of Reading; and Dr. Frederick Henninger of the University of Nebraska. I am also obligated to my colleague Professor Joseph Levine, who read the manuscript, and especially to Dr. Paul Ward, who contributed useful information, constant encouragement, and invaluable criticism all along the way. Last, but not least by any means, I am obligated to Sir John Neale, whose researches, writings, and insights have inspired and benefited those of us who dare tread the same paths of historical inquiry.

Abbreviations

APC	*Acts of the Privy Council.*
AHR	*The American Historical Review.*
BLO	Bodleian Library, Oxford.
BL	British Library.
BIHR	*Bulletin of the Institute of Historical Research.*
CJ	*Journals of the House of Commons.*
CSP Carew	*Calendar of State Papers, Carew.*
CSP Dom.	*Calendar of State Papers, Domestic.*
CSP Ire.	*Calendar of State Papers, Ireland.*
D'Ewes, *ACJ*	Sir Simonds D'Ewes, *A Complete Journal of the Votes, Speeches and Debates both of the House of Lords and House of Commons throughout the whole reign of Queen Elizabeth of Glorious Memory.*
DNB	*The Dictionary of National Biography,* ed. Leslie Stephen Lee (1885–1900, plus supplements).
EHR	*The English Historical Journal.*
EXRO	Exeter Record Office.
Gilkes, *TTP*	R. K. Gilkes, *The Tudor Parliament* (London, 1969).
HLQ	*The Huntington Library Quarterly.*
HMC	*The Historical Manuscripts Commission Reports.*

IHS	*Irish Historical Studies.*
JBS	*Journal of British Studies.*
LJ	*Journals of the House of Lords.*
LMP	*List of the Members of Parliament* in the Sessional Papers, vol. 62 (1878).
LP	Lambeth Palace.
Neale, *EHC*	John Neale, *The Elizabethan House of Commons* (London, 1963).
Neale, *EP*	John Neale, *Elizabeth I and Her Parliament*, 2 vols. (London, 1965).
PRO	Public Record Office.
Pollard, *EOP.*	A. F. Pollard, *The Evolution of Parliament* (London, 1926).
STC	*Short-Title Catalogue,* A. W. Pollard and G. R. Redgrave.
TCLD	Trinity College Library, Dublin.
TRHS	*Transactions of the Royal Historical Society.*

Introduction

John Hooker: Life and Writings

John Hooker (alias Vowell), antiquarian and editor of Holinshed's *Chronicles,* was born in Exeter in 1525.[1] His paternal forebears had been prominent landowners and officeholders in the Devon city for over a century.[2] His grandfather John Hooker (1440–93), bailiff in 1484–85 and mayor of the city in 1490–91, represented Exeter in five parliaments during the last third of the fifteenth century. His father, Robert Hooker, also served as mayor of Exeter for a one-year term in 1529, after enlarging his land holdings throughout the city. His mother, Agnes, daughter of John Doble of Woodbridge, Suf-

---

1. Most of the biographical information pertaining to John Hooker comes from his own writings and city records preserved in the EXRO and the Exeter Public Library. Of particular importance are his commonplace book, his biography of Sir Peter Carew, his history of Exeter, and his unfinished history of Devonshire, all of which have been published in part or in whole within the last century. In the absence of a complete biography one must rely upon John Prince, *The Worthies of Devon* (Exeter, 1810), pp. 505–06; George Oliver, *History of Exeter* (Exeter, 1861), p. 242; *DNB,* 9:1181–83; Edward Freeman, *Exeter* (London, 1887), pp. 102–04; W. T. MacCaffrey, *Exeter 1540–1640* (Cambridge, Mass., 1958), pp. 261–73; and Charles Carlton, "John Hooker and Exeter's Court of Orphans," *HLQ* 36 (1973): 307–16.

2. For the information about Hooker's ancestors and family I have relied upon J. L. Vivian, *The Visitations of the County of Devon* (Exeter, 1895), p. 479; J. C. Wedgewood and A. D. Holt, *Biographies of the Members of the House of Commons 1439–1509* (London, 1936), passim; J. J. Alexander, "Ancestors of John Hooker," *Devon and Cornwall Notes and Queries* 19 (1936–37): 222; *HMC Report on the Records of Exeter* (London, 1916), p. 361; Margery M. Rowe and Andrew M. Jackson, *Exeter Freeman 1266–1967* (Exeter, 1973), pp. 58, 59, 61; and Freeman, *Exeter,* p. 102. Vivian reprints the most complete pedigree. The name Vowell came into the family from Pembroke as a result of several marriages to heiresses. In the first half of his life John used the last name of Vowell and the alias of Hooker; during the latter part of his life he referred to himself as "John Hooker alias Vowell." In some documents and printed works the name appears as Hoker.

folk, and Robert Hooker's third wife, gave birth to several children after John, including Roger Hooker, the father of Richard Hooker, the theologian.

John Hooker lived within the shadows of Exeter Cathedral the first ten years of his life.[3] He was baptized in St. Mary Major, the parish church near the northeast corner of the cathedral yard, and the Hooker home was located in that parish. The Mayor's Court Rolls reveal that Robert Hooker owned tenements, shops, gardens, and stables scattered throughout the city and that he leased them to fellow citizens. He was a landlord, in short, an urban oligarch whose wealth came from rental properties located in and around one of England's larger provincial cities. Yet, the family possessed a coat of arms and John Hooker took great pride in his genteel status.[4]

Little is known about John Hooker's early years and education.[5] He became an orphan at the age of thirteen in 1538, when the plague struck Exeter and took away both of his parents, and the death of his older brother about the same time made him the eldest surviving male in the family. Being a minor, he did not immediately inherit any family properties; rather, he remained a ward of the city until he became of age. At the behest of his civic guardians (probably the mayor, Thomas Hunt) John Hooker commenced his formal education in the town of Menheniot, Cornwall.[6] Here he learned Latin

3. Walter J. Harte, *Gleanings from the Common Place Book of John Hooker, relating to the City of Exeter (1485–1590)* (Exeter, 1926), pp. 7–10.

4. John Hooker invariably entitled himself a "Gentleman" or "Gent." in his writings and official documents. His pedigree was registered in the College of Arms and his arms were recorded in the visitations of Devon made in 1565 and 1572. See Prince, *Worthies,* appendix I.

5. Harte, *Common Place Book,* pp. 7–9.

6. For this information see Hooker's "Synopsis Chorographical: Or, An Historical Record of the Province of Devon," manuscript in the Exeter Public Library (H. 783), especially ff. 105–17. Harl. MS 5827 seems to be a copy in Hooker's own hand; for a discussion of it see William J. Blake, "Hooker's Synopsis Chorographical of Devonshire," in *Transactions of the Devonshire Associ-*

in the grammar school operated by Dr. John Moreman, a Devonian who had taken his B. A. and M. A. degrees at Exeter College and enjoyed the patronage of Bishop Oldham of Exeter. Dr. Moreman, dubbed "the learned vicar of Menheniot," also held several livings in Devon and subsequently became dean of Exeter. In the words of Hooker, "he was of a very honest and good nature, loving to all men, and hurtful unto none . . . he was the first, in those days, that taught his parishioners and people to say the Lord's prayer, the Belief, and the commandments in the English tongue, and did teach and catechize therein."[7]

Next, taking the advice of Moreman, Hooker appears to have gone up to Oxford to continue his studies. According to Wood, he was "educated in grammar and logic for a time in this university either in Exeter or C.C. Coll., but whether he took a degree, our registers, which are in the time of K. Edw. 6 very imperfect, shew not."[8] Of the two colleges, Corpus Christi seems more likely. In his own writings Hooker draws special attention to that college and to one of its principal benefactors, Bishop Oldham of Exeter.[9] Similarly, in his commonplace book he alludes to Oldham in glowing terms.[10] More important, years later he and Bishop Jewell, also of Corpus Christi, persuaded Richard Hooker to enter that college; in fact, both rendered advice and financial assistance.[11] Like-

ation for the Advancement of Science 47 (1915), 334–48. For Moreman also see Frances Rose-Troup, *The Western Rebellion of 1549* (London, 1913), pp. 72, 107–09; A. L. Rowse, *Tudor Cornwall* (New York, 1969), pp. 151, 321–23; and G. C. Boase and W. P. Courtney, *Bibliotheca Cornubiensis* (London, 1874–82), 1:369.

7. From "Synopsis Chorographical" quoted in Prince, *Worthies*, p. 505.

8. Anthony Wood, *Athenae Oxoniensis*, 2 Vols. (London, 1691), 1:270.

9. See John Hooker, *A Catalogue of the Bishops of Exeter* (London, 1584), and Holinshed's *Chronicles*, (London, 1587). Also see Thomas Fowler, *The History of Corpus Christi College* (Oxford, 1891), p. 147.

10. Harte, *Common Place Book*, p. 7.

11. See Isaac Walton's account in John Keble, *The Works of that Learned and Judicious Devine Mr. Richard Hooker*, 3 vols. (Oxford, 1888), 1:8–11. Keble's critical remarks in the footnotes are quite helpful.

wise, John Hooker sent two of his own sons up to Corpus
Christi—Zachery in 1579 and Peter in 1587—and both were
designated as Devonshire scholars like their cousin Richard.
Moreover, Hooker donated to Corpus Christi a commemora-
tive tablet that contained a Latin inscription honoring the
founder of the college.[12] A benefaction of this type would
normally only be made by an alumnus of the college. Lastly,
Hooker's humanism—so evident in his translation of Erasmus,
who praised the Corpus Christi curriculum—reflects the
humanistically oriented studies and the faculty of that college.[13]

Hooker appears to have studied law at Oxford. Whether he
attended any lectures, participated in the disputations, and
took examinations as a regular student we cannot ascertain,
but in all likelihood he knew John Jewell, who was three years
older and entered Corpus Christi in 1539.[14] It is possible, in
fact, that Hooker read Latin with Jewell, who took pupils in his
chambers after receiving his B.A. degree in 1542, and that he
attended Jewell's lectures on Latin orators and poets. The
curriculum, in any case, included grammar, rhetoric, the
Greek and Latin classics, logic, and philosophy.

Hooker next traveled to the Continent to continue his studies. He first went to Cologne, where he read jurisprudence,
and eventually settled in Strasbourg, where he lived in the
residence of Peter Vermigli—the controversial humanist and
reformer—with whom he studied theology.[15] Vermigli, better

12. Anthony Wood, *Survey of the City of Oxford,* ed. Andrew Clark, 3 vols.
(Oxford, 1889–99), 1:551.

13. J. G. Milne, *The Early History of Corpus Christi College, Oxford* (Oxford,
1946), especially p. 37.

14. Hooker reveals nothing about his relationship with Jewel, but in his
biography of Richard Hooker, Isaac Walton alludes to the personal connections between Hooker and Jewel; see Keble, *Richard Hooker,* 1:9–13.

15. Harte, *Common Place Book,* p. 8. For Strasbourg and Peter Martyr see
Mariam Chrisman, *Strasbourg and Reform* (New Haven, 1967), especially pp.
260–69, and Donald R. Kelley, *Francois Hotman* (Princeton, 1973), pp. 71–98.
It is most interesting to note that among the Protestant exiles at Strasbourg

known as Peter Martyr, was a popular Florentine humanist who fled Italy in 1542 because of heresy charges and established a "university" in Strasbourg. Here, with the backing of Bucer and Zwingli, he gathered students from many Protestant countries and offered instruction in theology until 1547, at which time Archbishop Cranmer brought him to England and appointed him Regius Professor of Divinity at Oxford.

About the same time Hooker returned to Oxford and read civil law at Corpus Christi.[16] As civil law replaced canon law as a result of the Henrician Reformation the government established at Oxford several Regius professorships in civil law. Thereafter English students could read and take degrees in civil law at Oxford instead of being compelled to travel abroad to France, Germany, or Italy. John Hooker, though among the first to benefit from this academic innovation, does not appear to have received a degree in law, or any degree for that matter, from any English or European school. Rather, he appears to have returned to his native city early in the reign of Edward VI.

Hooker assumed his inheritance and soon thereafter married one Martha Tucker, the daughter of an Exeter citizen. She bore him one son named Robert before her untimely death. Hooker's second marriage was to Anastasia Bridgeman, by whom he had eight sons, including the aforementioned Zachery and Peter, and several daughters. It is interesting to note

during the reign of Mary were several figures associated with Hooker, including Francis Russell, later earl of Bedford. See below p. 27.

16. See Herbert Edward Reynolds, *An Original Manuscript of John Hooker* (Belfast, 1892), especially the editor's introduction. Reynolds has transcribed and reprinted portions of Hooker's unpublished history of Exeter, namely Hooker MS 3520 in the Exeter Cathedral Library, and the preface to an enlarged version, which was subsequently edited by W. J. Harte *et al.* and published in three volumes by the Devon and Cornwall Record Society (1914–1947) as *The Description of the Citie of Excester.* More than anything else these reveal Hooker's knowledge of ecclesiastical law and history. For his interest in civil law see the two dedicatory epistles reprinted below and my analysis of them.

that the Bridgemans had ties with the Russell family, especially
the earl of Bedford, Hooker's patron during the reign of Elizabeth I.[17] Hooker and his growing family lived in the ancestral
residence located in the parish of St. Mary Major. He was not
a merchant or directly involved in trading; nevertheless, in
1548–49 he sat on the board of the Exeter Company, which
traded with France, Portugal, and Spain.[18] One of his fellow
board members was Walter Ralegh, a gentleman landowner
and father of Sir Walter, another Hooker patron in late Elizabethan times.

In 1549 Exeter became the focal point of a provincial revolt.
The Western Rebellion (really a conservative reaction to the
Edwardian religious changes) began in Cornwall in spring and
picked up momentum as it spread eastward into Devon.[19] In
June, the Cornish insurgents, sparked by gentry and rural
clerics, fanned through the Devonshire countryside and garnered support by framing written articles demanding of the
Privy Council a reversal of the recent innovations prescribed
in the Prayer Book. Threatening to march on London, the
rebels, angry and armed, marched toward Exeter and during
the last days of June laid siege to the city.

John Hooker, then in his twenty-fourth year, participated in
the historic defense of Exeter. He experienced the long siege
and observed the deprivations and suffering of fellow Exonians. He witnessed the forays of Russell's troops, the raising of
the siege, and the final retreat of the rebels in mid-August. He
regarded the military defenders of Exeter, especially Lord
Russell and Sir Peter Carew, as saviors and promoters of
"God's true religion."[20] Soon thereafter John Hooker, at the

17. For Hooker's marriages and progeny see Vivian, *Visitations*, p. 479.
Bedford's circle included the Marian exiles Sir Peter Carew and Sir John
Chichester, both of Devon, and Sir William Fitzwilliam and John Jewell, all of
whom had connections with Hooker during the reign of Elizabeth I.

18. Freeman, *Exeter*, pp. 170–72.

19. For this rebellion see Rose-Troup, *The Western Rebellion*.

20. See John Hooker, *The dyscourse and dyscoverye of the lyffe of Sir Peter Carew*,
ed. John Maclean (London, 1857), pp. 14 and 53.

behest of the city magistrates, wrote the most complete and accurate account of the "Western Rising."[21] The intent behind this assignment—which paid the handsome fee of twenty shillings a day—is not clear. Perhaps it was to inform the public or serve some political purpose in Westminster. Whatever the case, Hooker performed the task and thus provided his countrymen and posterity with a firsthand history of the event. Years later he incorporated the account in the second edition of Holinshed's *Chronicles* and alluded to the events in his life of Sir Peter Carew.

About this time Hooker entered the service of Miles Coverdale, the biblical translator who had returned from the Continent in 1548 and succeeded Voysey as bishop of Exeter. We are not informed as to the precise nature of Hooker's "service."[22] Perhaps he assisted Coverdale in those theological writings and translations which subsequently appeared in print.[23] Perhaps he began his own diocesan history of Exeter at this time—a work that, though completed much earlier, was not published until 1584. Whatever the case, he labored on

21. Harte, *Common Place Book,* p. 8. Hooker later incorporated this account in his *Description of Exeter,* published along with the Exeter edition of his *Order and Usage* (1572).

22. Ibid. It is entirely possible that Hooker had met Coverdale on the Continent. We know that Coverdale corresponded with Conrad Hubert, a Protestant preacher in Strasbourg, and that between 1543 and 1548 he traveled to Strasbourg, where he stayed with Hubert and met Hooker's mentor Peter Martyr, with whom he discussed the education of English youth. Although Hooker may well have been in Strasbourg at the time, he makes no mention of Coverdale's presence there. See George Pearson, *The Remains of Myles Coverdale* (Cambridge, 1846), pp. 503–25.

23. Though he does not mention Hooker in any of his extant writings, very likely Coverdale used him as a translator. We know that Hooker translated St. Augustine's *Epistle to Dardanus* from Latin into English and that he subsequently presented it to the earl of Bedford. We also know that Coverdale not only used that source in the preparation of his *Hope of the Faithful*—a work written in Exeter and published in 1555—but that he twice quoted from an English translation. See George Pearson, *The Writings and Translations of Myles Coverdale* (Cambridge, 1844), pp. 128, 141, 152, 160, 203.

behalf of the bishop, whose life he later eulogized, and became associated with Robert Weston, Coverdale's assistant and lord chancellor of Ireland from 1567 to 1573.

John Hooker's commonplace book reveals a strong religious commitment to the Edwardian reformation.[24] He faithfully recorded the pulpit performances of reformer Hugh Latimer when he preached in Exeter, the suppression of several chantries in the diocese, the activities of Miles Coverdale, and the Western Rising. More important, his fragmentary comments indicate loyalty to the "Godly" like Coverdale and hostility toward those clergy still clinging to the old faith. He castigated Bishop Voysey for selling church lands and lining his own pockets. He considered goldsmith William Smith, mayor of Exeter in 1553, "a most inveterate papist and an enemy to all . . . suspected to be the true professors of the ghosple." He praised Mayor John Peryam, on the other hand, as "zelose in ye true religion of the gosple."

In 1551, while still in Coverdale's service, Hooker became a freeman of the city.[25] Two years later he was appointed chamberlain, a new office established by the common council.[26] As chamberlain, Hooker became custodian of the official records of Exeter and responsible for their preservation. Although this position paid only £4 per annum plus liveries, it was tailor-made for a man of Hooker's interests and abilities. To the disorganized accumulation of muniments he introduced order and systemization. He first established a civic archive and then devoted the rest of his life to the collection and preservation of Exeter's records. In fulfilling his duties Hooker extracted data, compiled lists, copied and translated, conducted several surveys of the records, and of course utilized these sources to write his descriptions and histories.

24. Harte, *Common Place Book*, pp. 17–21.

25. Rowe and Jackson, *Exeter Freeman*, p. 79. It is interesting to note that Robert Weston became a freeman the following year.

26. See Harte, *The Description*, 1:1–7. for a listing of the various positions he held in the city and for a description of his accomplishments as chamberlain.

During the reign of Elizabeth he acquired more responsibilities and additional offices. He served as collector of the tenths and fifteenths—taxes levied by Elizabeth's first parliament—and kept records of the same for over a decade.[27] In 1563 he became president of the newly established court of orphans—a court authorized by a royal charter granted by the queen—and in that capacity acted as official guardian to orphans and administered the estates of deceased citizens.[28] Five years later, serving on the admiralty court of Devon, he traveled to Sidmouth and other ports to adjudicate cases involving shipowners.[29] Also sitting on the court were Sir Arthur Champernowne and Gawen Carew, both Devon landholders, and Francis Russell, earl of Bedford, Hooker's patron and fellow Exonian.

In 1568 John Hooker's antiquarian skills and knowledge were retained by Sir Peter Carew, a fellow countryman from Mohun's Ottery, to recover some lands in Ireland.[30] Hooker first searched the Carew family muniments at Mohun's Ottery and informed Sir Peter that they contained documentary evidence of Irish lands once held, but long since lost, by his medieval ancestors. Sir Peter promptly secured from Queen Elizabeth I permission to attempt a recovery of the lands and authority to search the Irish records for substantiating evidence. He turned again to Hooker and persuaded the Exeter antiquarian to assist him. Hooker dutifully sought and received from the mayor and council a leave of absence from his

27. Ibid., p. 2.
28. See Carlton, "Hooker and the Exeter Court of Orphans," pp. 307–16; and *Court of Orphans* (Leicester, 1974), especially pp. 28–35.
29. *HMC Exeter,* p. 376.
30. In this section concerning Hooker's relationship with Carew, especially his service in Ireland, I have relied heavily upon the Carew Papers at Lambeth Palace, particularly MSS 605, 606, 610, and 635. MS 635 includes Hooker's biography of Sir Peter, his reports, and his correspondence, most of which have been published in extract form in J. S. Brewer and William Bullen, *Calendar of the Carew MSS,* 6 vols. (London, 1867–73). Also useful in this section were various miscellaneous manuscripts in TCLD and the PRO.

administrative duties in Exeter. On 20 May 1568 he proceeded
to Ireland and culled the records in Waterford and Dublin for
evidence supporting Carew's claim to the Barony of Idrone.[31]
He was eminently successful, for soon thereafter Sir Peter
Carew crossed to Ireland, assumed the title to barony, settled
upon his reclaimed lands, and rewarded Hooker with land and
patronage.

This association with Carew proved to be a turning point in
Hooker's life. Hitherto he had been a city-oriented officeholder, a provincial, but through Carew's patronage and
connections he became involved in national politics. Through
Carew he acquired important contacts in Dublin and Westminster—contacts with high officeholders, members of parliament, publishers, and scholars of national repute. While
searching the records in Dublin Castle he met James Stanihurst, recorder of Dublin, Speaker of the Irish House of Commons in 1557, 1559, 1568–69, and clerk of the parliaments. In
all likelihood Hooker also established a connection with the
recorder's son, Richard Stanihurst, Latinist and author of the
"Description of Ireland," which he included in the 1586 edition of Holinshed's *Chronicles*.[32] Through the Stanihursts and
Robert Weston, onetime chancellor to the bishop of Exeter
(Coverdale) and now lord chancellor of Ireland, Hooker no
doubt met other Dubliners.[33]

Instead of hastening back to Exeter after recovering Carew's
Irish lands, Hooker remained in Dublin and sat in the Irish
parliament convened by Lord Deputy Sir Henry Sidney in
January 1569.[34] We do not know how he secured the seat

31. The date comes from Harte, *Common Place Book*, p. 8. LP, Carew MS 606
contains the documents which Hooker garnered in support of Carew's claims.

32. On the Stanihursts see C. L. Falkiner, *Essays relating to Ireland* (London,
1909), p. 230.

33. On Weston see *DNB*, 20:1281–82.

34. For the best account of this parliament see V. Treadwell, "The Irish
Parliament of 1569–71," in *Proceedings of the Royal Irish Academy* 65C (1966–67):
55–89.

representing Athenry, a borough in Connaught. Perhaps he stood for election on his own initiative. More likely, he secured the seat through the influence of Sir Peter Carew or the Stanihursts—or perhaps even Weston. Whatever the case, he not only sat in the Irish House of Commons through the first session, that is from 17 January through 23 February, but he kept a diary of the most important proceedings.[35] In the absence of extant journals, which do not commence until 1613, Hooker's parliamentary diary—the first of its kind—serves to provide the inside story of this Irish parliament.

In his diary Hooker underscored the contentions and open hostility between the Irish and English members of the lower house.[36] The Irish MPs contended that the assembly was unlawful because of irregular electoral practices, while the English leaders staunchly defended both the procedures and the returnees. More particularly, Sir Christopher Barnwell attacked the election of nonresidents (especially Englishmen like Hooker), the self-nomination and selection process of mayors and sheriffs, and the return of burgesses from hitherto unrepresented towns, especially small and unincorporated towns. The bitter and rancorous debates over these matters led to several harsh confrontations between irate Irish MPs and uncompromising representatives of the crown—all of which, to the dismay of the leaders, culminated in the repeal of Poynings' Law by a very close vote.

Hooker incorporated a firsthand account of these parliamentary skirmishes in the 1587 edition of Holinshed's *Chronicles*.[37] From him we learn that discord and divisiveness prevailed; that orders and customs were violated; that

35. The diary, edited by C. L. Falkiner and published in the *Proceedings of the Royal Irish Academy* 25C (1904–05), was reprinted in Falkiner, *Essays*, appendix C.

36. Hooker's interpretation is confirmed in a letter from Nicholas White, master of the rolls, to William Cecil; see *CSP Ire.*, 1:403.

37. See 2:121 (1587 ed.). The account does not appear in Raphael Holinshed's original edition, published a decade earlier.

parliamentary procedures were flouted. Hooker used the words *mutinie* and *bearbaiting* to describe the deliberations. The Irish members, taking exception to the presence of nonresident English representatives, voted en bloc to prevent the passage of English-initiated bills and claimed that the assembly was not warranted by law. When the Irish members pushed for the repeal of Poynings' Law, as they did, Hooker himself delivered a lengthy speech on the benefits of Poynings' Law and the advantage of English rule. This lecture—so time-consuming that the house did not adjourn until well past the traditional hour—so offended the Irish MPs that Hooker feared for his safety and fled to the confines of his patron's house in Dublin.

Next day the opposition responded with vehemence. Under the leadership of Carew's avowed enemies, Sir Edward Butler and Sir Christopher Barnwell, they not only rebutted Hooker's arguments but "in a most disorderlie manner" inveighed against his person. In so doing, in Hooker's eyes, they violated the spirit and unwritten customs governing parliamentary deliberations. To forestall any further trouble the Speaker, backed by the consent of a majority in the house, ordered the dissident Irish members to be silent and suggested that they bring forward written charges against Hooker and then prove them in an open assembly. The whole incident was, to use Hooker's words, "more like to a bearbaiting of lose persons than an assembly of wise and grave men in parliament."[38]

These verbal skirmishes led several sober-minded members to petition the Speaker to "reform those abuses and disordered behavior." Speaker Stanihurst, a friend of both Hooker and Carew, responding favorably to the petition, requested the advice and assistance from all those members "acquainted with the orders of parliaments in England." At this juncture, it would appear, Hooker offered his services to Stanihurst and promised to produce a book covering "the orders of the parle-

38. Ibid.

ments used in England." Thus was born the idea which culminated in the publication of the *Order and usage of the keeping
of a Parlement in England.*

How Hooker intended to complete the project remains a
mystery. He had never before sat in an English parliament. He
may have observed some deliberations in Westminster as a
nonparticipating visitor—a very remote possibility—or he may
have acquired some knowledge of parliamentary procedures
from Exeter MPs. Among the Exeter records over which he
had custody as chamberlain were several letters and diarylike
reports addressed from Exeter MPs to the mayor and chamber.[39] It is also possible—though unlikely—that the records
contained a copy of the *Modus.* However, it is more likely that
he knew much about Exeter chamber procedures but little or
nothing about English parliamentary practice. If he had any
knowledge, it was hardly authoritative; instead, it was based
upon books or conversations rather than upon personal experience.

Shortly after the end of the tempestuous session described
above John Hooker received from the lord deputy and his
Privy Council a license to print a compilation of laws passed
by the Irish parliament.[40] In the course of his researches in
Dublin on behalf of Carew, it seems, Hooker discovered that
the Irish laws had never been collected and published, despite
their existence in manuscript form.[41] He had recently experienced in parliament the need for copies of laws in force,

39. *HMC Exeter,* pp. 32–35.

40. The license was granted on 20 March 1568/69; see LP, Carew MS 605,
f. 2. The best account of Hooker's role in the compilation is David B. Quinn,
"Government Printing and Publication of the Irish Statutes in the Sixteenth
Century," in *Proceedings of the Royal Irish Academy* 49C (1943–44): 45–79.

41. As early as 26 May 1568 Hooker wrote Sir Peter Carew that he had
perused records in Dublin Castle, that he had found some pertinent documents (especially the statute of 28 Henry 8 relating to the resumption of Irish
lands), and that he had copied the relevant documents. LP, Carew MS 605,
ff. 5–15, include the above-mentioned statute and his notes concerning other
muniments.

especially the semiorganic law named after Edward Poynings. Moreover, Speaker Stanihurst had suggested that a printed compilation would be desirable. Hooker labored on this project off and on for three years before his edition of the Irish laws (10 Henry VI through 13 Elizabeth I) came off the press.[42] They were printed in London by Richard Tottel, publisher of the English statutes, in the summer of 1572. The English Privy Council not only approved the project but called upon the lord deputy to foster the sale and distribution of the same. Although Sir Henry Sidney later claimed credit for the project —a project which he merely approved and advanced—Hooker and his assistants compiled the documents and edited the manuscript for the printer.[43]

Midway through this project John Hooker returned to England.[44] In April 1571, having been elected to represent Exeter in parliament, he arrived in Westminster and appeared in the House of Commons. He attended the daily deliberations but his role was that of a back-bencher. He served on two committees, both dealing with provincial legislation affecting Devonshire, but he made no formal speeches and took no part in the debates. Hooker attributed his insignificant role to an illness that impaired his speech, but perhaps he had been chastized into silence by his experiences in Dublin.[45] Certainly

42. A printed copy of the statute collection can be found in Cambridge University Library. A manuscript copy of the collection is located at the BL (Cotton MSS, Titus B. IX). One of the hands is Hooker's, this much seems clear, but the existence of several other handwritings indicates that he undoubtedly employed copyists to assist him. Also see J. Hardiman, *Tracts relating to Ireland,* Irish Archaeological Society (Dublin, 1843), pp. xx–xxii.

43. For Sidney's claim, made in 1583, see LP, Carew MS 605, f. 89.

44. The exact date of Hooker's return is not evident. We know that he left England in May 1568, that he spent three years there, and that he sat in the 1571 parliament in England, which convened on 2 April. In all likelihood he was back in Exeter for the elections, which took place sometime during the forty-day period before that date. It would appear that he assumed the place previously filled by Sir Peter Carew.

45. See the dedicatory epistle to the Exeter edition for Hooker's admission of silence and illness.

he was no match for experienced parliamentarians like William Fleetwood and Robert Bell.

Nevertheless, Hooker compensated for his passive role in the deliberations by keeping a record of the transactions, a parliamentary diary.[46] As chamberlain he was accustomed to record-keeping. He was, moreover, obligated to keep the Exeter oligarchy informed of actions in parliament. In earlier parliaments (1553 and 1566) John Prowse, Geoffrey Tothill, and Richard Prestwood had kept Exonians informed by means of "remembrances"—really newsletters commenting on the important deliberations.[47] As custodian of these records Hooker no doubt recognized their value both as contemporary news and as historic documents. Hooker was not the only diarist in the 1571 Parliament. As Sir Simonds D'Ewes and, more recently, Sir John Neale have demonstrated, someone else—an elusive "anonymous diarist"—kept a rather complete record of deliberations in the House of Commons through the first half of the session.[48] However, because the "anonymous diarist" stopped writing in late April, Hooker's record remains a unique source. Hooker's diary, though disappointingly ab-

46. This diary, part of Hooker's personal papers in the EXRO (book 6oh, ff. 1–9), was transcribed and edited by J. B. Davidson and published in *Transactions of the Devonshire Association for the Advancement of Science* (Plymouth, 1879), 40:442–92.

47. See EXRO, L. 31, for these "remembrances." It is possible that the diary or remembrance evolved from the expense records that MPs kept and submitted for reimbursement. In 1549 William Hurst kept a record of the expenses he incurred in Westminster and then submitted a statement to the Exeter government. A day by day record of deliberations would constitute a record to substantiate presence and insure reimbursement (see L. 28). It is interesting to note that in 1563 Hooker received from Geoffrey Tothill, MP from Exeter, letters describing bills before parliament. No doubt Hooker, then chamberlain, was expected to report this information to the mayor and common council of Exeter.

48. See D'Ewes, *ACJ*, p. 155 ff., and Neale, *EP*, 1:184. Both quote extensively from this diary. In addition to the two manuscript copies of this diary, which Neale used and cited, I located a third and more complete manuscript, TCLD, MS 535.

breviated and incomplete when compared with the uniden-
tified diarist, cannot be ignored. In the absence of official
returns from the 1571 parliament the diary establishes
Hooker's presence and thus verifies the single reference to
him in the official *Journal.*[49] It also corroborates Hooker's
claim to have been a firsthand observer to the "moderne form
and usage" of parliament.

After the end of the session, Hooker committed to paper,
using his own experiences, a description of parliament as it
existed in Elizabeth's England and searched for evidence of
procedures in earlier times. Finally, after locating a copy of the
Modus and preparing a translation for publication, he wrote
two prefaces to his work—one dedicated to the new lord deputy of Ireland, Sir William Fitzwilliam, and the other addressed to the governing authorities of Exeter—and published
two editions. The Fitzwilliam edition purported to provide the
Irish authorities with up-to-date parliamentary procedures,
which could serve to forestall any repetitions of unruly scenes
in the lower house. With the Exeter edition, to which he appended his "Description of Exeter," Hooker probably hoped
to win acclaim and, perhaps, another seat in the English parliament. Subsequently, when editing the second edition of Holinshed's *Chronicles,* he included in the volume on Ireland his
analysis of contemporary practice under the heading "The
Order and Usage how to keep a parlement in England in these
daies." These three publications of Hooker, when collated and
critically appraised, provide us with an insider's description of
parliament—its structure, composition, and procedures—in
Elizabethan England.

For our purposes the remainder of Hooker's career was
anticlimactic. In 1572, after the publication of the Irish statutes, he returned to Ireland and concerned himself with legal
questions relating to Sir Peter Carew's lands.[50] He attended

49. On 12 April 1571 Hooker was appointed to the select committee concerned with Bristol trade; see *CJ,* 1:84.

50. LP, Carew MS 605, ff. 20–38. Many are abstracted in the printed calendar.

Lord Deputy Fitzwilliam on a visit to Leinster and took custody of several properties attached to the Barony of Idrone. He kept Sir Peter, who was then in London, well informed by letter of his successes and retained lawyers to assist him in several suits growing out of Carew's reclaimed title. He appears to have been back in Exeter by the summer of 1573. Except for a final trip to Waterford to arrange for the funeral and burial of his patron, who unexpectedly died in November 1575, John Hooker spent the last portion of his life in England. Upon returning to Exeter, he erected in the cathedral church of St. Peter's a tablet commemorating Carew and then penned a biographical sketch of his patron.[51]

Hooker appears to have spent most of his time in Exeter, but he ventured to London when occasion demanded. He undoubtedly went to London to discuss with printers the publication of his several writings in 1584 and to complete arrangements for the reissue of Holinshed's *Chronicles* in 1586. We also know that he was in Westminster as an MP in the 1586 parliament.[52] He represented Exeter, as before, and assumed an inconspicuous role in the deliberations; at least, he was not appointed to any committees nor did he deliver any memorable speeches. In all likelihood he was extremely busy with his editorial responsibilities.

In short, Hooker remained a locally rooted and provincially oriented public servant and historian. In addition to the office of chamberlain, which he retained until his death in 1601, he held several other local offices. Between 1583 and 1589 he served as coroner and presided over several inquests; in 1590 he assumed the duties of recorder and in that capacity conducted the mayoralty election. In 1587 Sir Walter Ralegh ap-

51. Hooker's manuscript, part of the Carew Papers in Lambeth Palace, was first edited by Sir Thomas Philips and printed in *Archaeologia* 27(1840): 96–151. Subsequently, John Maclean reedited the manuscript and incorporated a critical introduction in his *Life and Times of Sir Peter Carew* (London, 1857) and J. S. Brewer included a transcription in his introduction to the *CSP Carew*, 1:vlxvi-cxviii.

52. *LMP*, 1:417.

pointed him the steward of Bradnich, a small manor attached
to the Duchy of Cornwall. The extant records detailing his
activities reveal a dedicated and public-spirited Exonian. Small
wonder that he served on the reception party appointed to
greet the earl of Essex and several other members of the Privy
Council who visited Exeter in 1589.[53]

These experiences as an officeholder coupled with his antiquarian interests help explain the nature and scope of
Hooker's writings. As chamberlain, he was responsible for
administering the court of orphans. To that end he acquired
and studied the charters and prevailing practices of other cities, especially London, and developed a set of principles and
guidelines for Exeter. In 1575, after two decades of experience, he committed them to writing and published them in
pamphlet form.[54] It is interesting that this short work, dedicated to the "Mayor and Senators of the Ancient and Honorable Citie of Excester," was printed by John Allde, a London
stationer known for printing ballads, almanacs, and other popular works.

Like numerous other Elizabethan scholars, Hooker took an
interest in translations. He translated an epistle of St. Augustine and Erasmus's "Detectio Praetigarum" into English and
presented them to Francis, earl of Bedford, no doubt in hopes
of receiving patronage.[55] In contrast to these writings, which
were never published, Hooker translated Giraldus's *History of
Ireland* for inclusion in the first edition of Holinshed's *Chronicles* (1577).[56] If nothing else, these scholarly activities reflect

53. *HMC Exeter,* pp. 58–60, 317.

54. The pamphlet, published on 4 July 1575 as *Orders enacted for Orphans,* is
replete with references to Greek, Roman, and Renaissance authors. Hooker's
records of the court of orphans, located in the EXRO, were used by Carlton
in "Hooker and the Court of Orphans" and *Court of Orphans.*

55. See Prince, *Worthies,* p. 506. He also dedicated "The Desplayenge of the
gulye Lyon of Berewicke" to the earl of Bedford; see *HMC 2nd Rept.,* p. 1. My
efforts to secure copies of these manuscripts were, unfortunately, not successful.

56. Raphael Holinshed listed Hooker as one of his authorities in the first

the influence of Peter Martyr and Miles Coverdale, not to mention the humanistic influence of Corpus Christi College.

Most of Hooker's remaining writings concern Exeter. In 1584 he arranged for Henry Denham, a well-known London stationer, to print his description of the Exeter government with details about laws, customs, and city offices.[57] That same year Denham also published Hooker's *Catalogue of the Bishops of Excester.*[58] If he used the city records under his custody to complete the former pamphlet, he utilized the diocesan records of the cathedral to write the latter. Two years later, as continuator and general editor of Holinshed's *Chronicles,* Hooker incorporated most of the above publications into the body of the work. As we have seen, he included his translation of Giraldus, his description of Exeter and the rebellion of 1549, his *Order and Usage,* his *Catalogue of the Bishops of Excester,* and accounts of several historic incidents involving Exeter and Ireland.[59] No doubt the space devoted to Sir Walter Ra-

---

edition of the *Chronicles* (see 2:1875), but he does not credit Hooker with the translation of Giraldus Cambrensis's *Irish Historie* from Latin to English. In all likelihood Hooker secured his copy of Giraldus from James Stanihurst, who also permitted Edmund Campion to use it in his *Historie of Ireland,* written while Hooker was in Dublin and dedicated to the earl of Leicester on 27 May 1571.

57. Written in 1583, *A Pamphlet of the Offices and Duties of Every Particular Sworne Officer of the Citie of Excester* was dedicated to the mayor of Exeter. This tract, along with the writings of R. Izack, was reprinted in 1765.

58. In this tract (also reprinted in 1765) Hooker claimed that while writing his description of Exeter at the behest of an unnamed "Minister" he discovered an outdated catalogue of bishops, presumably amongst the cathedral muniments, and considered it appropriate to update and publish the same. Copies of the *Catalogue,* dedicated to John Alleyn, then bishop of Exeter, were distributed to friends as New Year's gifts.

59. Hooker augmented the *Chronicles* with an account of the foundation of Corpus Christi College, Oxford, by Hugh Oldham, bishop of Exeter, and an account of Henry VII's expedition and defeat of Perkin Warbeck at Exeter in 1497 (2:784). Hooker went so far as to include his own coat of arms (2:108). For a full discussion of Hooker's role as editor see my critical introduction to the AMS Press reissue of the 1807 edition of Holinshed's *Chronicles,* 6 vols. (1976).

legh in the 1586 edition resulted from Hooker's decision.[60]

After the publication of this opus, which was promptly ex-
purgated, Hooker turned to several other projects. He compiled a definitive description of Exeter—including its history,
geography, political structure, and so forth—but did not live
to see it in print.[61] He penned short treatises on Exe Haven
and the Manor of Exiland, both of which remained unpublished, and he unsuccessfully labored to complete a monu-
mental description of Devon—a work modeled after William
Lambarde's study of Kent and his friend Richard Carew's description of Cornwall.[62] In 1601, while engaged in these labors, he died and was soon thereafter buried in the city he
loved.[63]

Most of John Hooker's manuscripts remained in the custody of his successor, namely Chamberlain William Tickell,
and became part of the official archives of the city. However, some original manuscripts and several copies of origi-

60. Hooker dedicated volume 2 of the 1587 edition to Sir Walter Ralegh,
then lord warden of the Stannaries. After some introductory comments on the
utility of history, he proceeded to trace Sir Walter's medieval ancestry to the
reign of Edward II. Finally, after discussing some of his patron's achievements
and explaining his reason for translating Giraldus, he concluded with a benedictory phrase and signature: "Your L. verie good friend and alie at command-
ment, John Hooker." I have found no evidence that Hooker was related to
Ralegh, as Arthur Cayley stated in his edition of Ralegh's *Works* (1:2); however, it should be noted that Hooker served Ralegh as steward of Bradnich
from 1586 until his death. In the text of the *Chronicles* Hooker incorporated
several references to Sir Walter's activities in Ireland and America (see 3:1369,
1401–03).

61. This work, completed in 1597 when Hooker was over seventy years old,
was more of a compilation of facts than a narrative history. It remained
unpublished until 1914.

62. See F. E. Halliday, *Richard Carew of Antony* (London, 1953).

63. Most of Hooker's unpublished manuscripts concerning Exeter and
Devon became part of the city archives, where they still remain; however, his
"Synopsis Chorographical" was placed in the hands of John Doddridge, a
Devon antiquary and judge, for proofreading and approval. Although Dod-
dridge approved the work and recommended its publication to Mr. Zack
Pasfield, a London stationer, the work was never published.

nals were scattered at the time of his death and because of
the laws of property and descent ended up in diverse
places and collections. A few manuscripts, such as his translations, remain in the private archives of the Russell family. The remainder are to be found in the British Museum,
the Bodleian Library, Queen's College, Cambridge University Library, Lambeth Palace, the College of Arms, and
Trinity College, Dublin. Many of Hooker's disseminated
manuscripts, it is most interesting to note, fell into the
hands of antiquarians and historians, who no doubt used
them in their own researches.

There is an obvious temptation to link Hooker with these
Elizabethan and Jacobean antiquarians.[64] He may well have
had connections with Archbishop Parker and his numerous
protégés who searched for those manuscripts lost during the
dissolution and published their findings through the patronage of the primate.[65] Hooker was aware of the work of Bale,
certainly, and he undoubtedly knew of Parker's efforts to re-

64. For the Elizabethan antiquaries see Joan Evans, *A History of the Society of
Antiquaries* (Oxford, 1956); Levi Fox, *English Historical Scholarship in the Sixteenth
and Seventeenth Century* (Oxford, 1956); Eleanor N. Adams, *Old English Scholar-
ship in England from 1566–1800* (New Haven, 1917); Levy, *Tudor Historical
Thought,* especially pp. 124–166; May McKisack, *Medieval History in the Tudor
Age* (Oxford, 1917), especially pp. 155–69; Thomas Hearne, *A Collection of
Curious Discourses Written by Eminent Antiquaries* (Oxford, 1720); and R. J. Scho-
eck, "The Elizabethan Society of Antiquaries and Men of Law," *Notes and
Queries* 199 (1954): 417–21.

65. For Parker's antiquarian activities see John Strype, *The life and acts of
Matthew Parker,* 3 vols. (Oxford, 1821), 3:210–38, 262–64, 279, 341, 414,
528–33; Matthew Parker, *Correspondence, 1535–1573,* ed. John Bruce and T. T.
Perrowne (Cambridge, 1853), pp. 298–301, 327, 406–11, 418–19, 448; and
W. W. Greg, "Books and Bookmen in the Correspondence of Archbishop
Parker," *The Library,* 4th ser. 16 (1935): 243–79. I have discovered no direct
connections between Hooker and the archbishop, although their antiquarian
searches were contemporaneous. However, Parker used some of the Saxon
manuscripts in the Exeter Cathedral, a collection that Hooker himself utilized,
and that he received a manuscript of Giraldus Cambrensis from the bishop of
St. David's. Parker did not uncover any copies of the *Modus,* it seems, at least
no references to it appear in his correspondence.

cover Anglo-Saxon and medieval manuscripts.[66] Yet, there seems to be no direct association between Hooker and the archbishop's private conclave of scholars. Similarly, Hooker was not a member of the Society of Antiquaries established in London in 1586.[67] True, he was in London during that year attending parliament and editing the second edition of Holinshed's *Chronicles* (which came off the presses shortly after the founding of the society), but he was not a founder nor does he appear to have attended the weekly meetings held at the College of Heralds. Hooker had associations with several members of the society and his interests ran parallel to topics considered by it, but he had no formal connection with the organization.

Nonetheless, his relationships with some individual antiquarians require comment. He was a close friend of Richard Carew of Antony, Cornwall, one of the founders of the society. In his *Survey of Cornwall,* Carew referred to Hooker as "the commendable painful antiquary, and my kind friend Master Hooker."[68] Hooker was also on good terms with Sir George Carew—a Devon cousin of Richard, successor of Sir Peter Carew and subsequently earl of Totness—who, though not a member of the society, was a genealogist, collector of manuscripts, and antiquarian.[69]

66. Hooker refers to Bale in his unpublished "Description of Exeter"—see BLO, Ashmole MS 762. For Bale see McKissack, *Medieval History,* pp. 7–25, and Honor McCusker, "Books and Manuscripts in the Possession of John Bale," *The Library,* 4th ser. 16 (1935): 144–65.

67. Evans, *Society of Antiquaries,* and Schoeck, "Society of Antiquaries." Hooker's name does not crop up in any of the documents touching upon the society. Also see L. van Norden, "Sir Henry Spelman on the Chronology of the Elizabethan College of Antiquaries," *HLQ,* 13 (1949–50), 69–78.

68. Halliday, *Carew,* pp. 130, 164, 184.

69. In 1575 Sir George Carew inherited from his cousin, Sir Peter Carew, the latter's lands, possessions, and literary effects, including Hooker's letters, memos, and notes. He used the material from both John Hooker and Joseph Holland to produce a scroll of arms, seemingly, at least the manuscript (Harl. 2129) contains several references to "Mr. Hooker." It would also appear that Carew requested and received information from Hooker, who as chamberlain

Hooker's relationship with several other antiquarians may well have been one-sided. In his study of West Country arms Joseph Holland, a Devonian antiquary, made several references to Hooker as an authority.[70] Similarly, Sir John Dodderidge, likewise a Devonshire native and graduate of Exeter College, Oxford, acquired Hooker's unpublished manuscript entitled "Synopsis Chorographical Descriptions of the Country of Devon," corrected it for publication, and recommended it to a publisher; more important, he appears to have freely used some of Hooker's researches in his own writings.[71] Though both of these Devonians represented a younger generation of scholars, in all likelihood Hooker had some acquaintance with them. It is also clear from his manuscript notes that William Lambarde relied upon Hooker's writing on parliament when gathering material for his *Archeion*.[72] Similarly, we know that Camden used Hooker's writings on Exe-

---

of Exeter had access to sources Carew utilized to construct his scroll and genealogies. For a printed version see J. Brooking Rowe, "Sir George Carew's Scroll of Arms, 1588," *Devon and Cornwall Notes and Queries* 1 (1900): 1–134.

70. BL, Harl. MS 5871, is replete with references to Hooker. In some cases, it would appear, Holland used Hooker's writings; in others, he personally contacted Hooker for information.

71. In Harl. MS 5827 there is a message from Doddridge to Mr. Zack Pasfield recommending publication. For Doddridge see Prince, *Worthies*, pp. 301–06. Although he does not give Hooker any credit, surely Doddridge used Hooker's unpublished writings on Cornwall, especially the "Synopsis Chorographical," in arguing a case; see TCLD, MS 807. Similarly, Doddridge probably used the *Order and Usage* in preparing his own essays on parliament's antiquity, at least he uses some of Hooker's terminology and arguments; yet, he makes no direct reference to Hooker. Doddridge's *True Presentation of Forpast Parliaments* and *Of the Antiquity of Parliaments*, were published posthumously in 1658; for manuscript versions see TCLD, MSS 850 and 853.

72. I have not discovered any personal relationship between these two antiquarians and yet it is clear that each was influenced by the other. Lambarde's "Noates" include references to Hooker's "Book of the Parliaments" and a transcription of the *Modus* and the *Order and Usage*. It is obvious that Lambarde used Hooker in the preparation of *Archeion*. Conversely, surely Hooker knew of Lambarde's *Chronicle called Brute* (1570) and his *Perambulation of Kent*, which served as a model for his own work on Devon.

ter.[73] Very likely Hooker had some acquaintance with William Fleetwood, legal antiquarian and recorder of London. They both sat in the 1571 parliament (in fact Hooker alluded to Fleetwood in his diary), and they both represented their respective cities in the 1586 parliament.[74]

As editor of Holinshed's *Chronicles* in 1586 Hooker's responsibilities brought him into contact with several other members of the Society of Antiquaries. No doubt he knew Francis Thynne, whose several contributions to the *Chronicles* sparked controversy and were duly excised by the Privy Council.[75] Hooker probably had some association with Robert Beale, clerk of the council and member of the society.[76] The precise nature of this relationship remains an unsolved problem. Most significant for our purposes, Beale possessed a manuscript copy of Hooker's *Order and usage of keeping a Parlement,* including the dedicatory letter addressed to the Exeter leaders.[77] Perhaps Beale received a printed copy from Hooker himself, as a gift from one antiquarian to another, but more likely he copied it in connection with his duties as clerk of the council. Perhaps it was a printer's copy that he perused either before or after publication. Whatever the case, the fact remains that Beale had some interest in Hooker's *Order and Usage,* either antiquarian or political—or both.

73. See BL, Cotton MS, Titus F. VI., which includes the manuscript copy of Hooker's *Description of Exeter* used by Camden in the preparation of his *Britannia.* Camden does not appear to have used Hooker's work on parliament.

74. They both served on the committee which perfected the Bristol trade bill in 1571. For Fleetwood see *DNB,* 7:269–71.

75. The excised sections were published in 1728 and incorporated in the 1807–08 edition of the *Chronicles.* On 1 February 1587 the Privy Council requested Dr. John Hammond, chancellor of London at the time, to examine the *Chronicles;* see *APC, 1586–87,* pp. 311–12, and *DNB,* 8:247.

76. On Beale see *DNB,* 2:3–7. It is interesting to note that Beale was from Woodbridge, Suffolk, the home of Hooker's mother Agnes Doble. He became clerk of the council in 1572 or thereabouts.

77. Beale's manuscripts descended to his son-in-law Sir Henry Yelverton, an early Stuart judge, and were eventually acquired by the British Library. The Beale manuscripts are identified as Add. MSS 48020 and 48025.

Thus, although not formally affiliated with the Elizabethan Society of Antiquaries, John Hooker knew several members and, more important, they knew of him and his researches.[78] Hooker represented an older generation and his scholarly contributions tended to be less national and more provincial in scope. Moreover, his writings reflect an uncritical Saxonist bias: he was bent on demonstrating the antiquity and continuity of Anglo-Saxon institutions.[79] Nevertheless, despite these limitations, Hooker possessed a national reputation as an antiquarian and archivist. This reputation no doubt accounts for his editorial role in the second edition of Holinshed's *Chronicles*.

The precise nature of Hooker's ties with an influence upon the puritans remain obscure. He regarded the leading protector of the puritans, namely the earl of Bedford, as his patron —this much is clear—and he associated with several Bedfordians, especially Carew and Fitzwilliam.[80] His in-laws the Bridgemans had connections with the Russells, as we have seen, and his younger sister Mary married one John Russell of Grantham. More significant, on 25 July 1580 his daughter Alice married John Travers, a "resolute" puritan minister whose activities in the West Country caused Bishop Woolton of Exeter no end of trouble.[81] Ironically, John's brother Walter Travers was Richard Hooker's principle adversary in the Temple sermon war. It is difficult to imagine John Hooker permitting his eldest daughter to marry without his consent. Yet, it is not evident from his writings that Hooker was a

78. Schoeck, "The Society of Antiquaries," pp. 417–21.

79. On Saxonism see T. D. Kendrick, *British Antiquity* (London, 1950), especially pp. 34–98; John Pocock, *The Ancient Constitution and Feudal Law* (Cambridge, 1957), especially pp. 57–64; and Adams, *Old English Scholarship.*

80. He had fought with Bedford (then Lord Russell) in the 1549 siege of Exeter and he dedicated some of his unpublished writings to Bedford. For the best discussion of these individuals and their relationship to the origins of Elizabethan Puritanism see Christina Garret, *The Marian Exiles* (Cambridge, 1966), especially pp. 104–08, 275–77.

81. Vivian, *Visitations of Devon*, p. 479, and Patrick Collinson, *The Elizabethan Puritan Movement* (London, 1967), pp. 441–43, 454.

puritan. He was committed to the episcopal system of church government, at least his pamphlet on the Exeter diocese reflects pro-Establishment views. He had few kind words for Roman Catholics, especially the Marian bishops, but he was not anticlerical as were many English puritans. He appears to have had friendly associations with several ecclesiastics in the diocese of Exeter, including Weston, Coverdale, and Woolton. But he had little in common with Thomas Cartwright.

Nevertheless, his tractate well suited the cause of parliamentary puritans. In the *Order and Usage* he claimed that the jurisdiction of parliament included matters pertaining to marriage and succession and that the House of Commons possessed authority to debate and legislate such matters. (see below p. 146). More important, he contended that parliament possessed the authority to "reform" the church. He elevated the role of the House of Commons in the lawmaking process and made broad claims about the rights and privileges of attendant members. He also underscored the authority of each house to judge and discipline its own members. No doubt these views explain why Hooker appealed to Elizabethan puritans like Beale and Yelverton, and to Leveller leaders like John Lilburne.

The Bibliographical Problem

Before proceeding to an analysis of John Hooker's *Order and Usage* it is necessary to unravel several knotty problems relating to its publication. First and foremost, unbeknownst to most scholars, Hooker published two different editions of his tract: (1) the Fitzwilliam edition, dedicated to the lord deputy of Ireland, Sir William Fitzwilliam, and (2) the Exeter edition, dedicated to the mayor and civic leaders of Exeter.[1] Second, since very few copies of these editions have survived, bibliographers have publicized what appear to be conflicting facts about the *Order and Usage* and scholars have not compared the different versions. To illustrate, the cataloguers of the British Museum, using their copy of the Exeter edition, listed the entry as "[London? 1575?]."[3] Joseph Ames, on the other hand, using the Fitzwilliam edition, dated the *Order and Usage* as 3 October 1572 but incorrectly suggested that it was published in Ireland.[4]. Following Ames and the British Museum

1. I have located only one copy of the Fitzwilliam edition, namely that in the Beinecke Rare Book and Manuscript Library at Yale University, New Haven, although the late Norah Evans's papers included a mutilated copy which has recently been acquired by the BLO. The full title page reads *The Order and Usage of keeping of the Parlements in England, Collected by John Vowel alias Hooker gentleman.* Copies of the Exeter edition are located at the Huntington Library and Art Gallery, the Houghton Library, BL, and BLO. The full title of this edition reads *The Order and Usage of the keeping of a Parlement in England, and the Description of tholde and ancient Cittie of Excester. Collected by John Vowell alias Hooker gentleman.* The signatures and pagination are different, see below p. 36.

2. *British Museum, catalogue of printed books,* 263 vols. (London, 1931–75), 105:643–44.

3. A. W. Pollard and G. R. Redgrave, *A Short-Title Catalogue of books . . . 1475–1640* (London, 1946), entry #24887 under John Vowell. The new edition of *STC,* fortunately, includes the Fitzwilliam edition and the date [1572?].

4. Joseph Ames, *Typographical antiquities: or an historical account of the progress of printing in Great Britain,* 3 vols. (London, 1790), 3:1524–25. The date came from the last page of the dedicatory epistle.

catalogue, in his article on Hooker in the *Dictionary of National Biography*, Thompson Cooper noted that in 1572 *Order and Usage* was issued separately and with the "Description of Exeter (London? 1575?)."[5] The ensuing discussion, focusing on the typographical congruities, similarities, and differences evident in the two editions, aims to untangle the twisted strands of interpretation.

Both editions of the *Order and Usage* were printed by the same stationer: this is clear from identities in type imprints, illustrative woodcuts, spacing, line endings, accidentals, direction marks, and printer's marks.[6] The roman capital letters on the title pages are identical—even to the raised H in the first word of the title—and the incidental marks at the top of the pages are congruous. Similarly, the three rectangular borders that frame the title and author's name—including the corner breaks and typographical faults—are identical. Although the contents of the dedicatory epistles vary greatly, the cursive italic typefaces appear to be from the same printer's fount. The two versions of Hooker's English translation of the *Modus* contain some minor differences in text and many typographical variations, but the type imprints and printer's marks are identical.

More important, the sections entitled "The Order and Usage how to keep a parlement in England in these dayes" of both editions are identical in every respect—as evidenced in the broken initial letter A on page 23a, the variant initial letter T on page 24a, the misspelling and spacing of the word "THE" on page 26a, the broken initial letter B on page 30a, the damaged printer's mark at the end of the text (page 35b), to mention but a few identifying congruities.[7] The same holds

5. *DNB*, 9:1181–83.

6. This comparison is based upon the Beinecke Library copy of the Fitzwilliam (or Irish) edition and the Huntington Library copy of the Exeter edition, which is identical to the copy in the BL. The type appears to be Basle Italic.

7. Since the Exeter edition has arabic pagination and the Fitzwilliam has none, I have used the Exeter edition for my point of reference throughout this introduction.

true for the annexed lists of "personages as ought to appear and be in the Parliament," on pages 36 through 39, including the damaged printer's mark on page 39. Thus, without doubt, the two editions came off the press of one printer and the concluding sections of both editions were from the same setting.

The data relating to the printer's identity and the date and place of publication were omitted from both editions of Hooker's *Order and Usage*. Normally the stationer placed his name or initials on the title page, usually toward the foot, or at the end of the text. Earlier in 1572, for example, Richard Tottel took credit for printing Hooker's edition of the Irish statutes and subsequently, in 1575, John Allde placed his name at the bottom of the title page of Hooker's *Orders enacted for Orphans*.[8] Similarly, in 1584 Henry Denham's name appeared on two of Hooker's pamphlets.[9] The absence of the printer's name from both editions of the *Order and Usage* raises several questions relative to the author's motive and purpose of the publication. Did the author wish to protect the identity of the printer? Was the printer fearful of printing an unauthorized tract concerned with parliament? Or did both author and printer conspire to exclude the latter's name? Whatever the case, the printer omitted his name and initials from the *Order and Usage*. Furthermore, he did not follow the generally accepted practice of registering the tract in the records of the Stationers' Company.[10]

Possibly Hooker arranged for a private printing of his *Order*

---

8. See D. B. Quinn, "The Bills and Statutes of the Irish Parliaments of Henry VII and Henry VIII," *Analecta Hibernica* 10 (1941): 76, and John Hooker, *Orders enacted for Orphans* (London, 1575).

9. See *A Pamphlet of the Offices and Duties of everie particular sworne Officer of the Citie of Excester* (London, 1584), and *A Catalogue of the Bishops of Excester* (London, 1584). For Denham see R. B. McKerrow, *Printers and publishers devices in England and Scotland 1485–1640*, Bibliographical Society Monographs (London, 1913), p. 88.

10. This is based upon a page by page search in E. Arber, *Transcript of the Registers of the company of stationers of London, 1554–1640*, 5 vols. (New York, 1949–50).

and Usage. This method of publication, when combined with a personal distribution, though rare, may explain the inclusion of Hooker's name as author and the exclusion of the printer's name. Archbishop Parker had privately printed and distributed some of his antiquarian writings.[11] Also, we know that in 1584 Hooker personally distributed several copies of his recently published pamphlets to friends in Exeter as New Year's gifts.[12] Private printing and personal distribution may also account for the paucity of extant copies of both editions of the *Order and Usage*. It provides, in any case, a feasible explanation for the coincidence of facts which otherwise appear inexplicable.

Nevertheless, private printing or not, it is possible to identify the printer. Of the three printers Hooker published with —Richard Tottel, Henry Denham, and John Allde—the last-named appears to have printed the *Order and Usage*. John Allde, after serving his apprenticeship with brothers Richard and John Kele, took up his freedom in 1555 and shortly thereafter established his own shop "in the Poultry at the stocks beside St. Mildred's church."[13] Between 1560 and 1582 he printed a great variety of popularly oriented works, including ballads, almanacs, devotional pamphlets, broadside epitaphs, and some theological treatises. Allde was lax in dating his publications, we are informed, and he had several brushes with authorities for printing violations. In 1568 he was imprisoned by the lord mayor of London for colluding with two Dutch emigrants to print a work about the duke of Alva.[14] Only after appealing to Sir William Cecil and promising to forward the

11. For a general discussion see John Martin, *A Bibliographical Catalogue of Books Privately Printed*, 2 vols. (London, 1834), 1:1–23. For particulars on Parker see his *Correspondence*, p. 410. For the private circulation of books see Greg, "Book and Bookmen," pp. 254–59.

12. EXRO, book 57, which is Hooker's memo and account book. We note that he had 75 copies of this pamphlet.

13. On Allde see R. B. McKerrow, "Edward Allde as Typical Trade Printer," *The Library*, 4th ser. 10 (1930): 121–62.

14. Arber, *Transcript*, 2:742–45.

secretary of state some foreign intelligence about Spain was Allde released from the "Counter in the Poultry" the following year. Subsequently, in 1577 he was fined by the Stationers' Company for breaking an order regulating apprentices and in 1578 for printing ballads without licenses.[15] The printer of the *Order and Usage,* then, was not above publishing controversial and unauthorized works.

To establish Allde as the printer of the *Order and Usage* one must rely upon internal typographical evidence in the absence of documentation in the Stationers' Company Registers. The type styles used by Allde in his two editions of the *Order and Usage* reappear in Hooker's *Orders enacted for Orphans,* for which Allde claimed publication credit.[16] Secondly, the frontispiece in the Exeter edition of the *Order and Usage* was reused as a frontispiece in the *Orders enacted for Orphans.*[17] Moreover, many of the damaged initial letters used in the *Order and Usage* reappear in the pamphlet on orphans, though they show increased wear. Likewise, Allde's star cluster decorative filler was used in both publications. Last, and most convincing, Allde incorporated in the *Order and Usage* a printer's mark, namely a small, decorative device depicting a strutting bird (perhaps an eagle) and what appears to be a scalding pot.[18] Surely this device was Allde's trademark indicating the location of his shop in the Poultry. Thus, both editions of Hooker's *Order and Usage* were printed in London (not Dublin or Exeter)

15. *Ibid.,* 843, 847.

16. I refer here to the italic type used in the body of each tract, not to the title page or the dedicatory epistles. For an excellent analysis of type styles see Francis Swinton Isaac, *English Printers Types of the Sixteenth Century* (Oxford, 1936).

17. This is an elaborate cut depicting the arms of the city of Exeter.

18. This device also appears in Allde's edition of Edward Gosynbill's *Heer Beginneth the Schoole House of Women* (1572). It is also interesting to note that Richard Kele, Allde's predecessor from whom he probably secured some type, also had a shop near the Stocks Market in Lombard Street and that his signboard depicted an eagle. It is possible that Allde assumed Kele's "syne of the Egle" as his own device when he bought him out.

by a controversial charter member of the Stationers' Company.

The date of publication is more difficult to determine with certainty. Since neither edition was recorded in the register of the Stationers' Company, one must rely primarily upon internal evidence in the dedicatory epistles to establish a *terminus ante quem* and a *terminus post quem.* In both epistles Hooker states that he attended the 1571 parliament and that he began writing after its dissolution—that is, after 29 May 1571. In the Exeter edition he alludes to "the right worshipful Sir Peeter Carew," as if his patron were alive.[19] Since Sir Peter died in November 1575, it is evident that the dedicatory epistle was completed before that date. In short, both were written and printed between 29 May 1571 and November of 1575.

Further evidence permits us to pinpoint more precisely when Hooker completed his manuscripts and when Allde printed them. During the 1571 parliamentary session Hooker, as noted in the dedicatory epistle of the Fitzwilliam edition, "did observe, consider, and mark all manner of orders, usages, rites, ceremonies and all other circumstances."[20] These firsthand observations plus his researches in the official records of parliament provided Hooker with the raw material for his description of parliament in "these days." He first committed to paper this description, shortly after the dissolution of that parliament, probably in the summer of 1571. In fact, Hooker retained an abbreviated rough draft of that description of parliament, actually the last section of the *Order and Usage,* and preserved it along with his diary of the 1571 parliament in the official archives of Exeter, where it has since remained.[21]

19. See p. 10a. Very likely the bibliographers of the British Library and Huntington Library who date the *Order and Usage* "1575?" base their assignation on the internal evidence relating to Carew.

20. The second page opposite the signatured page B.i.

21. EXRO, book 6oh, ff. 12–19. Although it is possible to ascertain Hooker's organization from the chapter headings and the contents of most chapters, the

Not content with only describing present procedures and curious about earlier practices, Hooker launched a probe into the past, probably during the summer or autumn of 1571: "I did then confer with the exemplars and presidents of tholde and aunicent Parlements used in times past within the Realme of England."[22] He uncovered two early treatises on parliament: one claiming to describe parliament during the reign of Edward the Confessor, the other dating from Edward I. Hooker rejected the latter and decided to publish the former along with his own description. Somehow he acquired the manuscript; at least he claimed to "have" what he called "an olde, and ancient Latin Record."[23] Hooker leaves us in the dark as to the details of acquisition. But, recognizing the significance of the "Record" and its relevance to his project, he proceeded to translate the *Modus* into English. Its translation and publication served the dual purpose, he claimed, of establishing the antiquity of parliament and providing precedents to those interested in the same.

After completing his translation of the *Modus,* Hooker then wrote his dedicatory epistle to the Exeter edition. Although he dated the first portion of that dedication 1571, he may well have completed it in 1572. The printer's copy of the Exeter edition, in any case, bears the date of 1571. However, when Allde set type for this edition he eliminated that date from the dedicatory epistle and did not include any other date. We can only surmise that he printed it the following year.

Several months lapsed before Hooker completed his dedicatory epistle to the Fitzwilliam edition. During these months, in all likelihood, he was involved in the publication and distribu-

---

manuscript is so badly mutilated at the bottom of each page that a complete text is out of the question. Moreover, it is replete with abbreviations, corrections, and interlinear words and phrases, all indicative of an early, if not the first, draft of the tract. The printer's copy and the two printed editions are longer and somewhat different in structure.

22. Page 2 of the Fitzwilliam edition.
23. Page 9a of the Exeter edition.

tion of the Irish Statutes. We know from several phrases in the Fitzwilliam edition that it was written in Ireland, for he repeatedly alludes to Ireland as "this land," and we learn from the epistle, which was completed on 3 October 1572, that the Irish statutes were already in print.[24] Thus, it would appear that Hooker completed the manuscript for the Fitzwilliam edition between the summer of 1572, when the Irish statutes were published, and 3 October of that year.

Conclusions regarding the order of publication are equally complex and difficult to ascertain, but the typographical evidence suggests that the Exeter edition was printed first. It is clear that the two editions were set by different compositors, for two different signature systems were used.[25] Moreover, some of the glaring typographical errors in the Exeter edition were picked up and corrected in the Fitzwilliam edition.[26] Conversely, one entire line dropped in the Fitzwilliam edition and not in the Exeter edition was surely made by a compositor who used the printed copy of the Exeter edition rather than a manuscript copy.[27] Similar uncorrected mis-

---

24. On signatured page A.ii Hooker referred to Ireland as "this Realm" and on the following page he used "this land." For the reference to the Irish statutes see B.ii.

25. *Exeter Edition Signatures*   *Fitzwilliam Edition Signatures*

Ai-ii	Ai-ii
Bi-ii	Bi-iiii
Ci-iiii	Ci-
Di-iiii	Ci-iiii
Ei-iiii	Di-iiii
Fi-iiii	Di-iiii
Gi-iiii	Fi-iiii
Hi-iiii	Gi-iiii
Ji-iiii	Hi-iiii
(Signatures Diiii and Iiiii	Ji-iiii
are blank)	

26. Compare the respective chapters entitled "Of places and seats in the Parlement," and "Of the porters of the Parlement." In each case the error in the Exeter edition is corrected in the Fitzwilliam edition.

27. In the chapter entitled "The Summons of the Barons of the Five Ports"

takes in the Fitzwilliam edition also support this conclusion.

These variations and the inferences based upon them suggest the following publication sequence. Compositor A first set and printed the *Modus* which appeared in the Exeter edition; he then set and printed enough copies of Hooker's *Order and Usage . . . in these Dayes* for both editions; he next set and printed Hooker's description of Exeter; and, finally, he set and printed the dedicatory epistle of the Exeter edition. The page numbers of this, the Exeter edition, were added later.[28] Compositor B, using a different system of signatures, reset the *Modus* section of the work, correcting obvious typographical errors in the process. He then set and printed the dedicatory epistle of the Fitzwilliam edition. These were then quired along with Compositor A's version of Hooker's *Order and Usage . . . in these Dayes.* This version, the Fitzwilliam edition, had neither arabic page numbers nor Hooker's description of Exeter.

Very likely the writing, setting, and printing processes described above overlapped so that while Allde was printing the Exeter edition Hooker was writing the Fitzwilliam edition. Internal evidence strongly suggests this conclusion. In his dedicatory remarks to the Fitzwilliam edition Hooker referred to the "Orders of the Parlments of England . . . *now inprint*" (emphasis mine).[29] Surely this refers to his own description in the Exeter edition, which was either in press or recently completed by Allde. In either case, it seems evident that Allde printed the Exeter edition before Hooker completed his dedicatory epistle to the Fitzwilliam edition. This deduction,

---

the line "coming to the Parliament, until the time of their departing and coming home" is omitted in the Fitzwilliam edition.

28. This practice of adding arabic page numbers after quiring was not unusual; in fact, the booksellers sometimes were responsible for quiring, binding, and pagination. See Philip Gaskell, *A New Introduction to Bibliography* (New York, 1972), p. 52. In 1584, Hooker appears to have received from the printer unbound copies of his pamphlets and forwarded a small number to bookbinders for binding in a separate operation; see EXRO, book 57.

29. See B.iiii verso.

if accurate, also permits us to date the two editions. The Exeter edition was published prior to 3 October 1572, probably shortly before that date, while the Fitzwilliam edition was completed and printed shortly after, certainly between 3 October 1572 and the end of the year.[30]

30. Regrettably, my limited and allotted time in the College of Arms did not permit a complete collation of the printer's copy (H.D.N. #41) with Hooker's manuscripts and the printed edition.

The Dedicatory Epistles

John Hooker used the dedicatory epistles to justify his publication and to promulgate his own views on the virtures of parliamentary government. He began each with a statement of purpose, which was customary, and ended each with a benedictory conclusion. Although writing for two different clienteles— one, the Anglo-Irish leaders in Dublin; the other, the mayor and MPs of Exeter—Hooker utilized similar arguments, employed some identical phraseology, and appealed to some of the same authorities. Thus, despite many differences, the contents of the two introductory epistles reflect similarity of tone and purpose.

Hooker was an avowed advocate of the English parliamentary monarchy, this much is evident, yet he neither put forward a theoretical justification of the monarchial form of government nor constructed a case for limited monarchy. Rather, he assumed a monarchical system and posited a king ("prince") as the head of state. He vigorously defended the English method of corporate lawmaking and repudiated the notion of a unilateral lawgiver. The English system was not unique in this respect, he argued, for the Israelites, the Athenians, the Spartans, the Romans, and even the Egyptians possessed constitutions that provided for collectively made laws. In citing these historical examples Hooker accepted the need for strong leaders like Moses, Solon, Lycurgus, and Justinian, and he recognized the value of one-man rule in the establishment of law and order.

Nonetheless, one-man rule possessed inherent weaknesses and limitations, Hooker contended; even some English sovereigns had been weak and imprudent. Rejecting the legal fiction "the king can do no wrong," he insisted that kings were imperfect and not immune from making bad laws and unwise

39

decisions. Certainly the Christian prince should be thoroughly educated in the Erasmian tradition and, in keeping with that tradition, he should strive to be virtuous, valiant, and wise. But, Hooker insisted, there is no assurance that a wise and virtuous leader will by himself propound good laws. Every king needs advice and counsel, especially from "the grave, auncient, wise and prudent elders."[1]

The earliest English monarchs, in their wisdom, had sought the advice, counsel, and consent of their subjects in the law-making process. Edward the Confessor had convened advisory assemblies, Hooker contended, and then, after a rather long interim occasioned by the Norman Conquest, Edward I revived and institutionalized them during his reign. Since then English sovereigns had relied upon parliaments to give counsel, approve new laws, and abrogate obsolete statutes. Thus, the judicious combination of kingly authority and the corporate wisdom of Englishmen in parliament accounts for the superiority and uniqueness of parliamentary monarchy in both England and Ireland.

To make their parliamentary system work smoothly and effectively, with a maximum amount of order and an absence of disorder, England's lawmakers devised operating rules and procedures. It was not enough to convene parliaments and deliberate upon new laws. Parliaments were composed of human beings, scores of Englishmen representing either themselves or their constituent interests, and the members possessed different motives and diverse objectives. To achieve orderly deliberations from such diversity parliament had its "orders and usages" dating back to pre-Conquest days. In short, parliament acquired its own constitution, its own internal rules for deliberating and making laws.

Yet, though superior and sanctified by time, these internal governing procedures remained unknown to all but a few. Ireland had never received the blessings of parliamentary

---

1. Signatured page B.i. of the Fitzwilliam edition; see below p. 206.

rules, in Hooker's view, at least there was little evidence of them during the 1569 deliberations in Dublin. In England, a different situation prevailed. Extant copies of the *Modus* existed—the clerk of the parliament, for example, possessed a copy—but the procedures detailed therein were outmoded and obsolete. More important were the unwritten rules and customs of parliament in general and of each house in particular. These "orders and usages"—conventions might be a better term—existed in the minds of experienced MPs and in the extant records of each house, especially the official journals. But, for all practical purposes, they remained "hidden" and unknown.[2] Just as the ancient rules governing parliament had been written down in the *Modus* centuries earlier so the modern procedures should be committed to paper and then published in the English language. Certainly the newly elected English MPs and the Irish representatives, even the public in general, would benefit from publication.

In England, parliament had developed over many centuries from a simple assembly described in the *Modus* to the more complex institution evident in Hooker's *Order and Usage*. In short, it had *evolved*. Hooker does not employ that word, of course, but nonetheless he recognized the validity of the concept. The *Modus* was outdated; it had been superseded by modern customs and usages, by different "manners and forms." Yet, the Elizabethan law and custom of parliament had never been reduced to writing and publicized. Thus did the present-minded antiquarian from Exeter justify the twin publication of the ancient and modern guides to parliamentary deliberations.

In Ireland, by way of contrast, the development of parliamentary institutions came later and evolved more slowly than in the mother country. The Irish parliament passed few laws, as Hooker well knew from his edition of the statutes, and instead of being printed they had remained "in a secret and

2. Exeter edition, page 8b; see below p. 125.

private place."[3] The arrested or fossilized development of the
Irish parliament, he believed, produced a chronic unrest and
general lawlessness so evident to the English rulers in Westminster. Similarly, because the Irish lacked parliamentary
procedures like those enunciated in the *Modus* or those in
Hooker's own description, disorderly deliberations and indecorous behavior prevailed in the Dublin assemblies. It is most
interesting to note, however, that Hooker did not attribute the
lawlessness to the national traits of the "mere Irish," as did
many Elizabethan and Jacobean commentators, rather he
faulted the Anglo-Irish governors for failure to enact, promulgate, and enforce the statutes.[4] If the rulers in Dublin would
reform and modernize the lawmaking process, Hooker contended, the Irish would become obedient subjects and tran-
quility would prevail. Hopefully, Sir William Fitzwilliam, the
new lord deputy would introduce the necessary changes and
usher in a new era in Irish history.

It is obvious from the Exeter edition that Hooker, despite
his approval of the English parliamentary system, perceived
some abuses and shortcomings, especially in the electoral process. Instead of adherence to the electoral laws passed in the
fifteenth century, particularly those pertaining to residents,
many English boroughs and some counties elected outsiders
—sometimes dubbed "strangers" or "foreigners"—to represent them in Westminster. By the reign of Elizabeth, as Neale
has so ably demonstrated, the demands of the gentry exceeded
the supply of seats in the lower house, thus forcing would-be
MPs to seek seats outside of their own counties.[5] They were
sometimes assisted by peers, who often possessed nomination
powers in the pocket boroughs, and by the sovereign, who
responded to the pressure and created new parliamentary

3. See the Fitzwilliam edition, signatured page B.iiii; see below p. 210.
4. Ibid. In his contribution to Holinshed's *Chronicles,* written nearly fifteen
years later, Hooker unsympathetically castigated the Irish for their rebellious-
ness (see 1808 edition, 6:321–461).
5. Neale, *EHC,* especially pp. 13–15, 19–51.

boroughs. In 1571 the House of Commons considered—but did not pass—a bill that would have legalized the election of nonresidents.[6]

Hooker disapproved of these electoral practices. He was a gentleman (at least he considered himself as such), he resided in Exeter, and he had represented that city in parliament.[7] The electors knew him. He knew the constituents and their needs and interests. This was true representation.[8] To change this system of parliamentary representation by legalizing the election of nonresidents was to court disaster. Worse yet were those nonresident MPs who violated the electoral laws to gain seats—how could lawbreakers be good lawmakers?

Hooker was also perturbed by other less obvious shortcomings and malpractices. Of late, he argued, Englishmen had returned to the House of Commons all too many inexperienced, rash, and simpleminded MPs. Some, in fact, were not mature men, but mere youngsters. These MPs fell short of Hooker's high standards. He believed that parliamentmen should be like Roman senators: grave, wise, experienced, levelheaded, public-spirited, and god-fearing. Only mature and wise men could write good laws. Hooker aimed his sharpest barbs at the youthful MPs. "If Salomon's wise and ancient senators ought to have place in Parlement," he asked rhetorically, "what shall rash and young councellors of Rohoboham

6. Ibid., pp. 150–53. From comments in the dedicatory epistle of the Exeter edition it is clear that Hooker favored the residency requirements and, very likely, opposed the bill which would have dropped them.

7. Like most status-conscious urbanites Hooker made much of his genteel origins. In his publication he invariably placed the word "gentleman" after his name and in several of his works he incorporated a woodcut of his arms. He also appears to have drawn a thick line between citizens like himself and burgesses.

8. Despite the contention of Neale (*EHC,* p. 14) that England lacked a constituency theory of representation, it is clear that Hooker defended and propogated such a theory. Moreover, in 1571 a majority in the House of Commons dashed a bill which would have undermined local constituency representation for national or virtual representation.

do then?"[9] "What shal be children, yungmen, and such as neither fear god nor hate iniquities, which are of no experience or knowledge sit in Senate of the wise; and give judgment among the grave and learned?" Parliament should be spared "punie, and rash hedders." One wonders, quite naturally, where Hooker drew the line and whether his criticism was aimed at Paul and Peter Wentworth.

No doubt these harsh strictures directed toward unqualified MPs resulted from Hooker's personal knowledge and experience. All of the abuses singled out in the "Epistle Dedicatory" were manifest in the 1571 parliament. There were numerous nonresidents in that parliament.[10] Among them were several younger sons of peers who secured seats through the influence of their fathers.[11] Also, there was one Thomas Long, a "simple-minded" gentleman from Wiltshire who foolishly bribed local officials to insure his election to the House of Commons.[12] More to the point, many of the members were young in years and inexperienced in public matters: Francis Hastings, a younger brother of the earl of Huntingdon, then in his twenties, occupied the "senior" seat of Leicestershire; Charles Somerset, a young son of the earl of Worcester, sat for Monmouthshire; Henry Knollys, the son of Sir Francis, who at the age of twenty-two, had represented Reading in the 1563 parliament.[13] No doubt there were others. Some members compounded the abuses in that they were young and inexperienced nonresidents who owed their seats to outside influence.

Hooker's denouncement of these practices represented a

---

9. See page 7a of the Exeter edition; see below p. 123.

10. There were enough to initiate and propel a nonresidency bill into its third reading; see Neale, *EHC,* pp. 150–53, and D'Ewes, *ACJ,* pp. 168–71.

11. For example, the two sons of Lord Burghley, who had only recently been created a baron; Sir Henry Radcliffe, son of the earl of Sussex; Charles Somerset, son of the earl of Worcester. No doubt there were others.

12. D'Ewes, *ACJ,* p. 164.

13. Neale, *EHC,* pp. 30, 37, 79.

typical "West Country" reaction. The western counties, according to Neale, disapproved of carpetbagging and parliamentary monopolies.[14] Moreover, in 1554 the council of Hooker's beloved Exeter passed a resolution restricting the election of MPs to resident citizens.[15] That same city government in 1563 rejected the nominee of the earl of Bedford and elected a local resident. Similarly, in 1570 the Plymouth council resolved that only "town-dwellers" should be chosen to sit in the House of Commons.[16] Hooker's conservative and legalistic reaction to electoral practices becoming prevalent throughout England reflected the pride and prejudice of a loyal Devonian.

The numerous allusions and authorities cited by Hooker in the two dedicatory epistles reveal that many of his political views derived from humanistic sources. He cites several Latin and Greek classics, as one might expect, and refers to several historical figures from classical times. He alludes to such Spartan leaders as Lycurgus, Chilon, and Archidamus; to Heraclitus of Ephesus, a historian; and to Xerxes of Persia—all of whom appear in Plutarch's *Lives*, Polybius's *Histories*, and Livy's *History of Rome* (see below pp. 122, 208). He is most favorably impressed with the Spartan constitution under Lycurgus and the Roman constitution during the middle years of the Republic.

Hooker also refers to several Renaissance humanists. In both dedicatory epistles he paraphrases the "Prince of the Humanists," Erasmus of Rotterdam, in each case the *Institution of the Christian Prince* (see below p. 118). Having studied at Corpus Christi, where Erasmian ideals had been incorporated in the curriculum, this comes as no surprise. Similarly, in both epistles, Hooker quotes directly from *De Institutione Reipublicae,* a political treatise written by the fifteenth-century Italian humanist Francesco Patrizi, also known by his Latinized surname

14. Ibid., p. 51.
15. Ibid., p. 191.
16. Ibid., p. 171.

Patricius.[17] Very likely Hooker first encountered the writings of Patrizi while studying law in Cologne or through the influence of his Strasbourg mentor, Peter Martyr.[18] Possibly he acquired a copy of Patrizi's *De Institutione Reipublicae,* which was published in England in 1559.[19] Whatever the case, the Platonic and Ciceronian political ideas of Patrizi left their imprint on Hooker.

Though trained in the civil law, Hooker seems oblivious to common law and English authorities.[20] We find no allusions to Bracton, Littleton, or Fortescue. We see no reference to statutes, cases, Year Books or precedents. Yet Hooker may have been more indebted to some English commentators than his sources reveal. Some of his phraseology and allusions bear resemblance to Fortescue, others to Ponet and Foxe. In his *De Laudibus,* to illustrate, Fortescue likens the House of Commons to the Roman Senate and lauds the corporate system of lawmaking.[21] Hooker's quotation from Justinian is almost identical to one appearing in *De Laudibus*;[22] likewise his allusions to Moses, the Egyptians, and Diodorus resemble those of Fortescue.[23] Fortescue also subscribed to Saxonist mythology: he accepted the Brutus legends and believed in the pre-

17. For Patrizi see the writings of Leslie F. Smith, especially "Members of Francesco Patrizi's Family appearing in his Letters and Epigrams," *Renaissance Quarterly* 29 (1974): 1–7, and Charles Schmitt, *Cicero Scepticus: A Study of the Influence of the Academica in the Renaissance* (The Hague, 1972), pp. 43, 46, 48, 49–51, and 171–77.

18. It is also possible that Hooker's interest in Erasmus, who borrowed from Patrizi, led him to the writings of the Italian humanist.

19. It is most interesting to note that in his description of the Exeter court of orphans Hooker also cites Patrizi and that Sir Edward Coke makes a passing reference to Patrizi in his *Institutes* (lib. 5, p. 9).

20. On page 4b of the Exeter edition Hooker, though little versed in the common law tradition, quoted one of the inscribed maxims of the "professors of the common laws"; see below p. 120.

21. S. B. Chrimes, *Sir John Fortescue: De Laudibus Angliae* (Cambridge, 1942), pp. 41, 87.

22. Ibid., pp. 4–5. See below p. 119.

23. Ibid., pp. 32–33, 158.

Roman antiquity of English law.[24] It is entirely possible, though not demonstrable, that Hooker was influenced by Fortescue whose writings were available in two editions.

Also Hooker may have been indebted to John Ponet, the onetime bishop of Winchester who fled to Strasbourg during the reign of Mary and published in 1556 his *Short Treatise of Politique Power*. In the latter we note that Ponet alludes to the misery that followed the Norman Conquest and to the virtues of corporate lawmaking.[25] We also know that Ponet was influenced by Erasmus and Thomas Elyot, both of whom had borrowed heavily from Patrizi, and that he knew several of Hooker's exiled friends in Strasbourg, including Sir Peter Carew.[26] Yet, the fact remains that Hooker attributes nothing to Ponet. Nevertheless, Hooker does reveal his Protestant sympathies: he included many Biblical allusions and cited Melanchthon to verify a point regarding Solon (see below p. 121).

More to the point, the dedicatory epistles reveal a fusion of three different views of the English parliament. As a Renaissance humanist steeped in Greek and Roman history, Hooker perceived parliament as the English version of the Roman senate and the elected MPs as senators. "The order (therefore) among the Romains was that none should be received or allowed to be of their Senate house," he wrote in the Exeter edition, "unless he were grave in yeers, and wel experienced in common affairs of the publique welth" (see below, p. 116). On the first page in the same edition he addressed the Exeter common councillors as "Senators" (see

24. Ibid., p. 33. For discussion of Fortescue's political ideas see S. B. Chrimes, *English Constitutional Ideas in the XV Century* (Cambridge, 1936), especially pp. 62–73, and B. Wilkinson, *Constitutional History of England in the Fifteenth Century* (London, 1964), pp. 199–203.

25. See W. S. Hudson, *John Ponet (1516?–1556), advocate of limited monarchy* (Chicago, 1942), p. 168.

26. Ibid., pp. 94, 148–54. Also at Strasbourg during the Marian exile were Francis Russell (later earl of Bedford), John Bodley, and Miles Coverdale. For the influence of Patrizi on Erasmus and Elyot see John M. Major, *Sir Thomas Elyot and Renaissance Humanism* (Lincoln, Nebr., 1964), pp. 40–43, 156–60.

below, p. 115). Furthermore, he makes several references to Roman concepts and customs in his own description of the English parliament.[27] Without doubt Hooker ascribed to the English parliament—as did contemporaries like Sir Thomas Smith—some classical features worthy of respect and imitation.[28]

At the same time, as a provincial Devonian imbued with Saxonist interpretations of England's early history, Hooker perceived a thread of continuity from the early advisory assemblies of the Anglo-Saxon sovereigns to the Elizabethan "high court of parliament." His uncritical Saxonism, though less obvious, is implicit in several instances. He regards the *Modus* as an Anglo-Saxon document dating from the reign of Edward the Confessor; at least, he does not question the statement in the proem of the *Modus* claiming that the procedures were "used in the time of King Edward the Confessor."[29] In accepting the pre-Conquest date for the *Modus* Hooker rejects the Vergilian interpretation and perpetuates the anachronistic assumption that parliaments began and developed in pre-Norman England.[30] It was relatively easy for an Exonian who believed in the Brutus legend to accept this assumption uncritically, but in so doing Hooker fostered the "Norman Yoke" myth so evident in the writings of Sir Edward Coke. More important, in publicizing these views along with the *Modus,* he sparked a debate over the antiquity and structure of the "high court of parliament"—a debate that con-

27. See below p. 189. He attributes to the Romans the practice of wearing long robes.

28. For Smith's allusions see L. Alston's edition of *De Republica Anglorum* (Cambridge, 1906), pp. 49–58.

29. Page 12b of the Exeter edition and signature page C of the Fitzwilliam edition. Also, later in the dedicatory epistle to the latter Hooker refers to the *Modus* as used in the days of "King Edgar (or as some say, King Edward the Confessor)." See below p. 206.

30. Polydore Vergil's history of England had become the more or less authorized version in that it was used by the sixteenth-century chroniclers. See Levy, *Tudor Historical Thought,* pp. 53–68, passim.

tinued among legal scholars and antiquarians long after Hooker's demise.[31]

Third, as an observant Englishman who had participated in Elizabethan parliaments, Hooker believed that the English parliament was unique.[32] Though bearing some resemblance to the Roman senate and originating during the reign of Edward the Confessor, it had become a complex and sophisticated lawmaking body. The time-tested system was not perfect, he fully realized, for there were abuses in the electoral mechanism and shortcomings in the deliberative process. Yet, parliament was "an honorable assembly" in a "noble state" and as such should be preserved by adherence to proven parliamentary procedures and by the election of "grave, wise, ancient, and expert" Englishmen (see below, pp. 125, 183). The resultant amalgamation of these three views in Hooker's mind accounts for some of the distortions and anachronisms in his introductory comments. Yet, such views, however distorted, supported an emergent political mythology which elevated the place of parliament in English society and the role of Commons in parliament.

31. See below pp. 87–110 and Pocock, *Ancient Constitution*, especially the chapters concerned with Spelman and Brady.

32. A comparison of Hooker's diary of the 1571 parliament and the *Order and Usage* reveals that he probably used the former while writing the latter. The lord keeper's speech guaranteeing the freedoms of parliament, which he reports in the diary (EXRO, book 6oh, f. 2), is very close to his description in the *Order and Usage* (see below p. 179).

Hooker and the *Modus*

To establish the antiquity of parliamentary procedures and demonstrate the continuity between the early practices and those of his own day, John Hooker published for the first time the *Modus*. Although his source was a Latin manuscript in his possession, he did not reproduce the *Modus* in Latin; rather, as stated in both dedicatory epistles, he translated it into English. It is not clear whether the original, referred to as "the olde and ancient Lattin Record," from which he made the translation, was his personal copy or whether it belonged to someone else.[1] He suggests ownership in the words "which I have," yet more likely he had only temporary possession of a manuscript borrowed from a friend or government official.

In 1572 there were several copies of the *Modus* from which Hooker could have made his translation.[2] The 1510 transcription, prefixed to the manuscript journals of the House of Lords and regarded as the authoritative version, remained

1. See below p. 125.
2. In this discussion of the *Modus* I have consulted M. V. Clarke, *Medieval Representation and Consent* (New York, 1936); John Taylor, "The manuscripts of the *'Modus Tenendi Parliamentum,'* " *EHR* 83 (1968): 673–88; M. Bémont, "La Date de la Composition du *Modus Tenendi Parliamentum in Anglia,*" *Mélanges Julien Hart* (Paris, 1895), pp. 465–80; W. A. Morris, "The date of the *Modus Tenendi Parliamentum,*" *EHR* 49 (1934): 407–22; V. H. Galbraith, "The *Modus Tenendi Parliamentum,*" *Journal of the Warburg and Courtauld Institutes* 16 (1953): 81–99; D. E. Hodnett and W. P. White, "Manuscripts of the *Modus Tenendi Parliamentum,*" *EHR* 34 (1919): 209–25; Olive Armstrong, "Manuscripts of the *Modus Tenendi Parliamentum* in the Library of Trinity College, Dublin," *Proceedings of the Royal Irish Academy* 36 (1921–24): 256–64; John Taylor and Nicholas Pronay, "The Use of the *Modus Tenendi Parliamentum* in the Middle Ages," *BIHR* 47 (1974): 11–23; and J. S. Roskell, "A Consideration of Certain Aspects and Problems of the English *Modus Tenendi Parliamentum,*" *Bulletin of the John Rylands Library* 50 (1968): 411–42.

with the clerk of the parliament.[3] There was at least one copy in the Tower of London.[4] When Thomas Egerton wrote his treatise on the statutes in 1569, he possessed a copy of the *Modus*.[5] We also know that Robert Dudley, earl of Leicester, owned a copy dated 1554 and that W. L. (probably William Lambarde) later utilized a copy for his researches.[6] The recent research of John Taylor reveals the existence of several others in the possession of lawyers and officials.[7]

Certain circumstantial evidence points to the Tower of London as the source of the *Modus* from which Hooker made his translation. In 1572 William Bowyer, keeper of the records in the Tower, completed an inventory of the parliamentary records under his custody and, seemingly, began to make abstracts of some of the rolls.[8] Then on 16 September 1572, while Hooker was working on his *Order and Usage*, Sir Peter Carew, Sir Thomas Wroth, William Fleetwood, and Henry Knollys were authorized to enter the Tower for some undisclosed "things to be done."[9] Was it to secure for Hooker the records of early parliaments which he sought and alluded to in the dedicatory epistle completed on 23 October 1572? Did they uncover the copy of the *Modus* that Hooker used? Did they remove the Vetus Codex which bears Fleetwood's name

3. See A. F. Pollard "The Authenticity of the Lords' Journals in the sixteenth century," *TRHS*, 3rd ser. 7 (1914): 17–40.

4. Hodnett and White, "Manuscripts," p. 224, and D'Ewes, *ACJ*, p. A2. The latter, writing in 1629, noted the presence of two copies (one Latin and one French) in the Tower of London, and he also commented upon one in his own possession (a Latin manuscript).

5. See Taylor "Manuscripts," p. 683n, and S. E. Thorne's edition of Egerton entitled *A Discourse upon the exposition and understanding of the statutes* (San Marino, 1942), especially pp. 109–13.

6. See BL, Add. 15,091 and Domit. xviii. In the latter, which ended up in Cotton's possession, we note on f. 92 the initials of William Lambarde and the date, 1574.

7. "Manuscripts," and his article with Pronay on "The Use."

8. H. G. Richardson and George Sayles, *Rotuli Parliamentorum Anglie Hactenus Inediti*, Camden Society, 3d ser. 51 (London, 1935): xx and 231.

9. *CSP Dom. 1547–1580*, 1:290, 292, 450.

and which, according to John Stow, was "restored to the Tower" sometime after 1576, when Michael Heneage succeeded Bowyer as keeper?[10]

The evidence is neither clear nor conclusive, but the circumstances appear to be more than coincidental. We know that between June 1571 and October 1572 Hooker was searching for evidences of early procedures. We know also that between these dates he located a Latin copy of the *Modus* and some early records of parliament during the reign of Edward I (see below p. 206). The composition of the group lends weight to this argument. Sir Peter Carew, then constable of the Tower, was Hooker's patron and friend; moreover, he was indebted to Hooker and acquainted with the project. William Fleetwood, recently appointed recorder of London, had served on the same committee with Hooker in the 1571 parliament.[11] Wroth and Knollys were MPs from well-known families.[12] Within six weeks of their visit Hooker had completed his translation of the *Modus* and his dedicatory epistles to the *Order and Usage*.

Internal evidence permits some concrete deductions and conclusions. From the proem it is clear that Hooker did not copy from an Irish version of the *Modus*.[13] Whereas copies of the Irish version refer to Henry II in the proem and contain only twenty-four chapters, Hooker follows the English ver-

---

10. See Richardson and Sayles, *Rotuli,* p. xix, and Frederic William Maitland, *Memoranda de Parliamento,* Rolls Series 98 (London, 1893): xi. From his speeches in parliament we know that Fleetwood professed knowledge of England's early legal and constitutional history; see Neale, *EP,* 1:196.

11. They served together on the committee concerned with a Bristol trade bill. Fleetwood was appointed recorder through Leicester's influence in 1571.

12. See the "List of members of the 1571 Parliament," Cheshire Record Office, DLT, Unlisted #6, ff. 38r–41r. Also see Neale, *EHC,* pp. 298, 301–02.

13. See Clarke, *Medieval Representation,* pp. 70–124, for a discussion of the Irish *Modus;* and see Robert Steele, *Tudor and Stuart Proclamations, 1485–1714,* 2 vols. (Oxford, 1910), 1:clxxxviii–cxcii for a printed version. The manuscript that Steele used had been seen by Cotton, Selden, and Hakewill and had been printed in 1692 by Anthony Dopping, bishop of Meath.

sion, which alluded to "regis Edward filii Ethelredi regis" and generally contained at least twenty-six chapters. Thus, while Hooker had access to the official archives of Ireland and actually used them for other purposes, he did not use any Irish versions that may have been available to him. In fact, all the evidence points to the conclusion that Hooker knew nothing about the Irish *Modus* and that the manuscript he used came from England not Ireland.

The English versions of the *Modus* available to Hooker can be divided into two groups on the basis of organization, chapter order, and textual variations. In both groups of manuscripts, according to the system devised by Hodnett and White and accepted by most scholars, the order of the first seven chapters is identical, while the remaining chapters are arranged along two different lines.[14] The first seven chapters detail the composition of parliament, while the others are concerned with parliamentary procedures and official personnel.

Hooker's *Modus* is an English translation of a Latin manuscript that is similar, but not identical, to the Gruthuyse MS 6049 printed by Duffus Hardy in 1846 and reprinted in Stubbes's *Select Charters*.[15] The proem is identical. The text is nearly identical. Hooker omits the chapter entitled "De Stationibus Loquentium," which sets forth the rules of debate in very brief and general terms. Hooker's rendition also contains more chapter headings. First, he separated the introductory statement on the summons to parliament from the section concerning clerical summons. Secondly, he separated the last sentence of the chapter entitled "De Inchoatione Parliamenti" and entitled it "Of the Proclamations." Similarly, he took the last paragraph of chapter XXVI, "De Partitione Parliamenti," and made it a new chapter entitled "For Billes and Petitions

14. Hodnett and White, "Manuscripts," especially pp. 210–11.
15. This version, first printed by D. L. D'Achery in *Spicilegium* (Paris, 1675), part xii, pp. 57–59, was edited by T. D. Hardy for the Record Commission (London, 1846). William Stubbs incorporated the latter in his *Select Charters* (Oxford, 1881), pp. 502–13.

of the Parliament." He also made minor changes in the text
and appended a short concluding statement that does not
appear in any other versions I have consulted.[16]

In his chapter "Days and Hours" Hooker omits a phrase
stating that parliament was to meet in a public place, not a
private or secret place. This seems to indicate, to borrow assumptions made by Hodnett and White, that Hooker used a
manuscript with a copyist error.[17] It is clear that Hooker's
Latin manuscript lacked the phrase that other versions possessed, including that from which Hakewill later made his
translation, to wit "et parliamentum debet teneri loco publico
at non in privato nee in occulto loco."[18] Hooker makes a
similar error in his chapter entitled "The Forme of Parliament":

> And also it is to be noted that the two principal Clarks of
> the Parliament for the king and his Councel, and other
> secondary Clarks, of whom and whose mencion *shalbe*
> heerafter made [see below p. 137].

As both Hardy and Hodnett have noted, the clerks had been
discussed in earlier chapters. Thus, it is evident that Hooker
used an old, uncorrected derivative of a manuscript in the B
category.[19]

English translations of the B type are more plentiful than the
A type.[20] At least three fifteenth-century B type manuscripts
are extant, but these must be rejected as Hooker's source on
grounds that he found and used a Latin manuscript rather than
an English transcript. At least six sixteenth- and seventeenth-
century English transcripts have been identified by Taylor:[21]

---

16. I have consulted the texts in the BL and MS E.L. 7976 at Huntington
Library.

17. Hodnett and White, "Manuscripts," p. 212.

18. Compare Stubbs, *Select Charters*, p. 508, and Hooker's translation.

19. Hodnett and White, "Manuscripts," pp. 210–12.

20. See Taylor, "The Manuscripts," p. 685.

21. Ibid., p. 688.

1.	Harley	1309
2.	"	2208
3.	"	3504
4.	"	7371
5.	Egerton	985
6.	Add.	12227

Of these, numbers 2, 3, and 6 bear close resemblance to the printed edition (Exeter) and the printer's copy in the College of Arms.[22] Of these three, Harley 2208 seems to be Hooker's translation of the *Modus*, seemingly a preprinter's copy.[23] The course of the manuscript's migration from 1572 to 1724, when it was purchased by Edward Harley from Nathaniel Noel, a London bookseller, remains an unsolved problem.[24]

The omission of the chapter on speaking in parliament demands further explanation.[25] It is possible, though unlikely, that Hooker merely copied from a manuscript version of the *Modus* that lacked that chapter. Or perhaps his omission was an oversight, a copyist error. However, there remains the possibility that Hooker excluded the chapter because he objected to it. In both Irish and English parliaments, it will be recalled, he was involved in incidents relating to speaking. In Ireland, his long-winded defense of the crown evoked criticism and hostility. In England, his voice was so inaudible that he did not deliver any formal speeches. One wonders if Hooker took offense at this rule and deliberately excluded it from his version.

---

22. Norah Evans completed collations of these but did not publish the results of her findings before her death in 1973. Her papers and notes were recently acquired by the BLO, but I have not yet had the opportunity of comparing her results with mine.

23. Very likely Harley 2208 is a copy of the translation rather than the original draft.

24. See Cyril Ernest Wright, *Fontes Harleiani* (London, 1972), pp. 253–55.

25. That chapter requires the peers to remain seated except when speaking, to enter and exit from one door, and to always speak from a standing position and give judgment from a sitting position.

Hooker's concluding statement, really a transitional phrase linking the two tracts on parliament, clearly reveals his views on the evolving nature of parliament:

> These orders in process' of time did surcesse and were out of all use, few or no Parlements beeing kept, from the time of William the Conqueror, until the reign of king Edward the first, who by the advise of his wise and learned Counsailers prescribed a forme and order how Parlements within this Realme should be observed and kept; whiche orders also in the course of certain yeeres grew out of use in many points, and the order heer ensuing is that which is in our dayes received and used [see below, p. 144].

Whereas Polydore Vergil and most other sixteenth-century historians traced the first parliament to the reign of Henry I or his Plantagenet successors, Hooker rejected this interpretation and accepted the attribution in the proem of the *Modus*.[26] In so doing he reflected the Saxonism of Archbishop Parker and his coterie of antiquarians. Just as the monarchy and the church could point to the impeccable ancestry of Saxon antiquity so could parliament. Just as legal antiquarians like William Lambarde could establish the pre-Conquest origins of England's laws so could Hooker substantiate the Saxonist beginnings of parliament with his publication of the *Modus*.

Hooker's concluding remarks plus the proem to the *Modus* contributed to the "Norman Yoke" legend later popularized by Sir Edward Coke in his parliamentary speeches and published writings.[27] In so doing, Hooker betrays a consistent provincial bias. Like countless other Elizabethans, he sub-

---

26. See Evans, "The Antiquity of Parliaments," pp. 206–08; Levy, *Tudor Historical Thought*, pp. 57–63 and passim; and McKisack, *Medieval History*, pp. 26–101.

27. See Christopher Hill, *Puritanism and Revolution* (London, 1958), pp. 50–122.

scribed to the Brut legend and its diverse implications.[28] The dissolution of the monasteries and the acquisition of medieval manuscripts by both ecclesiastical and secular scholars reinforced some of the fantastic legends associated with Brut and the founding of Britain. Moreover, those Elizabethans who perpetuated these legends believed what they read and wrote. Second generation antiquarians like Spelman and Selden, both more sophisticated and critical, would question these political myths and reject them for more accurate and reasonable interpretations.[29] But, when Hooker published his two tracts on parliament these mythological explanations prevailed.

Devonians like Hooker were particularly susceptible to these fictitious interpretations of Britain's past for they played on provincial pride. King Brut, the legendary founder of Britain, landed neither in Kent nor near London but in Devonshire near Totnes. Athelstan promulgated his laws in Exeter not Westminster. Similarly, parliament began not with William the Conqueror and his Norman successors but with the Anglo-Saxon kings, especially Edward the Confessor. In Hooker's view, in fact, William the Bastard destroyed those parliamentary practices which predated the Conquest. This distorted view of English political development proved most propitious, for it meant that the Elizabethan parliament was blessed with unquestionable ancestry and sanctified by centuries of time: the antiquity of parliament dated from Edward the Confessor; the continuity of parliamentary procedures dated from the days of Edward I, the English Justinian.

28. That Hooker subscribed to the legend is evident in his other writings, especially his history of Exeter and his pamphlet on the bishops of Exeter.

29. See Evans, "The Antiquity of Parliaments," pp. 216–19, and Pocock, *Ancient Constitution,* pp. 107–14, 137.

An Analysis of the *Order and Usage*

In his *Order and Usage how to keep a Parlement in England in these dayes* John Hooker provided his readers with an up-to-date description of parliament—its purpose, composition, structure, personnel, and modus operandi. Fully cognizant of the fact that the medieval *Modus Tenendi* was obsolete and, for all practical purposes, useless as a guide to contemporary proceedings in parliament, he sought to render an accurate portrayal of parliament in Elizabethan times. In publishing the two accounts side by side any literate Englishman could readily perceive the differences in medieval and modern parliaments. Hooker himself was influenced by the medieval *Modus,* this much is clear, for one can detect some similarities in organization, chapter headings, and phraseology. Yet, it is also evident that he did not slavishly imitate the medieval model, for he readily added, omitted, rearranged, and combined chapters and, more important, he changed the contents and emphases so much that his indebtedness to the *Modus* was minimal.

Instead of opening with a discussion of the composition of parliament—as did the *Modus*—Hooker began with an introductory section on the general nature and purpose of parliament. In his first chapter, entitled "By whome and for what cause a Parlement ought to be summoned and called," Hooker observed that parliaments were convened by the king—"by God's anoynted beeing the hed and cheef of the whole Realm" —and by him alone (see below, p. 145). Hooker did not employ the word *queen* or a neutral abstraction such as *sovereign* or *monarch.* Nor did he use the term *prince,* as did Sir Thomas Smith.[1] Rather, throughout his tractate Hooker utilized such

---

1. *De Republica Anglorum,* especially the second book. Though a contemporary of Hooker, Smith's work was published in 1583, six years after his death; however, his manuscript was circulated and portions of it were incorporated

masculine nouns and pronouns as *king, his,* and *he* to denote monarchial authority.

The king should summon parliaments for important matters affecting the nation: for those "weightie and great causes" requiring the "advice and counsel of all the estates of his Realm" (see below p. 146). In Hooker's eyes the first and foremost cause was religion. Because the king was God's "deputye and vicar in Earth"—a phrase strikingly similar to that later used by James I—he must provide leadership and laws to insure that God was honored in England by profession to the "true religion." To that end parliament should be called to reform the church and stamp out all "idolatries, false religions, heresies, schismes, errors, supersticions."[2] The phraseology confirms what we know about Hooker's Protestantism.

Next to religion were those vital secular matters relating to royal marriage, the succession, suppression of traitors, war, rebellion, civil wars, and the levying of taxes to preserve the monarchy. Lastly, parliament should be called to establish good laws and repeal those laws made obsolete by time. While Elizabeth never summoned a parliament specifically to deliberate on succession of her marriage—in fact, she attempted to prohibit all discussion of such matters!—the fact remains that these issues aroused great national concern and precipitated several petitions and much debate in the House of Commons. In truth, most Elizabethan parliaments were summoned to provide the crown with funds to sustain its ongoing military operations on the Continent and in Ireland. Nevertheless,

---

in the first edition of Holinshed's *Chronicles.* Hooker did not have access to the manuscript—at least there is no evidence of his being influenced by it—while Lambarde did.

2. See below p. 146. For the role of religion in Elizabethan parliaments see the writings of Neale, especially, "Parliament and the Articles of Religion, 1571," *EHR* 67 (1952): 510–21. Also see Hooker's "Journal," p. 490, for Lord Chancellor Bacon's speech, which touched upon the religious issues in that parliament.

Hooker's emphasis is understandable, for parliament passed
many pieces of ecclesiastical legislation between 1558 and
1571 and the lower house devoted a large portion of its deliberations to religious matters.

On this point the contrast between Hooker and the *Modus*
is most striking. In the *Modus* this whole topic was dealt with
superficially in a short chapter, "Of Matters of the Parliament," embedded in the middle of the tractate. Therein the
first and foremost purpose of calling a parliament was "warres
if there be any, of matters concerning the King or Queenes
person and of their children" (see below, p. 136). The second
purpose was to deliberate on "matters concerning the common weale, and to ordain new Lawes, debarring the olde
Lawes made in times past whose execution have been prejudi-
tiall"—a phrase that Hooker paraphrased toward the end of
his first chapter. The third and last purpose mentioned in the
Modus—namely, to adjudicate private matters—does not even
appear in Hooker's first chapter, although he was fully aware
of private bills.[3] To Hooker the overriding purposes of calling
a parliament were to give advice and counsel to the sovereign
on matters of national concern, to provide the crown with
funds, and, most important, to provide laws for the "great
causes" of religion, succession, heresy, rebellions, and civil
wars.

Hooker then proceeded to describe the composition of parliament and to spell out the different methods by which the
various groups were summoned. But, rather than follow the
Modus and devote six separate chapters to the topic—one to
each group summoned—he covered the subject in three chapters. In chapter two, short and general, he simply listed in
descending order the groups receiving writs of summons (see

3. Admittedly, Hooker does not discuss private legislation as such, but from
his comments on the fees paid to various personnel for assistance in the
passage of private bills it is clear that he knew of such legislation. Moreover, his experience in the 1571, as revealed in his "Journal" (especially pp.
490–92), exposed him to private bill legislation. See below p. 160.

below, p. 147). In chapter three he delved into a detailed description of how the lower clergy were selected to attend Convocation and in chapter four he explained the mechanics of county, city, and borough elections (see below, p. 149). Both of these chapters, besides being technical in nature, reflect the influence of the *Modus* upon the author.

In chapter five Hooker borrowed the title "Of the degrees of the Parliament" from the *Modus* and then proceeded to update the contents (see below, p. 150). Instead of the "six degrees or estates of the Parlement" in the *Modus*, he delineated only four degrees: (1) the king; (2) the lords, both spiritual and temporal; (3) the commonalty, including the knights, citizens, and burgesses; and (4) the clergy, meaning only the lower clergy, who met in Convocation and "have no voice in the Parlement." These four degrees sat in three separate "houses," as Hooker explained in chapter six (see below, p. 153). Thus, in Hooker's view, England had neither a unicameral nor a bicameral but a tricameral assembly. However, these houses were not coequal partners in the lawmaking process—even though they met and deliberated at the same time—for the "Upper house," which included the king and the lords, and the "Lower house," which included the knights, citizens, and burgesses, outranked the "Convocation house," composed only of the clergy. Nonetheless, though limited in scope to ecclesiastical matters, Convocation could not be excluded from any description or analysis of parliament.[4] In fact, Hooker devoted an entire chapter to Convocation and he touched upon that house in two other chapters. Yet, his relegation of Convocation to a subordinate place accurately reflects the changing constitutional structure of post-Reformation England.

4. On this score it is interesting to note that Sir Thomas Smith glossed over Convocation and the role of the clergy in parliament. For the importance of the clergy in 1571 see Neale, "Articles of Religion," pp. 511–14. The articles debated in that parliament had been considered in the 1566 session of Convocation.

Having asserted the tricameral structure of Parliament, Hooker next discussed each of the three houses. After briefly describing the "higher house" in general terms, he devoted separate chapters to the official personnel of that body: the Speaker, the chancellor or record keeper, the two clerks, the sergeant at arms, and the porters.[5] In a similar manner, after making several generalizations about the House of Commons, he allotted separate chapters to the Speaker, the clerk, and the sergeant of that house (see below, p. 164). His chapter on Convocation, though significant in being singled out for separate treatment, was short and succinct (see below, p. 174). The detail in these chapters, though quite accurate and exceedingly instructive, was not as well organized as the material in the early chapters.

The last five chapters of the tractate, though essential to the discussion, were not closely interrelated. Hooker devoted a chapter to those attending parliament by virtue of writs of assistance—"extraordinary persons"—and detailed their particular duties and functions (see below, p. 176). He borrowed from the *Modus* the title of his next chapter, "Of the Days and Hours to Sit in Parlement," but the contents differed considerably because of changed practices regarding plenary sessions of parliament (see below, p. 178).

In chapter nineteen Hooker analyzed the role of the king of parliament. He had touched upon the king's role in chapter one and listed the monarch as the first and foremost degree in chapter five. But, instead of proceeding to the king's role in chapter six, as one might expect, he dealt with the inferior

5. See below pp. 155–63. Hooker devotes two chapters to the responsibilities of the lord chancellor. In chapter 8 he details those duties connected with the speakership of the House of Lords. In chapter 9 he describes those clerical activities incumbent upon the lord chancellor after the session, namely those connected with the construction, preservation, and distribution of "the records of the Parlement and the Acts whiche be past." In his clerical capacity as recorder the chancellor was, according to Hooker, "the principall Clark of the higher house." This phrase disturbed Robert Bowyer; see below p. 159.

degrees and their respective "houses" first and then, as in the *Modus,* considered the king. To Hooker, the function of the king in the parliamentary process, while not central to the lawmaking process, was essential. The authority of the sovereign was necessary to initiate the summons and convene the component parts. The royal authority must be exercised in the approval or rejection of bills. The king was "the beginning and the ending of Parliament" and "without him and his authority nothing can be doon" (see below, p. 178).

Moreover, to insure the success of the deliberations the king must adhere to certain customs of the realm. Hooker used the words "ought to see to be kept" (see below, p. 178). Reflecting the medieval conception of kingship, that the king is bound by certain customs, Hooker then listed and commented upon the specific responsibilities and functions of the king-in-parliament. He must summon the appropriate individuals and groups at least forty days before the opening day and he must appoint certain parliamentary "officers." However, the king should not interfere in the local elections and he should not choose either the speaker of the House of Commons or the prolocutor of Convocation. Rather, to use Hooker's apt phrase, "they must be elected and chosen by the lawes, orders and customs of the Realme, as they were want and ought to be." Furthermore, the king should grant to every member of parliament the "auncient freedoms, priviledges, immunities, and customes during the Parlement." Hooker did not immediately elaborate upon these rights and privileges which the king should grant in response to the speaker's request; instead he treated them in the next chapter (see below, p. 183). However, he specified the times when the sovereign should be present either in person or by commission. Some of the phraseology in this chapter comes from the *Modus,* especially from the chapter entitled "Of the King's Absence."[6] Finally, the sovereign was also obliged to inform parliament in writing "all such

6. Compare pp. 140–41 with pp. 179–80.

things and matters of charge, as for which he calleth the said Parliament." This undoubtedly refers to the opening speech made by the sovereign's spokesman, usually the lord keeper or lord chancellor. This formal speech, besides establishing the purpose and parameters of the deliberations, was incorporated in the official records of parliament.

In the next chapter, the twentieth, Hooker proceeded to wax eloquently on "the dignitie, power, and authoritie of the Parlement" (see below, p. 181). Here, in his longest and most original chapter, he was less bound to the *Modus* and more openly committed to parliamentary government, although his organization leaves much to be desired. To Hooker, as to his emulator William Lambarde, parliament was a court: "the hiest, cheefest, and greatest Court that is or can be within the Realm."[7] Having established the juridical supremacy of parliament, he then demonstrated how the component parts of that body cooperated and concurred in the lawmaking process. Just as every inferior court has its own set of procedures governing its deliberations so the highest court has its own "laws and customs." These orders of parliament—to use Hooker's phrase—determine how the three estates of England, "the king, the Nobles and the Commoners," shall make their laws.[8]

The principle of concurrence was clearly enunciated by Hooker in the second paragraph of this chapter. The king by himself cannot declare the law. The king and either the Lords or the Commons cannot make laws. Similarly, the Lords and Commons cannot by themselves enact laws without the royal assent. Rather, only the three estates in concurrence can transform petitions (bills) into statutes. However, Hooker hypothecated an exception to this general rule and in so doing

7. See below p. 181. In *De Republica Anglorum*, Sir Thomas Smith touches upon parliament's judicial powers in his short paragraph-chapter entitled "Trial or judgement by parliament" (p. 64). Neither Hooker nor Smith allude to impeachment per se.

8. For a discussion of Hooker's concept of "estates" and its importance see below p. 103.

promulgated a doctrine bordering on political heresy. If duly summoned lords do not respond to the summons; or, if they absent themselves from the daily deliberations; or, if they obstruct the deliberations: then, under these extraordinary circumstances, the king and the lower house may concur and "establish any Act or Law." It is difficult to imagine an upper house so depleted by either the sessional or daily absentions that the deliberations there would grind to a halt, though one must admit that the low daily attendance during the last parliaments of Henry VIII and the depleted ranks during the Puritan Revolution (1643–48) argue for the plausibility of such a situation.

However, his contention that the upper house can be circumvented by the king and Commons when the Lords abstain or obstruct must have been deemed unorthodox in Elizabethan times. Here was an argument—an argument based upon the *Modus*—that one might expect to find in 1647 or in 1909. But Hooker goes even further, for he also promulgates the doctrine in positive terms:

> The King with the concent of his Commons (who are represented by the knights, citizens and burgesses) may obtain and establish any Act or Law, which are as good, sufficient and effectual: as if the Lords had given their consents [see below, p. 182].

Thus, under certain conditions, which must have seemed farfetched and unrealistic, two of the three estates involved in the lawmaking process could legislate without the assent of the third.

Does this same principle apply to the king and the upper house? Or, suppose the lower house abstained from coming to a session or obstructs, could the king ignore the Commons and combine with the Lords to make laws? Hooker's answer was an emphatic negative for both historical and logical reasons. In early days there was, in Hooker's view, no upper house—"there were no Prelats or Barons of the Parlement, and the Temporal Lords were very few or none"—and, consequently, "the King and his Commons did make a ful Parliament" (see below, p. 182). This antiquarian argument, however inaccurate, reflected Hooker's Saxonist views on the antiquity of English institutions in general. Hooker also employed logic to buttress his argument. Members of the upper house are summoned individually and, as such, they represent only themselves. Together they may possess common interests, they can be labeled an estate or class, but they cannot speak for the "Commons of the Whole Realme" or, to use a more modern term, the nation. Only the duly elected knights, citizens, and burgesses can speak for the "Commons of the Whole Realme." When sitting in parliament they do not represent themselves, as the Lords, rather they represent the "Commons of the Whole Realme."[9] When an MP consents to a law, he does so not only for himself, "but for all those also whom he is sent." Thus, on both historic and logical grounds the king and Commons are justified in making laws without the consent of the upper house. The priority and supremacy of the commonalty is implicit in Hooker's view which is at once reactionary and prophetic.

Hooker moved on to propound other modern-sounding political doctrines. The two predominant houses of parliament are coequal: neither is superior to the other. In times past all members summoned to a parliament met together, in one house as it were, but in due time "for the avoiding of confusion" they separated into two houses.[10] Nevertheless, even though the upper house reflected higher social rank and status

9. The *Modus* of course speaks of the essential role of the commonalty in parliament (see below p. 142), while many medieval documents dating from before and after the *Modus* used such phrases as "Community of the Kingdom" and "Community of the Realm." For a detailed discussion of the concept of *communitas* and its several derivatives see H. M. Cam, "The Theory and Practice of Representation in Medieval England," *History* 1 (1953): 11–26. Also see Clarke, *Medieval Representation*, pp. 154–77.

10. Hooker does not assign a date or reign to this bifurcation. Most historians, following McKisack and Chrimes, place the bifurcation in the late fourteenth and fifteenth centuries.

than the lower house, the two bodies "are of like and equall authoritie," according to Hooker. Not only are the two houses equal, but the persons summoned are also equal: all are peers of the realm. Both before and after parliament these individuals are unequal, but during the session all attendees were equal. The opinion of the lowest burgess, to borrow from Hooker, counted as much as the judgment of the greatest lord. One wonders how many other Elizabethans, especially MPs, shared these assumptions and conclusions.

Hooker then returned to a topic emphasized in the dedicatory epistle—namely the qualities of a good parliamentman—and reiterated some of his arguments. All members of parliament, irrespective of rank and status, should be "grave, wise, learned and expert men of the land, for such were the Senators of Rome" (see below, p. 183). These political virtues, so evident in the "Patres conscripti" who ruled Rome, should be present in those who make laws in England. Good laws, in effect, emanate from good men. But alas! The electoral processes of Tudor England did not insure the return to parliament of men possessing these virtues—this much we have learned from the dedicatory epistle—and herein is one of the inherent weaknesses of England's parliamentary monarchy. The responsibility for the return of wise and public-spirited lawmakers rested with the electorate. To these electors Hooker issued an appeal:

> They, therefore which make choice of knights, Citizens and Burgesses, ought to be wel advised that they doo elect and choose such as beeing to be of that assemblye, and therby equall with the great estates: should be grave, auncient, wise, learned, expert & careful men for their commonwealth [see below, p. 183].

If the electors do not return members with these qualities to Westminster, they harm not only themselves but the sovereign and the nation as well.

Once elected to parliament the member had certain rights, privileges and responsibilities, which Hooker then delineated.[11] The duly elected MP had the right of access and attendance or he was free "from all troubles, arrests and molestations." During the deliberations the MP was not actionable except in "causes of Treason, Murder and Fellony." Each member had the right to speak his mind and vote his conscience. He must speak to the matter under consideration— that is, his speech must be germane to the matter before the house—and he must only speak once per reading per bill. Moreover, he possessed the right to introduce bills and put forward petitions. Finally, a duly admitted lay member had the right to attend the deliberations or, to put it conversely, he cannot be disabled by his peers unless he is "excommunicated, outlawed or infamose."[12] If a cleric was returned to the lower house, somehow elected by oversight, he "ought and shalbe dismissed," Hooker writes; the proper place for the lesser clergy was Convocation.

Hooker then detailed the forms of political behavior expected of responsible members of parliament. An MP should be honest, sober, gentle, and attentive at all times. MPs should not taunt or deprecate each other in words or deeds. They should speak with a minimum of emotion and a maximum of reason. If a member violated these standards of behavior, he could be corrected and punished "by the advise and order of the residue of the House" (see below, p. 185). In Hooker's view each house—not the sovereign!—should judge and discipline its own members. If a member was found guilty of reprehensible conduct that required imprisonment, parliament possessed the authority to commit him.

11. See below p. 184. For a discussion of this subject see Neale, *EHC*, pp. 347–49, 362–64, and G. R. Elton, *The Tudor Constitution* (Cambridge, 1965), pp. 243–81.

12. In 1571 an attempt was made to expel John Garnons, an MP from Herefordshire who was excommunicate at the time of his election, but the final disposition of the case is not clear; see Neale, *EHC*, p. 150. Another MP, Thomas Long of Wiltshire, was found guilty of bribing two officials of Westbury to secure his seat; in all likelihood he was expelled, but again conclusive evidence is lacking.

At this juncture Hooker digressed for three paragraphs to discuss some of the judicial powers of parliament.[13] If parliament decides to commit one of its members, it possesses authority through the whole realm. Normally parliament used the Tower of London, but in fact it could utilize any and "all the Prisons, wardes, gailes within the Realme and the keepers of the same." Similarly, if any member was served or arrested by a lesser court, even chancery or common pleas, parliament possessed the authority to stay any legal action and release the party until the end of the session. Hooker's rationale was very simple: The Parlement beeing the hiest court, all other Courts yeeld and give place to the same (see below, p. 186). Sir Edward Coke's debt to Hooker for both the words and the arguments is obvious.[14]

Hooker devoted the remainder of the chapter to short statements and brief comments upon parliamentary procedures and privileges. Servants of members, like the members themselves, were free from molestation and arrest.[15] No nonsummoned persons were to attend the deliberations and all violators of this order could be punished as each house saw fit.[16] Deliberations in parliament were considered secret or, to use Hooker's language, "every person of the Parlement ought to keep secret and not to disclose the secrets and things spoke

13. Though he discusses some of the judicial functions of parliament, Hooker says nothing about attainder, impeachment, or the appellate jurisdiction of the upper house, all of which figure large in the writings of Sir Edward Coke. However, it should be noted that Smith and Lambarde have little more than Hooker on this subject.

14. See C. H. McIlwain, *The High Court of Parliament and Its Supremacy* (New Haven, 1910), and Pollard *EOP,* especially pp. 20–43, 61–63. William Lambarde was a very important link between Hooker and Coke; in particular, see his *Archeion: or a commentary upon the high courts of justice in England,* ed. C. H. McIlwain and P. L. Ward (Cambridge, Mass., 1957).

15. In the 1571 parliament there were several cases involving the servants of members; see D'Ewes, *ACJ,* p. 181.

16. In 1571 two visitors, both lawyers from Inner Temple, were removed from the lower house and committed to the Sergeant's Ward for violating this rule.

and doon in the Parlement."[17] Duly summoned MPs shall not
absent themselves unless they obtain a leave from the speaker.

Furthermore, each house had its own internal code of behavior and each member was expected to comply with its tenets. In the upper house each lord, before taking his place,
"ought to do his obeysance before the cloth of estate."[18]
When speaking, each lord must remove his hat, stand, and
speak his mind "plainly, sensibly, and in decent order." Messengers must remain outside the inner door until properly
identified and summoned; upon entering, they must follow a
series of ritualistic actions before approaching the bar with
their message. It would appear that Hooker obtained his information either by personal observation or from someone in the
upper house well acquainted with such details.

The lower house, similarly, possessed its formal code of
behavior.[19] Each member, before taking his place, must genu-
flect before the Speaker's chair. Once seated, he should be
"grave, wise and expert." Moreover, he should be properly
attired, that is, in nonmilitary garb consistent with his role as
lawmaker. Even though those commoners with the highest
rank and status, namely the knights of the shire, were supposed to be "girded with the sword" and skillful in feats of
arms, as parliamentary writs so demanded, when the duly
elected knight entered parliament he appeared without his
sword and military apparel. Hooker's reasoning is sound and
his words are grandiloquent:

17. See below p. 187. This rule was of course broken in various and sundry
ways. Privy councillors in both houses informed the queen, as one might
expect, while members of the House of Commons kept their constituents
informed through letters and reports. Also, it is clear from the correspondence and reports of foreign ambassadors that news about parliamentary
deliberations was leaked out by those in attendance.

18. See below pp. 187–88. These and other orders of the House of Lords
were studiously garnered by a select committee in 1621 and approved by the
plenary body as Standing Orders; see *Manuscripts of the House of Lords,* ed.
Maurice F. Bond (London, 1953), pp. xxxix–xlvi, 1–27.

19. See below p. 188. The lower house, in contrast to the upper, did not
authenticate Standing Orders until the eighteenth century.

> . . . the Parliament house is a place for wise, grave and good men, to consult, debate, and advice how to make Lawes, and orders for the common welth, and not to be armed as men redy to fight, or to trye matters by the Sword [see below, p. 188].

Parliament, in short, was a lawmaking court: good laws resulted from a contest of words not swords.

Hooker next turned to the procedures governing the passage of bills into statutes.[20] He does not give as many details as William Lambarde nor does he arrange his six short paragraphs into a perceptible pattern. Yet, his comments instructively reveal that the process was much like that used in a modern legislature.[21] Each bill introduced must be read three times on three separate days. A bill could be rejected or approved at any stage. If a bill was unanimously rejected on the first or second reading, or if it was "overthrown" by a majority after the third reading, it could not be reintroduced during the same session. If a bill met general approval but required some emendations to meet objections, it was committed—that is, assigned to a group of members empowered to recommend changes to the whole house. The committee, however, did not possess the authority to conclude; rather, "onely to order, reforme, examin and amend the thing committed unto them," after which the bill was returned to the house for further consideration (see below, p. 189). If the committee altered the bill's substance, the whole house must treat it as a new bill and read it three times; if, on the other hand, the committee merely changed words, the house could treat it as the original bill and proceed to the final reading. After the third reading, the bill was either rejected or approved and then forwarded to the other house.

20. Hooker's comments are not as complete as those of Lambarde, but they are more detailed than those of Sir Thomas Smith. However, their writings were published posthumously, Smith's in 1583 and Lambarde's in 1641.

21. Sir John Neale used Hooker's "Journal" and knew of the printed edition of the *Order and Usage,* but he preferred the early draft in the EXRO.

The rules of debate dovetailed with the above procedures. At any stage in the process, that is, after any of the three readings, a member could speak for or against the bill. However, though his words had to be germane to the subject, only the Speaker could intervene with a reminder or reprimand. As in the upper house, each commoner was expected to stand "with all reverence, gravitie and seemly speech and declare his mind" (see below, p. 190). However, when the member was judging, that is when he was voting to allow or reject a measure, he was to remain seated, for he was a judge in the high court of parliament. A member might change his opinion; he might, in fact, speak for a bill in committee and against it in a plenary session.

Hooker concluded his longest and most significant chapter with a paragraph that logically belonged near the beginning. Every commoner, he stated, before entering parliament should be sworn in and take an oath acknowledging the king to be the supreme and only governor of the realm and to renounce all foreign sovereigns. This "order" of parliament, first put into practice in 1571 as a result of the 1563 Act of Supremacy, had the effect of eliminating all Roman Catholics from the House of Commons.[22] No doubt Hooker was among those to whom the lord steward administered the oath during the opening days of the session.

Hooker devoted his last chapter to procedures governing the beginning and ending of parliament. In so doing he combined two chapters of the *Modus* and rendered an updated account of the Elizabethan practices (see below, p. 191). He described the formal ceremonies connected with the opening of the session, especially those ceremonies involving members of both houses, and then detailed the more functional activities of the second and third days such as the presentation of the Speaker of the lower house to the king and his acceptance speech. Hooker then switched, without any transitional sen-

---

22. See D'Ewes, *ACJ*, p. 156. For a discussion see Neale, *EHC*, pp. 338, 375. This law did not apply to the members of the upper house and, consequently, Roman Catholic peers could and did attend the deliberations.

tence or paragraphs, to the formal procedures prevailing at
the end of each session: the final oration of the Speaker of the
House of Commons; the answer of the Speaker of the House
of Lords; the reading of the bills which have passed both
houses; the assent or disapproval by the sovereign; and the
final prorogation or dissolution pronouncement by the lord
chancellor. "And this is called the last or end of the Parlement," Hooker concluded, "and every man is at libertie to
departe homewards" (see below, p. 194).

To maximize the utility of his tract John Hooker appended
a list of those "personages as ought to appear and be in the
Parlement (see below, p. 195). The first portion, composed of
those summoned to appear in the House of Lords, began with
the king and ended with those summoned by writs of assistance (namely the judges, the king's attorney, the sergeants at
law, the king's solicitor, and the king's learned counsel). Below
the king Hooker placed "the Lord Speaker," as one might
expect, but he then listed proctors from France, Scotland, the
Duchy of Aquitaine, the Duchy of Guisne, and the Duchy of
Anjou. Why Hooker included these as summons-worthy and
dubbed them proctors is not clear. Perhaps he confused them
with the "auditores" or "triers of petitions"—that is, those
lords appointed to hear petitions from the non-English do-
mains. Perhaps he misunderstood the role of the triers and
auditors and, not being a member of the upper house, mis-
judged their function. Whatever the case, he then went on to
list in descending order the spiritual lords, the temporal lords,
and finally those summoned by writs of assistance. Lest some
of his contemporaries question his list of temporal lords,
Hooker appended two short but significant paragraphs explaining criteria for membership in the upper house. Each
baron ought to be summoned to parliament and assume a
place "according to his degree." At the same time, Hooker
explained, those sons of dukes, marquesses, and earls who are
barons while their fathers were alive had no right to a summons unless they received a special summons from the king or
were advanced to a higher rank by marriage.

Hooker's list of members summoned to the House of Com-

mons is based upon rank (see below, p. 198). He could have
listed the members along geographical or alphabetical lines.
But, instead, following the contemporary criterion of status so
evident in the body of the tractate, he divided his list of commoners into several categories:

    1. Knights of the Shire
       a. English counties
       b. Welsh counties
    2. Citizens
    3. Barons of the Five Ports
    4. Burgesses
       a. English boroughs
       b. Welsh boroughs

Within these groupings there is no perceptible rationale for
the arrangement unless it be a garbled alphabetical one. Nowhere in either the body of the tract or his appendix did
Hooker give the reader a numerical picture of either house: his
observations and analyses were invariably qualitative in nature. Nonetheless, he fully realized that the House of Commons like the House of Lords had grown in size and could be
enlarged.[23] The king possessed the authority to create a new
country, to incorporate a new borough, and to send parliamentary writs to these newly established electoral units. Those
duly elected representatives from the new counties and
boroughs, he concluded, possessed all the rights and privileges of the older constituencies sending members to "the
high Court of Parlement."

    In conclusion, Hooker neither propounded a general theory
of government or law nor did he put forward a theory of
legislation. Rather, he provided his readers with a descriptive
analysis of lawmaking in Elizabethan England. In this description, though superficially resembling the *Modus,* Hooker rendered a fairly accurate depiction of parliament—its structure,

23. For Hooker's comments at the end of each list see below pp. 198, 204.

composition, personnel, and modus operandi. His analysis of
the House of Commons, though somewhat repetitious, is quite
comprehensive and complete. His account of Convocation is
very brief, as one might expect, and his description of the
House of Lords contains some minor inaccuracies. Hooker's
rhetoric, his arguments and organization, and his conclusions
all reflect a past-conscious citizen strongly committed to parliamentary monarchy and partial to the preeminence of the
House of Commons in the lawmaking process. Moreover, the
Order and Usage, when placed in the context of the dedicatory
epistles and the English *Modus,* is more than simply a descriptive analysis. Implicit therein is a theory of corporate lawmaking. English laws are made in a court, "the high Court of
Parlement," which had evolved from a unicameral body in the
reign of Edward the Confessor to a multicameral assembly
involving hundreds of Englishmen. The lawmaking process
involves four degrees and three estates. Each house possesses
its own modus operandi, distinct functions, and powers in the
making of laws. The personal role of the monarch and the
influence of the clergy are declining, it is evident, while the
collective power and privileges of the third estate, represented
in Commons, is increasing. Also implicit in Hooker's tract is
a theory of representation—a curious blend of classical ideals,
medieval practices, and West Country prejudice. Such were
the "modern" views of an intelligent civilian lawyer from the
provincial city of Exeter.[24]

24. Hooker's methodology and point of view bore a closer affinity to civil-
ians Sir Thomas Smith and Sir Thomas Wilson than to William Lambarde, Sir
Edward Coke, William Hakewill, and Henry Elsyng, all trained in common
law. He did not search the journals for precedents, as did Lambarde; he did
not probe the rolls of parliament, as did Coke; he did not cite cases, as did
Hakewill and Elsyng. Rather, he searched for earlier analyses like the *Modus*
and consulted other treatises on government; in so doing he reflected the
preconceptions of an antiquarian trained in civil law. Nevertheless, his tractate
served the interests of those trained in the Inns of Court.

The Influence and Significance

If John Hooker hoped to reap any immediate political benefits from his twin tracts on parliament, as has been suggested above as a possible motive, he was disappointed. He was not elected to the next English parliament; nor did he sit in any subsequent Irish parliament. Moreover, his hope that Sir William Fitzwilliam would introduce his up-to-date guide to English parliamentary procedures as the official model for Ireland went unfulfilled. In fact, during Fitzwilliam's short tenure as lord deputy (1571–75), he did not even convene a parliament and, therefore, had no need for Hooker's advice and guide.[1]

However, Hooker did live to see the fruits of his labors utilized in the next Irish Parliament. In April 1585 Sir John Perrot convened Elizabeth's third and last Irish Parliament, which met off and on for over a year. Using his authority as lord deputy, Perrot sought to Anglicize the proceedings from beginning to end.[2] He insisted that English dress be used

1. Sir William held several high offices in Ireland under the earl of Sussex and Sir Henry Sidney, but during the latter's administration he unsuccessfully sought permission to return to England for reasons of health and poverty. Instead, he was appointed lord deputy 11 December 1571 and sworn in office 13 January 1572. It was during his administration that Sir Thomas Smith and the earl of Essex attempted to subdue and colonize Ulster. Sir William himself was obliged to wage war in Munster against the earl of Desmond, who was released from prison in 1573. After capturing Desmond in 1574, Sir William became so seriously ill that he was replaced by his predecessor, Sir Henry Sidney, and returned to England soon thereafter. See *DNB*, 7:232–34, which is based upon vols. 55–58 of the Carte Papers in the BLO. Unfortunately the Fitzwilliam Papers, while containing much information on Ireland, reveal nothing about Hooker or the *Order and Usage*. Also see Richard Bagwell, *Ireland Under the Tudors*, 3 vols. (London, 1890), 3:140–52.

2. See F. J. Routledge, "The Journal of the Irish House of Lords in Sir John Perrot's Parliament," *EHR* 29 (1914): 104–17, and C. Litton Falkiner, "The

during the deliberations—a requirement which caused embarrassment to some Irish leaders who were ridiculed by the Dublin masses. He also encouraged some unsummoned Irish nationals to observe the parliamentary deliberations—"to see *the order thereof*"—a move probably designed to educate them in English ways.[3] Several pieces of legislation reflected this same policy. Perrot's plan also involved the formal adoption of Hooker's *Order and Usage* as the official guide to parliamentary procedures. The evidence of this adoption derives from several sources. In his capacity as continuator of Holinshed's *Chronicles* Hooker took it upon himself to incorporate in the volume pertaining to Ireland a version of his *Order and Usage*. After reprinting the title from the Exeter edition, which credited him as author, he added the phrase: "and the like used in hir majesties realm of Ireland."[4] He included only the *Order and Usage* in this reprint, omitting all the introductory material in the two editions published in 1572, and he did not include his rendition of the *Modus*.

The anachronistic context in which the *Order and Usage* appears in Holinshed's *Chronicles* has produced both misunderstanding and misinterpretation. Hooker inserted his *Order and Usage* in the narrative encompassing Sir Henry Sidney's administration and the parliament convened in 1569 rather than

Parliament of Ireland Under the Tudor Sovereigns: with some notices of the Speakers of the Irish House of Commons," in *Proceedings of the Royal Irish Academy* 25 (1904–05): 508–41.

3. See Rawlinson D. 922, f. 49. The phrase comes from "Advice and directions for summoning a Parliament in Ireland," written by an undisclosed lawyer between 1585 and 1601, taken from Dublin to England by Sir William Gerrard and later found among Selden's papers. It is described and briefly extracted in *Analecta Hibernica* (Dublin, 1931), pp. 83–84.

4. (1586 ed.), 2:121. Between this phrase and the first paragraph of the *Order and Usage* Hooker incorporated the following: "And here you must note, that what the kings and queenes of England do in their persons in England, the same is done in Ireland by the lord deputie, and who in the like parlement robes and under the like cloth of estate representeth her maieste there in all things."

in the section covering Sir John Perrot's administration. His insertion at this point in the narrative, though anachronistic, is understandable for it demonstrated the personal motives behind his research and the causal factors leading to the ultimate adoption of the *Order and Usage* by the next Irish parliament. Nonetheless, some commentators have erroneously assumed that the *Order and Usage* was adopted in the 1568–70 parliament and others, not finding any record of that adoption, apparently have completely ignored Hooker's claim.[5]

However, this claim is verified in some documents preserved in the Rolls Office in Dublin.[6] These include two summons lists, one for the 1560 parliament and another for the 1585 parliament, both held in Dublin. Attached to the latter is a fragment entitled "Orders to be kept and observed in the Lower or Common House of Parlyament." All nine paragraphs were extracted from Hooker's *Order and Usage* and, as the following clearly indicates, many of the words and phrases are identical:

> Ffirst, that every knyght, cyttizen, and burgesse, at his entre into the howse, make his dutyfull and humble obeisance, and after to take his place.
>
> Item, that every knyght, cyttizen, and burges, during the tyme of his abode in the said howse, be apparayled in his gowne, having no armor nor weapon about him.

5. The perpetuator of this misunderstanding was Viscount Mountmorres, who in his *History of the principal transactions of the Irish Parliament (1634–66)*, 2 vols. (London, 1792), entitled his section "Mr. Hooker's Account of the Method of Proceeding in the Parliament which was held by Sir Henry Sidney, in the eleventh Year of Elizabeth" (1:68–86). Immediately after this account, which is borrowed from Holinshed, Mountmorres reprinted the *Order and Usage* (pp. 87–152). In "Sir John Perrot's Parliament," p. 105, Routledge falls into the same error in attributing Hooker's "rule of procedure for the guidance of *this* parliament," meaning 1568.

6. These documents, first found and published by William Lynch, *A View of the Legal Institutions . . . in Ireland* (London, 1830), pp. 341–51, were reprinted by James Hardiman in appendixes II and III of his *Tracts relating to Ireland* (Dublin, 1843).

Itm, eche knyght, cyttizen and burges, in uttering his mynd to any bill, to use and frame his speache after a quyet and curtyous maner, without any taunts or wordes tendyng to the reproche of any person in this said howse assembled.

Itm, as eche person, here assembled, hath graunted unto hym free libertie of speach, in declarying his mynd and opynion to eche matter proponed, so likewise he is to speake but ones to every reading of any bill.

Itm, if any offend or mysbehave hymself in this howse, his punyshment ys to be consydered of, and assygned by the speaker, with thadvise and assent of the residue of the howse.

Itm, that no cyttizen, knyght or burges of this howse absent or departe from the same, ether for cause of sicknes or otherwise, without notice given to the speaker, and lycence had, and such lycence to be recorded.

Itm, any knyght, cyttizen, or burges mynding to speck to any bill, most, duryng the tyme of the said speche, stand and remayne uncovered.

Itm, no knyght, cyttizen, or burges disclose the secretes, either spoken or done in this said howse, to any stranger not being of the same howse, under payne of souche punyshment, as by the specker, with thassent of the residue of the howse, shalbe lymyted.

Itm, yf during the tyme of parlyament, any of this howse, his servantes or goods, be sued, arested or vexed, contrary to the auncient customes in souche cases used, the speaker ys, upon informacon thereof to hym gyven, to send the serjant at armes to souche courte, to declare the person so troubled to be of the parlyament, and therupon requyring the officers thereof to stay in further proceeding therin; whiche, being dysobeyed, the party or officer so doyng ys by auctoritie from the speaker, to be sent for, and to be imprysoned, and receive punyshment, according the

discrecyon of the howse, to be assigned and laid
downe.[7]

It would appear that this was a fragmentary portion of a larger
document drawn up by some official attending Perrot's parliament of 1585, either a clerk or the master of the rolls, in whose
office they were uncovered.[8]

The details surrounding the official adoption of Hooker's
Order and Usage elude us. Perhaps Perrot himself imposed
these parliamentary rules as part of his Anglicizing program.
Perhaps an Irish official or English MP recommended their
introduction. Perhaps Perrot or one of his subordinates received instructions from English officials or recommendations
from Sir William Fitzwilliam. Perhaps Hooker himself persuaded Perrot to use his *Order and Usage*. The two men knew
each other, evidently, at least they had met earlier when Perrot
was president of Munster and Hooker served as Sir Peter
Carew's solicitor.[9] We also know from the laudatory remarks
in Holinshed's *Chronicles* that Hooker, if not a personal friend,
idolized Perrot and admired his policies and administration.[10]
Yet, there is no evidence that Hooker himself was in Ireland
when Perrot convened his parliament, therefore the *Order and
Usage* was introduced through an intermediary whose identity
remains unknown.[11]

7. Ibid., p. 143. "The orders are endorsed on the preceding list of the
Parliament of A. D. 1585," he added in a footnote.

8. Sir Nicholas White was master of the rolls in 1585.

9. Sir John Perrot, a natural son of Henry VIII and hence a brother of
Elizabeth I, enjoyed royal favor throughout the reign. He sat in the 1566
English parliament, where he undoubtedly acquired first-hand experience and
knowledge, but it would appear that he did not sit in any Irish parliaments
before 1585. For Hooker's connection see Holinshed, *Chronicles* (1808 ed.),
6:368–69. Also see Herbert Wood, *Sir James Perrot, The Chronicle of Ireland
1584–1608* (Dublin, 1933), and S. E. C. *The The Governance of Ireland Under Sir
J. Perrot* (London, 1626).

10. Ibid., pp. 371, 456.

11. Hooker was in England working on the revised edition of Holinshed's
Chronicles at the time.

The absence of an official journal of the House of Commons in 1585–86 precludes an inquiry into the actual application of Hooker's *Order and Usage* in the lower house. However, the existence of a short account of deliberations in the upper house affords additional verification and some insights into the status of parliamentary procedures.[12] The account differs from Hooker's diary for the 1568–69 parliament, for it is a formal record of the official acts of the House of Lords written in the third person. It has the characteristics of a journal; in fact, its editor calls it "the earliest fragment of the original journals of the Irish parliament."[13] Here, it should be recalled, Hooker included in his chapter entitled "Clerk of the Parliament" the mandatory requirement: "He must keep true records and true entries of all things there doon and to be entred" (see below, p. 160). Thus, if not before, in the third and last parliament of Elizabeth an official record was made and retained by a clerk in the Irish House of Lords.

It is possible to extract from this journal certain facts and deductions pertaining to procedures and personnel. The two houses met separately.[14] The lord chancellor presided over the upper house, as in England, and the lord deputy appeared at the beginning and end of each session. Each bill was read three times on separate days before putting it to the question for final approval. The lords voted by voice, it seems, and abided by the majority principle. Some bills were "dashed," while others were passed and then either sent to the House of Commons or held for the lord deputy's decision. Contrary to rules embedded in Poynings' Law, they even amended bills by adding a "proviso." Bills were engrossed after their second reading. Some bills originated in the Commons, others in the

---

12. Routledge reproduced this journal in "Sir John Perrot's Parliament," pp. 111–17.

13. Ibid., p. 105.

14. Ibid., especially pp. 111–17, for the points raised in this paragraph. For a more general discussion of procedures see Falkiner, "The Parliament of Ireland," pp. 508–31.

Lords, but all had to be read thrice in each house before presentation to the lord deputy. We also learn that the upper house had select committees and that the two houses held a joint conference during the second session. The clerk's use of the phrase "manner and forme," when added to the above facts, leads one to conclude that the Irish House of Lords followed English procedures and to infer that Hooker's *Order and Usage* served as the guide.

During the last week of Perrot's parliament a petty dispute erupted over the fees allotted to certain parliamentary personnel. The nature and significance of this dispute cannot properly be understood without reference to the *Order and Usage*. In the English House of Lords, to quote Hooker,

> there is but one Sergeant whiche hath the charge of keeping of the doores . . . he must attend and go alwaies with his mace before the Speaker, unless he be Lord Chauncellor, or keeper of the great Seale, for then he hath a Sergeant of his owne [see below, p. 162].

This statement could evoke an ambiguous interpretation. To begin with Hooker says there is "but one Sergeant," but he then goes on to state that the lord chancellor also has "a Sergeant of his owne."

In Ireland, this ambiguity was not at first apparent. The lord chancellor by custom appointed a gentleman usher to attend him, it would appear, and the sergeant at arms attended to routine duties in the upper house as outlined by Hooker. However, in May 1586, when it came time for the payment of fees and rewards assigned to the office, the ambiguous statements in Hooker's *Order and Usage* provoked different interpretations and a dispute. The sergeant at arms laid claim to the "benevolence given from the lords," whereupon the gentleman usher countered with his own claim.[15] The lords, in any case, were not about to pay double. A select committee appointed to

15. Ibid., p. 116.

resolve the differences decided against the former and for the latter. The lord chancellor should have had his own sergeant but "hathe none," the committee reported, but in effect the gentleman usher served in that capacity and thus deserved the fees and rewards. But they went even further. The sergeant at arms should be serving in the House of Commons, they insisted, attending the needs of the Speaker of that house and receiving his compensation from that body—not the House of Lords. The committee appealed to Hooker to resolve the problem, evidently, for the phrase "that the chauncellor should have a serjant at armes of his own," thus recorded in the journal, came from the *Order and Usage*.[16]

It would appear from the above evidence that the introduction of Hooker's *Order and Usage* constituted an integral part of Perrot's Irish policy. In all likelihood Perrot knew of the unruly and unparliamentary behavior which had prevailed in Sir Henry Sidney's parliament. Most likely he had a copy of the *Order and Usage,* probably the Irish edition dedicated to Sir William Fitzwilliam, and hoped that its imposition would produce a less hostile and more congenial parliament. If he hoped that the *Order and Usage* would induce subservience, however, he was mistaken indeed, for the House of Lords dashed seven bills out of nine and the House of Commons opposed his scheme to commute cess into a more equitably levied tax.[17] Moreover, Perrot's attempt to repeal Poynings' Law, while squeaking through the upper house by one vote, was rejected by the lower house by a rather large majority. Nevertheless, it would appear that Elizabeth's third and last parliament, if not accommodating to Perrot and his masters in England, proved to be more decorous and less disorderly than the second parliament.

That the Irish parliament needed a set of rules, a modus operandi, had become obvious in 1569. The old rules embed-

16. Ibid., p. 117.
17. Ibid., p. 106.

ded in the Irish *Modus* were obsolete, of course, as was the English *Modus*.[18] In England, parliament met frequently enough during the sixteenth century so that the unwritten rules of usage, which had in effect superceded the *Modus*, were transmitted from one parliament to the next by experienced MPs, leaders, and clerical personnel. In Ireland, however, parliament met less frequently and the turnover of personnel was considerable.[19] Moreover, from the newly created county and borough seats came not only inexperienced MPs but backwoodsmen with grievances aplenty. One might expect that the initiative which the leaders in Dublin and Westminster possessed would have forestalled the appearance and growth of a parliamentary opposition, but such was not the case. There was a hostile antigovernment faction in 1569, as we have seen, and there were similar groups in 1585 and 1613.[20] Thus, while Hooker hoped that more decorous deliberations would result from reliance upon his parliamentary code, very likely the lord deputy and his cohorts looked to Hooker's *Order and Usage* as a means to contain and restrain opposition in the Irish parliament.

Once adopted, Hooker's *Order and Usage* remained the basis for parliamentary procedures in Ireland—at least in the House of Commons—for decades thereafter. The manner and form of the next parliament, that of 1613–14 in which Sir John Davies was Speaker of the lower house, evidently followed Hooker. The Irish *Journals of the House of Commons* contain references to "Rules of Parliament," presumably those borrowed from Hooker, and to precedents in the "last Parliament," meaning Perrot's 1585 parliament.[21] The committee

18. On the Irish *Modus* and its significance see Clarke, *Medieval Representation*, pp. 70–124; H. G. Richardson and G. O. Sayles, *The Irish Parliament in the Middle Ages* (London, 1967).

19. D. B. Quinn, "Parliaments and Great Councils in Ireland, 1461–1586," 3 (1942–43): 60–77.

20. See Moody, "Irish Parliament under Elizabeth and James I," pp. 42–71.

21. *The Journals of the House of Commons of the Kingdom of Ireland*, 20 vols. (Dublin, 1796–1800), 1:23, 62. Also see William Farmer, *A Chronicle of Lord*

system seems to be more mature, for there is one committee concerned with disputed elections and another "Grand Committee" dealing with privileges. The daily meetings take place in the morning, as in England, and the committees sit in the afternoon. Besides a Speaker, the Commons has a clerk of the house and a sergeant at arms. There are references to precedents, privileges, and per diem wages. The Irish House of Commons in 1613–15, like its English counterpart during the reign of Elizabeth, was maturing into an independent and self-conscious body. On one occasion the lower house expelled, committed, and fined one of its own members; on another it ruled that a Star Chamber subpoena violated parliamentary privilege.[22] The opposition complained of the presence of royal officials, especially judges and the king's learned counsel, and of nonresident MPs in the lower house; however, they did not succeed in excluding them from parliament. Nevertheless, it is clear that the introduction of Hooker's *Order and Usage*, while providing for a more orderly assembly, not only served the interests of the Anglo-Irish Establishment. Rather, the *Order and Usage* also provided the opposition with an arsenal of parliamentary procedures, privileges, and rights that could be turned to their advantage.

A generation later, in 1634, the Irish House of Commons reaffirmed its commitment to the procedures established by Perrot and Davies. Under the date of 18 July 1634 the clerk entered in the journal the following order:

Chichester's Government of Ireland (London, n.d.), especially pp. 167–77, and *Historical Tracts by Sir John Davies* (Dublin, 1787), pp. 187, 293, 313. It is clear from his tract, *A Discovery*, that Sir John Davies, Speaker of the Irish House of Commons in 1613–15, was acquainted with Holinshed's *Chronicles*, Giraldus Cambrensis, and the Irish parliament of 1568. In all likelihood his knowledge of the last-mentioned came from Hooker's account which preceded the *Order and Usage*.

22. For a discussion of parliamentary procedure see J. R. O'Flanagan, *The Lives of the lord chancellors and keepers of the great seal of Ireland*, 2 vols. (Dublin, 1870), 1:298–301, 318–19, 371–72.

It is ordered by the House, for avoiding of Disorder in the
Proceedings of the House, that the Orders and Usages of
the House be entered with the Clerk; and that he shall give
Copies thereof unto such as desire them, to the end those
that have not been formerly acquainted with the Orders
of Parliaments, may the better inform themselves how to
demean themselves in the House.[23]

To cure the chronic maladies of the Irish parliament—namely,
a few sessions, newly created seats, inexperienced MPs, and
the threat of unparliamentary behavior—once again the *Order
and Usage* was affirmed by the lower house and became part of
the official record. This explains why Lord Mountmorres prefaced his edition of the Irish parliamentary journals with a
copy of Hooker's *Order and Usage*.[24]

Hooker's influence in England proved to be less direct and
more diffused in nature. Among antiquarians and historians
Hooker possessed an enviable reputation. His researches on
Exeter were used by Francis Godwin, bishop of Hereford, in
his ecclesiastical writings.[25] In his *Britannia* William Camden
relied upon Hooker for his description of Exeter and lauded
his erudition.[26] Sir Thomas Wilson, author and royal archivist,
considered Hooker one of the "best writers" to contribute to
Holinshed's *Chronicles*.[27] And, as we have seen above (p. 22),
his scholarship won the praise of Sir Richard Carew. In short,

23. *CJ*, 1:90.
24. See his *History*, 1:87–155. He uses the Holinshed version, this much is
evident from internal evidence, and he seems to be unaware of both the Exeter
and the Fitzwilliam editions.
25. *A Catalogue of the Bishops of England* (London, 1601), p. 315, and the Latin
translation *Ad Commentarium de Praesulibus Angliae* (London, 1643), pp. 452,
457, 465–71.
26. See BL, Cotton MS, Titus F. VI. ff. 88–93 for the manuscript copy of
Hooker's description of Exeter used by Camden in the preparation of *Britannia*. Camden also praised Hooker's erudition: "vir eruditus, et de antiquita-
tis studio optime meritus"; see Arthur Cayley, *Sir Walter Ralegh* (London,
1805), p. 2.
27. See Dean Gunter White's memo on the Carew MSS in LP.

Hooker's reputation as a civic archivist and provincial antiquarian is easy to document.

Yet, it is more difficult to pinpoint his place in parliamentary history. He never became a leader in the lower house. He never served parliament in a clerical capacity. Though an MP in two parliaments, he served on few committees and rarely spoke. His was the role of a silent, methodical, and observing back-bencher. Very likely he commingled with other MPs, especially those from the West Country who shared his prejudices and the antiquarians who shared his interests, and possibly he worked behind the scenes or in the public houses, but again there is no record that he propagandized his views through these means. In all likelihood he regarded the earl of Bedford as his patron and the puritans in the lower house as political allies, but the evidence is inferential in nature.[28]

Despite his obscurity as a member of parliament, Hooker occupies a unique niche in parliamentary history. He was the first MP to record and preserve his experiences in diaries. He was the first political commentator to publicize the antiquity of parliament through an English translation of the *Modus*.[29] Moreover, he was the first Englishman to provide his contemporaries with a reasonably accurate insider's view of "the high court of Parliament"—its composition, structure, and inner workings. And, most important, he put forward in his twin editions of the *Order and Usage* a vigorous apology for the

28. I have found no direct connections between Hooker and Bedford, but we know that Hooker lived near Bedford's residence in Exeter. We also know that Hooker praised Bedford (then Lord Russell) in his history of Exeter and that he dedicated two unpublished manuscripts to him. Moreover, Bedford's circle of influence included several of Hooker's friends: Sir Peter Carew, Sir William Fitzwilliam, and Edward Bridgeman. Unfortunately, my efforts to search the Russell papers for connections and for information about Bedford's circle were frustrated.

29. Other Elizabethans such as Thomas Egerton used the *Modus* before Hooker, but he was the earliest to print and distribute his English translation. He antedates Hakewill, whose translation was published posthumously in 1641.

preeminence, powers, and privileges of the House of Commons.

Nonetheless, in spite of these achievements, Hooker's activities have been obscured, neglected, and frequently misunderstood. The reasons for this oversight and lack of acclaim are several. As a political commentator, Hooker was overshadowed by Sir Thomas Smith, whose *De Republica Anglorum* was published posthumously and in part reproduced in a conspicuous place in Holinshed's *Chronicles.*[30] Hooker broke into print earlier than Smith, but he did not publicize views on parliament widely enough to draw lasting attention. In 1572 he wrote and published for a limited audience, as we have seen, and in 1587 as continuator of Holinshed, he received a wider press, but the *Order and Usage* appeared in the volume concerning Ireland.[31] Quite possibly his reputation suffered adversely because of the government-ordered excisims.[32] Moreover, as a recorder of parliamentary procedures, Hooker was subsequently overshadowed by precedent-conscious common law lawyers like Lambarde, Coke, and Hakewill. Thus, his direct influence was somewhat ephemeral and his labors were subsumed in the more detailed and intensive researches of those who superseded him. Within this context, then, what can be said about Hooker's influence and importance?

30. In his *Description of England,* which was incorporated in the 1577 edition of Holinshed's *Chronicles,* William Harrison borrowed heavily from Sir Thomas Smith; see George Edelen's edition, *The Description of England* (Ithaca, 1968), pp. xxi, 152, 170n, 187.

31. Whereas Smith's description of parliament appeared in the introductory section of the first volume, Hooker's account was buried in the narrative section of the third volume (pp. 121–29).

32. On 1 February 1587 the Privy Council directed the archbishop of Canterbury to prohibit the sale of the second edition of the *Chronicles* and to examine those portions containing sensitive material, especially the new insertions pertaining to matters of state; see *APC, 1586–87,* pp. 311–12. Large sections were castrated before further publication and sales, thus placing the continuators under a cloud; however, Hooker's insertions were not among those deleted. The excised pages, which came into the possession of William Cecil, were published separately in the eighteenth century.

Hooker's publication of the *Modus,* though limited by a private distribution, sparked a chain reaction of interest and a century-long controversy over parliament's antiquity, original structure, and early composition. In 1572 the *Modus* was an obscure and obsolete document known only to a handful of Englishmen. Shortly thereafter William Lambarde made notes on the *Modus* and included it in a short bibliography.[33] Within a decade the House of Commons expelled Sir Arthur Hall for political heresies which included aspersions on the antiquity and composition of parliament.[34] In 1593 Sir Edward Coke, then Speaker of the House of Commons, alluded to the *Modus* in a speech and paraphrased Hooker on the pre-Conquest origins and composition of parliament:

> At first we were all one House and sat together, by a precedent which I have of a Parliament holden before the Conquest by Edward the Son of Etheldred. For there were Parliaments before the conquest. This appeareth in a Book which a grave Member of this House delivered unto me, which is Intituled *Modus tenendi Parliamentum;* out of that Book I learn this, and if any man desire to see it, I will shew it him. And this Book declareth how we all sat together, but the Commons sitting in presence of the King and amongst the Nobles disliked it, and found fault that they had not free liberty to speak. And upon this reason that they might speak more freely, being out of the Royal sight of the King, and not amongst the great Lords so far their betters, the House was divided and came asunder.[35]

---

33. Add. MS 5123, f. 1, and TCLD, MS 852, ff. 17–47. Although Lambarde's authorship of this bibliography has been accepted by Sir John Neale and Paul Ward, it has been rejected by Retha Warnicke in her biography *William Lambarde* (London, 1973), pp. 17–21. I think the weight of the evidence argues for Lambarde's authorship.

34. D'Ewes, *ACJ*, pp. 291–98.

35. *Ibid.*, p. 515. Surely Sir Edward's memory was playing tricks upon him at this point. The only *Modus* in book form was Hooker's English translation in the *Order and Usage;* moreover, there is nothing in the *Modus* supportive of

Soon thereafter the Society of Antiquaries began to probe into the antiquity of parliament.[36] In short, Hooker rescued the *Modus* from the dustbins of history and recycled it into a useful instrument which served the interests of legal antiquarians and political mythologists of the late Elizabethan and Jacobean eras.

I shall not detail the controversy over the *Modus*—that has been done in John Pocock's superb study—but will merely make a few observations.[37] Initially the legal antiquarians and proparliament mythologists accepted the *Modus* and most Hookerian arguments uncritically. Sir Edward Coke used the *Modus* without reservation throughout his *Institutes.* The *Modus* was cited in parliament, as one might expect, and it was used more or less uncritically by Cotton, D'Ewes, Elsyng, and Hakewill in their researches. In 1641 Hakewill published a second version of the *Modus*—an English rendition different from that published by Hooker—and some of his own comments on parliament.[38] Small wonder that John Milton accepted the

---

Coke's statement. However, the following statement (see below, p. 153) in Hooker's description would appear to be the source of Sir Edward's contention: ". . . th' olde usage and maner was that all the whole degrees of the parlement, sat togither in one house, and every man that had there to speak: did it openly before the king and his whole Parlement, but heerof did growe many inconveniences, and therefore to avoid the great confusions which are in such great assemblies: also to cut of th' occasions of displeasures which eftsoones did happen, when a mean man his conscience freely, either could not be heard, or fel into the displeasure of his betters, and for sundrye othergreat greefs, did devide this one house into three houses, that is to wit, the higher house, the lower house and the convocation house." It would appear that the "grave" member was Hooker, that the book was the *Order and Usage* or, possibly, Holinshed's *Chronicles,* and that Coke was acquainted with Hooker's interpretation. Although Coke's library did not contain a copy of Hooker, it did contain the *Chronicles.*

36. See F. L., *The Opinions of Several Learned Antiquaries* (London, 1685), and Joan Evans, *The Society of Antiquaries* (London, 1956).

37. Pocock, *Ancient Constitution,* passim.

38. Actually, early in 1641 a London printer brought out an unauthorized edition of Hakewill's treatise and the *Modus* (type A), using one of several copies of the manuscript then in circulation. In July of that year Hakewill

Modus as a bona fide document and some of the Hookerian assumptions regarding the pre-Conquest origins of parliament.[39]

These assumptions and the validity of the *Modus* came under attack in due time. Both Sir Henry Spelman and John Selden cast doubts on the proem of the *Modus* and questioned the pre-Conquest date assigned to it.[40] During the Puritan upheaval William Prynne, taking issue with Coke, labeled the *Modus* a forgery and proceeded to demythologize the political doctrines derived from it.[41] Others joined in the fray and the controversy lingered on into the reign of William and Mary. Meanwhile, adding fuel to the controversy, were the publication of Henry Elsyng's *Ancient Method and Manner of holding Parliaments in England* in 1660 and Dom Jean Luc D'Achery's collection of documents in the *Spicilegium* (1677), which included a Latin version of type B.[42] Ironically, by this time—a century after the publication of Hooker's twin booklets—the prime activator of the chain reaction was all but forgotten.

In England, Hooker's *Order and Usage* was never formally adopted and officially sanctioned—as it was in Ireland—this much is clear. In fact, during the reign of Elizabeth there was no written modus operandi such as Thomas Jefferson's *Manual*, Erskine May's *Treatise*, or General Robert's *Rules of Order*.

---

himself issued a second edition along with an explanatory preface and corrections. For a discussion of this matter see Ward, *Archeion*, pp. 147–48.

39. See his *Defensio Prima* in *The Works of John Milton*, ed. Frank A. Patterson, 18 vols. (New York, 1931–38), 7:424–25.

40. Evans, "The Antiquity of Parliaments," pp. 210–12.

41. See the preface to *An Exact Abridgment of the Records in the Tower of London* (1657), in which he cites Hooker's *Order and Usage* and attacks Sir Edward Coke for spurious interpretations concerning the antiquity of parliament.

42. See Geoffrey Bing's introduction to his edition of Elsynge's *Manner of Holding Parliaments in England* (Shannon, 1971), pp. vii–xix, and Elizabeth Read Foster, *The Painful Labour of Mr. Elsynge,* in *Transactions of the American Philosophical Society*, new ser. 62 (Philadelphia, 1972). Elsynge's work went through several editions before the revolution of 1688. I have used the second edition of D'Achery, 3 vols. (Paris, 1723), 3:394–97.

Rather, there were unwritten rules *(lex et consuetudo parliamenti)*
and orders recorded in the *Journals* which governed the deliberations in both houses.[43] The guardians of these rules, and
those in the *Journal* called "ancient orders," were the Speakers, the clerical personnel, and the older, experienced members. In due course the upper house would reduce its orders
to a written code and circulate them as *Standing Orders;* and
eventually the lower house would regard the works of Hatsell
and May as authoritative; but throughout the sixteenth and
seventeenth centuries the House of Commons lacked an authoritative guide to procedure and behavior. The *Modus* may
have been alluded to as a historic document, as it was in 1593
and again in the 1620s, but it was obsolete for all intents and
purposes.[44]

In the absence of a definitive set of rules Hooker's *Order and
Usage* served several MPs, seemingly, as a unofficial guide. It
was not cited in the *Journal,* nor did the diarists allude to it as
such. We have no way of ascertaining how many MPs in the
House of Commons possessed copies of the *Order and Usage,*
yet it seems reasonable to assume that there were printed
copies in Exeter and the Devonshire area.[45] It is also safe to
assume that Sir William Fitzwilliam possessed a copy and that
he had occasion to use it in the English House of Commons.
We also know that William Lambarde had access to a copy of
the Exeter edition and that Robert Beale had access to a copy
of the same edition. There seems to have been a copy at
Lincoln's Inn. Thus, even before its republication in Holinshed's *Chronicles* brought about a wider distribution, the

43. Coke, *Institutes* (book IV, cap. I).

44. For 1593 see above p. 89; and for 1621 see Wallace Notestein et al.,
Commons Debates 1621 7 vols. (New Haven, 1935), 2:403, 352; 3:138, 192,
340n; 4:388.

45. We know that in 1584 Hooker distributed seventy-two copies of two
other publications to friends in Devonshire and sent three copies to the
bookbinders. It would appear that he printed at least seventy-five copies. See
EXRO, book 57.

Order and Usage was available to several important figures in the lower house.

More important, however, were the manuscript copies in the hands of members. There was the printer's copy which ended up in the College of Arms, probably through the earl of Arundel or another member of the Howard family.[46] There were two manuscripts available to Exonians.[47] There were also several manuscript copies of the printed Exeter edition:

1. The manuscript of Robert Beale which descended first to Christopher Yelverton, MP and Speaker of the House of Commons, in 1597, and then to his son Henry Yelverton, who represented Northampton in several Jacobean parliaments;[48]

2. A manuscript made by a copiest for William Lambarde and now in Lincoln's Inn Library;[49]

46. This MS, labeled H. D. N. #41, is a printer's copy.

47. Both are in the EXRO. Book 60h, ff. 12–19, is a preliminary draft of the *Order and Usage,* while book 52, ff. 234–36, was an abridgement of the version appearing in Holinshed's *Chronicles* designed to be incorporated in Hooker's unpublished history of Exeter.

48. BL, Add. MS 48,020, includes the *Modus* in English (ff. 26–32) and Hooker's *Order and Usage* (ff. 33–52). Add. MS 48,025 includes (ff. 154–62) Hooker's dedicatory letter to the mayor of Exeter followed by the English *Modus.*

49. Harper 18. Circumstantial evidence points to the presence of a printed copy of the Exeter edition at Lincoln's Inn during Elizabethan and Jacobean times, for several common law lawyers associated with Lincoln's Inn either cited and/or copied the *Order and Usage,* including William Lambarde, Jerome Alexander, John Glanville (the younger), and William Prynne. Unfortunately, I have not been able to establish the authorship and provenance of Harper 18. It appears to be a late sixteenth-century hand; but, according to Paul Ward, it is not Lambarde's handwriting. The manuscript was acquired by Lincoln's Inn Library in 1915 as a gift from one H. Stuart More. The copiest, whoever he was, rendered a shortened version of Hooker's chapter on Convocation and he did not copy the list of lords and MPs; nevertheless, it is clear that the copiest used the printed Exeter edition.

3. A manuscript copy acquired by Jerome Alexander during the reign of James I;[50]

4. Sampson Lennard's copy which passed to Camden and eventually to Sir Robert Harley.[51]

There is also a manuscript copy of the Fitzwilliam edition in the Hatton MSS at Beinecke Library.[52] In addition, a manuscript copy of the Holinshed *Chronicle* version ended up in the papers of John Glanville, presumably made by either the elder, who sat in several Elizabethan parliaments, or the younger, who sat in several early Stuart parliaments and served as Speaker of the House of Commons during the Short Parliament.[53] No doubt there were others which have been lost.

---

50. TCLD, MS 852, ff. 17–47. This appears in material collected by or for Jerome Alexander. The latter, a graduate of Caius College, Cambridge, was admitted to Lincoln's Inn in 1616 and became a barrister-at-law. He went to Ireland in 1626 and ten years later was named an assize judge by Lord Chancellor Loftus over the protests of Strafford. In 1660 he was knighted and appointed judge of common please (Ireland), an office which he held until his death in 1670. See O'Flanagan, *Lives of the Lord Chancellors*, pp. 305, 325–29, and J. Venn, *Alumni Cantabrigiensis*, 4 vols. (Cambridge, 1922–27), 1:15. Folio 29 is a copy of William Lambarde's bibliography, while ff. 36–42 are Hooker's translation of the *Modus*. Folios 56–68 contain the *Order and Usage* copied from the Exeter edition. The pages between these two sections contain a miscellany of matters pertaining to the English parliament, especially the passing of bills and privileges. It appears to have been written in England during the 1630s.

51. BL, Harleian 1178, ff. 19–26. Very likely Lennard, Camden's deputy responsible for the visitations of Devon and Cornwall in 1620, came upon Hooker's *Order and Usage* in the course of his heraldic researches and copied it. However, this appears to be a copy of the Holinshed edition rather than the 1572 edition.

52. Beinecke Library, Osborne MS fb. 23 ff. 138–72. This is a seventeenth-century copy of various manuscripts in the Hatton family collections, probably copied by a secretary of antiquarian Christopher Hatton between 1628 and 1640. The latter may have used it in the Short Parliament. The volume also includes copies of *Leycester's Commonwealth* and Ralegh's *Discourse*.

53. Queen's College MS 172, ff. 289–327. This seems to be that portion of John Glanville's papers which descended to Joseph Williamson. Glanville was very active in Caroline parliaments, especially 1628, and earlier he had served as secretary to the earl of Essex.

Very likely the paucity of extant printed copies of the *Order and Usage* accounts for the fairly large number of manuscript copies.

These interrelated facts indicate that Elizabethan and early Stuart antiquarians and politicians, especially those trained in common law, regarded Hooker's *Order and Usage* as a useful authority of sorts. One of the earliest to so regard it was William Lambarde who composed a short bibliography of six entries and incorporated it in his treatise on the House of Commons. The second entry, following a reference to the *Modus,* referred to "Hoker's book of ye Parliamt."[54] Lambarde does not borrow heavily from Hooker; in fact, some statements contradict those in the *Order and Usage.* Nonetheless, in his *Archeion,* Lambarde accepts Hooker's view on the antiquity of parliament and uses some of his terminology.[55] It is also interesting to note that Lambarde's treatise was utilized by others, at least several copies of it have survived.[56] In all likelihood Lambarde's copy of Hooker's *Order and Usage*

54. BL, Add MS 5123, f. 1.

55. In her *Lambarde,* Warnicke rejects Lambarde's authorship of the bibliography on grounds that none of the books listed therein were ever in his possession. Yet, we know that Lambarde had used a copy of the *Modus* as early as 1574 (see above p. 89). Moreover, with a library at Lincoln's Inn—a library large enough to have a librarian in 1646—he did not have to personally possess all the works cited, for borrowing from individuals and institutional collections was very common. Furthermore, Lambarde may well have given some of his books to his friends prior to his death. Regarding the *Modus,* Lambarde noted (p. 257) that it was "to be seen in many hands." Like Hooker, he considered parliament an assembly which dated back to pre-Conquest times, particularly to the West Saxons. He also subscribed to Hooker's "estate theory"—that is, he regarded parliament as composed of three estates: the king, the nobility, and the commons. Compare *Archeion* (1635), pp. 116, 243–45, 247, 257, 272–73, and below p. 103. When Lambarde deemed parliament "our chiefe and Highest Court," as he did on p. 273, he must have been quoting or paraphrasing p. 31 of the Exeter edition (see below p. 181).

56. TCLD, MS 852, f. 17, and BL and at least ten others, although no text of any authority has yet been identified. I am deeply indebted to Paul Ward for much of this information on Lambarde.

was known and used by his fellow lawyers of Lincoln's Inn.

It is tempting to suggest a direct causal relationship between Hooker's views on the preeminence of Commons and the assertion of rights and privileges in the session of parliament which followed the publication of his *Order and Usage*. In that session the lower house witnessed Peter Wentworth strike a blow for freedom of speech, the contempt proceedings against Arthur Hall in a very complicated case involving freedom from arrest, and the incarceration of an observer who violated the custom of the lower house.[57] It is entirely possible that some MPs were influenced by Hooker's strong advocacy of parliamentary power and privilege, but direct causal links are not in evidence.

However, it is possible to demonstrate connections between Hooker's *Order and Usage* and some personnel who served in subsequent parliaments. The Yelverton manuscripts contain copies of all three parts of the 1572 edition: (1) the dedicatory epistle, (2) Hooker's *English* translation of the *Modus,* and (3) his *Order and Usage*.[58] These manuscripts, actually transcribed copies of the Exeter printed edition, form part of the Yelverton papers attributed to Robert Beale, brother-in-law of Sir Francis Walsingham.[59] Through the patronage of Walsingham and the earl of Bedford, Beale was appointed clerk of the council in 1572 and selected to represent the Devonshire borough of Totnes in the 1575 session of parliament.[60] As clerk of the council he might have come into the possession of either the manuscript or the printed version of Hooker's work, al-

57. See Neale, *EP,* 1:241–368.

58. BL., Add. MSS 48020, ff. 26–52, and 48025, ff. 154–62.

59. For a printed calendar see *HMC 2nd Rept.,* pp. 39–46. The collection includes much material on Anglo-Irish affairs during the Elizabethan era, including the communications of Sir Thomas Smith and Sir Francis Walsingham. Beale took his orders from his brother-in-law Walsingham, apparently, and sometimes filled in for him.

60. *DNB,* 2:3. It is possible that Beale and Hooker knew each other: Hooker's maternal relatives came from Beale's village (Woodbridge, Suffolk) and both had connections with the earl of Bedford. It is very possible that Bedford used his influence in Devon to secure the Totnes seat for Beale.

though there is no evidence of this in his papers or in the *Acts of the Privy Council*.[61] Yet, we know he had access to the printed 1572 edition, for he possessed a manuscript copy of the same. It is conceivable that Beale knew of Hooker's *Order and Usage,* and that he acquired a manuscript copy of it to acquaint himself with procedures in conjunction with his sitting for Totnes in parliament. Very likely he, a novice and back-bencher in 1575, made use of it in that session and subsequent parliaments.

Another explanation is also feasible. Beale had connections with Sir Christopher Yelverton (1535–1612), a promising lawyer who represented Northampton in the 1572–81 parliament.[62] In fact, Beale's daughter Mary married Sir Christopher's eldest son Henry, thus explaining how Beale's literary effects became part of the Yelverton family papers. It is possible that Sir Christopher, a staunch proponent of parliamentary privilege in 1572 and active in 1575, came into possession of Hooker's *Order and Usage* and passed it on to Beale. Whichever possibility approximates the truth, the fact remains that Beale and possibly Yelverton had access to the *Order and Usage.* The extent to which either or both used it remains conjectural, but it should be remembered that the *Order and Usage* was the best guide to parliamentary deliberations prior to the compilations of Hakewill and Scobel.[63] In fact, except for the descriptive

61. Beale did considerable investigative work for the Privy Council, as evidenced in his own papers, and he may have acquired Hooker's *Order and Usage* as an agent for Walsingham and/or the Privy Council, but there is no official record of Hooker being examined or investigated by the Privy Council. It is also possible that Hooker gave a copy of the *Order and Usage* to the earl of Bedford—as he gave him unpublished manuscripts—and that Bedford, a prominent member of the council, turned it over to Beale.

62. See *DNB*, 21:1230–32.

63. Hakewill's manuscripts may have been in circulation in late Elizabethan times, but they were not published until 1641. Henry Scobel's *Rules and Customs* was not published until 1692. Some of the legal treatises and law reports touch upon parliament, but most of the material in them concerned the legal aspects of the summons and election law, such as Richard Crompton, *L'Authoritie et jurisdiction des courts* (London, 1594).

work of Smith and the unpublished writings of Lambarde, Hooker's parliamentary manual was the only work available to parliamentary officials and MPs.[64]

During the preliminaries to the 1581 session of parliament the House of Commons, while not mentioning Hooker by name, took actions which seemed to sanction several practices recorded in the *Order and Usage*.[65] The newly selected Speaker, John Popham, lectured his fellow members on the need for orderly and decorous behavior. He called upon MPs to be discreet and reverent in their speeches, to forbear speaking after the first reading of a bill, to forbear unnecessary arguments and motions, and to make certain "that they would see their Servants, Pages, Lackies attending them kept in good order." Commons next approved a motion by Sir James Croft, comptroller of the queen's household, which called for orderly adjournment procedures. Commons also exercised more control over its members through various measures. After heated debate, a majority voted to permit a burgess indicted for a felony to retain his seat on grounds that he was innocent until proven guilty. They also passed orders aimed to assure better attendance. The House of Commons, as these measures reveal, gradually assumed and asserted internal control over its own deliberations and composition.

The most significant action taken by Commons in this session involved the disablement of Arthur Hall.[66] This cantankerous MP from Grantham, a relative of Lord Burghley who

64. Smith's work circulated in manuscript from its completion in 1565 to its publication in 1583. Subsequently it went through numerous editions and parts of it were incorporated in Holinshed's *Chronicles*. Lambarde's short treatise entitled "Some Certaine Notes of ye Order, Proceedings, Punishments, and Privileges of the Lower House of Parliament," though perhaps started in the mid-1570s, was certainly not completed until 1587; but it was not published until forty years after his death in 1641. The *Archeion* had little to say about parliamentary procedures.

65. This paragraph is based on D'Ewes, *ACJ*, pp. 277–310.

66. Much of the information on Hall is based upon Herbert Wright, *Life and Works of Arthur Hall of Grantham* (Manchester, 1919).

had antagonized the lower house in both the first and second sessions of this parliament, had been in contempt since 1575. In a well-planned act of defiance and revenge aimed at his political enemies, in 1579 Hall had published a defamatory pamphlet in which he criticized the lawmaking process in England and called into question some of the fundamental assumptions of MPs. The attack received little attention at first, but in 1580 the author was summoned before the Privy Council, censured for his action, and ordered to cease distribution of the libel.[67] But, even after this judgment, he continued to publicize the pamphlet, whereupon on 4 February 1581 he was reproached in parliament by Thomas Norton, taken into custody, examined by a committee of the lower house, and eventually disabled and punished by the whole house.[68]

The composition of the committee is most significant, for it included at least two MPs who had access to Hooker's *Order and Usage:* Sir William Fitzwilliam, the ex-lord deputy of Ireland, to whom Hooker had dedicated his *Order and Usage,* and Robert Beale, clerk of the council, who appears to have assumed a more conspicuous role in the session than in 1575.[69] The committee chairman was Secretary of State Sir Thomas Wilson.

This committee charged Arthur Hall of being in contempt

67. *APC, 1579–80,* pp. 306, 313, 327.
68. D'Ewes, *ACJ,* pp. 291–2, 296–98.
69. Ibid. The original committee, appointed on 4 February 1581, included "Mr. Vice-Chamberlain, Mr. Chauncellor of the Exchequer, Mr. Secretary Wilson, Mr. Treasure of the Chamber Sir Henry Lea, Sir Thomas Cecil, Sir William Fitzwilliam, and Sir Henry Gate" (p. 291). On 6 February, after the above members interrogated the printer and other implicated parties and reported their findings, the lower house agreed to add to the original group "all the Privy-Council being of this House, Mr. Knight Marshal, Mr. Recorder of London, Mr. Sergeant Flowerdewe, Mr. St. Leger, Mr. Cromwell, Mr. Atkins the Master of the Jewel-House, Sir Thomas Browne, Sir Thomas Smith, Mr. Nathanael Bacon, Mr. Beale, Mr. Norton and Mr. Alford" (p. 292). It is possible that Sir Christopher Hatton, then vice-chamberlain, also had a copy of the *Order and Usage,* for one of his heirs had access to a manuscript copy of the Fitzwilliam edition.

of the House of Commons for ignoring a summons, publicizing speeches made at a conference, publishing a libel and
counterfeiting the authorship, slandering particular MPs, im-
pugning the authority of the House of Commons, defying a
Privy Council order, and committing perjury.[70] Hall's most
grievous crime, in the eyes of the committee, involved his
aspersions of the House of Commons. He had questioned the
orthodox mythology of the House of Commons, in particular
its antiquity, structure, and composition, as the following quotation indicates:

> And not herewith satisfyed, hathe in some parte thereof
> conteyned a false and sclaunderouse discourse against the
> Antiquytie and Aucthoritie of the common howse or
> thirde estate of the parliament, wherein he hathe falsely
> sought, as muche as in hym is, to impugne, deface,
> blemyshe, and dymynyshe the power, antiquity and auc-
> thoritie of this howse and the Interest that this howse
> hathe alwayes, and in all ages had, to the greate Impeache-
> ment of the auntyent order and government of this
> Realme, the rights of this howse and the forme of makinge
> lawes.[71]

In short, Hall had called into question those orthodox doctrines expounded in Hooker's *Order and Usage* and brought
upon himself charges of political heresy.

Hooker does not seem to have had any direct role in the Hall
case. He was not an MP at the time; rather he was residing in
Exeter and carrying out his numerous responsibilities as civic
archivist and antiquarian. None of the pertinent documents
mention him or his *Order and Usage* by name. Hall was charged
with violating "the ancient Orders of this House," which probably meant the unwritten rules that Coke later called *lex parliamenti* rather than the *Modus*, but there were no references to

70. Wright, *Hall*, p. 70.
71. Ibid., p. 188.

the modern rules propounded by Hooker and dedicated to Fitzwilliam.[72] Yet, it seems that Hookerian assumptions and arguments were advanced and that they prevailed. It should be underscored that in his twin publications Hooker had made much of the antiquity of parliament, of the evolution of parliament from a small unicameral body to a complex tricameral institution, of the preeminence of the House of Commons in ancient and modern times, and of the necessity for orderly deliberations and courteous behavior. Hooker had also alluded to the secretive nature of the deliberations and enunciated the rule against revealing anything about the proceedings in St. Stephen's Chapel.

When the committee reported, as it did on 14 February 1581, the whole house accepted its findings and pronounced Hall guilty.[73] The vote was unanimous. The victim was then committed to the Tower, fined, and expelled from the House of Commons. Moreover, the case was digested and entered into the *Journal* so that subsequent parliaments could cite it as a precedent. And thus did the lower house authenticate several political doctrines which Hooker had put forward in his *Order and Usage.*

Hookerian nomenclature also left its imprint on posterity. As noted above Hooker deemed the English parliament a court, in fact, "the hiest, cheefest, and greatest Court that is or can be within the Realm" (see above, p. 181). It was the sovereign's court, the ultimate court of appeal, and all duly summoned Englishmen possessed the obligation to attend. The *Order and Usage* is replete with judicial and legal terms. Hooker speaks of "trials," "causes," "summons," "fines," "fees," and "actions." The personnel include the highest judicial officers in the realm, sergeants at arms to maintain order and sergeants at law to give counsel in "doubtful causes." These terms and concepts were not novel, to be sure, for as

72. See D'Ewes, *ACJ,* p. 295.
73. Ibid., pp. 296–97.

Chrimes has ably demonstrated, in the fifteenth-century parliament was considered a high court of law and many of its
forms were judicial in nature.[74] It was regarded as the king's
court by petitioners, by attendant commoners, and by lawyers
and judges. Their views were recorded in the rolls of parliament, unpublished speeches, sermons, and Year Books.
"Whatever the full facts of the parliamentary practice may
have been," wrote Chrimes, "there can be no doubt that the
theory of parliament as a court was flourishing throughout the
century; and the acceptability of this theory ensured its continued vogue for several centuries.[75] These terms were current
in Elizabethan times and we confront them in legal treatises
and law reports. Hooker's principal role was to transmit and
publicize the terms and concepts. We know that Lambarde
used Hooker and that Coke borrowed from both Hooker and
Lambarde. And, as McIlwain has demonstrated, the concept of
parliament as a court prevailed in the official records of the
upper house.[76] It was indeed a useful concept to those serving
in parliament—especially the common law lawyers and antiquarians in the lower house and the judges in the upper
house—who looked to the pre-Tudor past for precedents to
bolster their claims to power and prestige. In depicting parliament as England's highest lawmaking court Hooker sketched
a skeleton which was subsequently filled in by William Lambarde and Sir Edward Coke.[77]

In like manner Hooker publicized the concept of "estates."
In the dedicatory epistle to the Exeter edition he spoke of "all
degrees and estates of people" and "with advise and consent
of all the estates and sages of the same" (see below, p. 123).
In his rendition of the *Modus* he employed the word thrice, in
each case as a synonym for "magnates" (see below, p. 135ff.).

---

74. Chrimes, *English Constitutional Ideas*, pp. 70–76.
75. Ibid., p. 75.
76. McIlwain, *High Court of Parliament*, pp. 109–245.
77. See Lambarde's *Archeion*, pp. 254–75, and Coke's *Institutes*, Book IV,
especially cap. I.

In his *Order and Usage,* however, Hooker used the term liberally as a synonym for degree. In the chapter entitled "The degrees of Parliament," to illustrate, he writes, "In times past there were six degrees or estates of the Parlement . . . but now the same are reduced to foure degrees" (see below, p. 152). Throughout the remainder of the tractate this usage prevails, although he reduces the number of estates to three, as we shall see.

Again, Hooker's nomenclature was not novel except in its publicized form. Chrimes has shown how the "estate theory" of a representative assembly emerged more or less simultaneously with the judicial conception treated above in pre-Tudor times.[78] The term *estates* generally denoted "degree" or "order," although it also connoted a condition ("Estates of the Realm") or a landed interest. When used to denote a degree of society, as it was in the writings of Wyclif and in the rolls of parliament, it was usually fused with a trinitarian concept and then gradually came to denote the three "estates of parliament." However, in pre-Reformation England and France the three estates were more often than not delineated as follows: first estate, prelates or lords spiritual; second estate, lords or lords temporal; third estate, commoners. The king, it should be noted, was not deemed an "estate."

Hooker depicted parliament as both a court and a representative assembly, this much is clear, and he accepted the trinitarian notion of three estates. However, he redefined and modified the component parts of the trinity. He rejected the well-known organic concept which viewed the king as the head and the three estates (prelates, lords, and commoners) as the body of society.[79] He also refused to regard the prelates as the first estate. To him the clergy constituted a degree in society. They were summoned to parliament, but in Hooker's view they were not an integral part of the lawmaking process. They

78. Chrimes, *Constitutional Ideas,* pp. 79–126.
79. For the medieval organic view see Ruth Mohl, *The Three Estates in Medieval and Renaissance Literature* (New York, 1933).

met separately in Convocation; they voted their own subsidies; they possessed a voice in ecclesiastical legislation. But, he did not consider them to be one of the three estates: they had no veto power; they were not essential to statute making. Rather, for Hooker the king was the first estate, the lords comprised the second estate, and the commons constituted the third estate (see below, p. 152). Here was a different political trinity —king, lords and commons—refashioned from medieval times to fit the realities of Elizabethan England.

The source of Hooker's trinitarian concept of estates is not altogether clear. It is entirely possible that he consulted the rolls of parliament and other medieval documents in the Tower of London. He stated in his dedicatory epistle that, after using the records of the 1571 session, "I did confer with exemplars and presidents of tholde and auncient Parlements used in tymes past, within the said Realme of England" (see below, p. 206). It is also possible that he consulted others better versed than he on such matters. But who? Fleetwood? Lambarde? Egerton? Beale?—all contemporary common law lawyers with antiquarian interests. Unfortunately, there is no evidence of any direct connections with these contemporaries. It is likewise possible that Hooker was influenced by contemporary Continental literature and/or other compatriots who themselves were influenced by Continental theories and events. The influence of the French constitutional theorists on English political thought has been well documented.[80]

Among those contemporaries whose writings may have influenced Hooker were Ponet and Aylmer. In his *Short Treatise* Ponet stated his preference for limited monarchy, corporate lawmaking, and government by consent.[81] Many of his authorities and some of his arguments were later used by

---

80. W. F. Church, *Constitutional Thought in Sixteenth Century France* (Cambridge, Mass., 1941); Pocock, *Ancient Constitution*, pp. 1–29; and Donald R. Kelley, "History, English Law and the Renaissance," *Past and Present* 65 (November 1974): 24–51.

81. Hudson, *John Ponet.*

Hooker. We also know that Ponet, a Marian exile, had lived in Strasbourg and known some of Hooker's friends there. In fact, Ponet used one of Sir Peter Carew's books and cited it in the *Short Treatise*.[82] Very likely he also knew Francis Russell and other Devonian friends of Hooker. Whatever the case, despite the affinity of some ideas, Ponet neither viewed parliament as a court nor utilized the "estates theory." Moreover, Hooker gave no indication of having read the *Short Treatise*.

A second and more likely possibility is John Aylmer, Marian exile and subsequently bishop of London, who wrote *An Harborowe for faithful and trewe Subjects*.[83] This defense of Elizabeth's succession—really an answer to John Knox's first *Blast*—was dedicated to Hooker's patron, the earl of Bedford. He too had spent his exile in Strasbourg and no doubt knew some of Hooker's associates. Alymer noted that England is a mixed government composed of three parts: the king, the aristocracy, and the commoners. He also used the concept of estates. Moreover, he was very pro-Saxon and anti-Norman in his portrayal of England's early history. But again, the evidence is circumstantial and inferential.

Other possibilities remain. Perhaps Hooker himself acquired the writings of French Huguenots like Beza who enunciated popular sovereignty and representative government in his writings.[84] Perhaps he had access to some of the early writings of Hotman or other humanists partial to representative government.[85] Perhaps more concrete evidence will turn up. Meanwhile, despite the lack of conclusive information relating to sources, it should be noted that Hooker frequently

82. Ibid., pp. 94 and 207.

83. This was printed in Strasbourg on 4 February 1559. It is interesting to note that the Huntington Library copy of this tract has the signature of "Ralfe Rookbye," Lambarde's friend and client.

84. Church, *Constitutional Thought*, pp. 123–26.

85. See Kelley, *Francois Hotman;* Gordon Griffiths, "Humanists and Representative Government in the Sixteenth Century," in *Representative Institutions in Theory and Practice* (Brussels, 1970), pp. 59–83; and Ralph Giesey and J. H. M. Salmon, *Francogallia by Francois Hotman* (Cambridge, 1972).

used the word "estates" and the French spelling of "Parlement":

> . . . it consisteth of the whole Realme, which is devided into three estates, that is to wit, the king, the Nobles, and the Commons, every of which estates are subject to suche orders as are concluded and established in Parlement.
>
> These three estates may joyntly and with one consent or agreement: establish and enact any Laws, orders, & Statutes for the commonwelth [see below, p. 181].

The significance of the "estates theory," particularly in its trinitarian form, has been underscored by several scholars, yet Hooker's role in its diffusion has been overlooked. Subsequent to the publication of the *Order and Usage* we confront it in the writings of Lambarde.[86] We find Lord Burleigh alluding to the "three estates" and by that meaning the queen, the House of Lords and the House of Commons.[87] In due time Doddridge, Tate, Camden, and Selden all used Hooker's version of the concept while Cotton and Holland employed a similar version in their writings on parliament.[88] Sir Edward Coke reverted to the medieval form when writing of "the king and these three estates are the great corporation or body politic of the kingdom."[89] Yet, he did follow Hooker when noting that the three estates sat together in one house.

If not before, in 1581 Hooker's trinitarian interpretation of the "three estates" acquired orthodox status in the Arthur Hall case. The latter had aspersed not only the antiquity of

---

86. *Archeion* (1635), pp. 123, 126, 128, 139.

87. D'Ewes, *ACJ*, p. 350.

88. See *The Opinion of Several Learned Antiquaries . . . touching . . . the High Court of Parliament in England* (London, 1685), pp. 6, 14, 34–36, 43, 47–49, 53–55. For a discussion of the seventeenth-century proponents see Corinne Comstock Weston, "Concepts of Estates in Stuart Political Thought," in *Representative Institutions*, pp. 87–131.

89. *Institutes*, book IV, cap. I. While Coke did not refer to Hooker, he cited Holinshed's *Chronicles* as a source.

parliament, but he also questioned the composition and structure of pre-Conquest parliaments. Hall, in the words of Sir Francis Bacon, "said the Lower House was a *new* person in the Trinity, and (because these words tended to the derogation of the state of the House, and giving absolute power to the other) he was therefore committed."[90] In short, Hall had committed the political sin of blasphemy—he denied the omnipresence of Commons in early parliaments—a sin which demanded not simply a penalty, but a recantation. It would appear that those members of the house who were privy councillors drafted the retraction which Hall signed after spending seven weeks in the Tower. It read as follows:

> And wheare I am charged to have practicyed to discreditt the aucthoritie of the lawes and proceadinges of the parliament, I doe most humbly require that if my particuler speaches in sum thinges that concerned, as I than thought, mine owne cause, have been the cawse of that generally charging of me to discredit the aucthoritie of the lawes and procedyngs in ye parlement, I maie not for thos particuler thyngs yt concerned my self be charged with such a generall offence to the whole, for I doe from the botome of my hart reverence the lawes and proceadings in the Parliaments in both ye houses and Counsills, *and doe allowe of the ancient aucthoritie of the common howse, wherein the third estate of the whole Realme is duelie represented,* and so may it largely appeare in my said Book what a great accompt I mak both of the whole Parliament in generall and of the aucthoritie of the common howse, representing the third Bodie of the said Parliament, Requiring that my large writing uppon the matter in my said Book maie serve as well for my awnswer and excuse unto this genrall charg, as for an expressing of my good, reverent meaning both to ye sayd laws and procedyings.

90. Francis Bacon, *Collected Works,* ed. J. Spedding, 14 vols. (London, 1857–74), 3:37.

Finallie, I doe submitt my self first to the Quenes most
excellent Majesty, the head of all the Bodies and Councells of this Realme, and I doe reverence in theire degrees,
both in generall and particuler, all the membres allowed
in thos Councells, both in the higher howse and in the
common howse, and doe affirme to my poor understanding that theare cannot be anie better order by witt of man
devised for the making, abrogating, or changing of lawes,
to gouverne the Realme and everie particuler member
from the highest to the lowest, *then is already provided for,*
and of ancient time hath been practicyed in this Realme, by calling
and assembling the thre Estates of ye realme, as they are called, to
give advise, Councell, and aydes to the Quenes Majesty as ye head
of the whole Realme, in all cawses to them expounded on the
behalfe of the Realme.[91]

A close examination of this recantation reveals an author
versed in Hooker's *Order and Usage.* Note the trinitarian concept of the "three estates." Note also that the purpose—that
is, "to give advise, Councell, and aydes"—appears to be lifted
from the first chapter of the *Order and Usage.* In that chapter
Hooker wrote:

And y King having this authoritie, ought not to summon
his Parlement: but for weightie & great causes, and in
which he of necessitie ought to have the advise and counsel of all the estates of his Realme [see below, p. 146].

It would appear from the above evidence that some figure in
the Privy Council regarded Hooker's *Order and Usage* as the
authoritative statement on the antiquity, structure, composition, and power of the House of Commons. In all likelihood
that "figure" was the clerk of the council, Robert Beale.

In the decades following Hall's recantation Hooker's views
on parliament were espoused by more and more Englishmen.
The inclusion of the *Order and Usage* in Holinshed made those

91. Herbert, *Hall,* p. 188 (emphasis mine).

insights more readily available to literate Elizabethans.[92] The debates of the members of the Society of Antiquaries on the origins of parliament also reveal an awareness of the *Modus* and a widespread use of Hooker's views and nomenclature.[93] John Doddridge, Hooker's friend and countryman, traced the English parliament to Saxon times and alluded to the three estates, as did Francis Tate and John Selden. Sir Robert Cotton, though citing Sir Thomas Smith, referred to "the High Court of Parliament." Few of the discussants indicated their sources and none of them mentioned Hooker, yet their papers reflect the terminology, the concepts, and the assumptions embedded in the *Order and Usage.* Thus, through a process akin to osmosis, Hooker's views slowly but steadily permeated the membership of parliament during late Elizabethan and early Stuart England.

On the eve of the Puritan Revolution Hooker's views on the antiquity, composition, and power of parliament prevailed in both houses. The Speaker of the House of Commons during the Short Parliament, John Glanville, possessed a copy of the *Order and Usage,* and members of the lower house used Hooker's terminology and subscribed to the political doctrines embedded in the Elizabethan tract.[94] Equally important, a majority in the House of Lords also affirmed those doctrines in the Short Parliament. On 16 April 1640, when Archbishop Laud sought special concessions for the bishops to attend Convocation, he encountered a hostile majority, sparked by Lord Saye, who refused to regard the bishops as coequals in the lawmaking process.[95] Two days later the issue cropped up again and produced some verbal clashes over the composition and structure of parliament. The prelates in the upper house, it seems, claimed that they constituted one of the estates of the

92. Several of the antiquaries and Sir Edward Coke cite that *Chronicle* as an authority on parliament.
93. *Opinion,* passim.
94. On Glanville see *DNB,* 7:1291, and above p. 93n.
95. Gardiner, *History,* 9:100–02.

realm and that they were an integral component in the legislative mechanism. Lord Saye, rejecting their claim, contended that parliament was composed of three estates and no more: king, Lords, and Commons.

Like Hooker, Lord Saye's trinity excluded the clergy as a separate estate and included the king as the first estate. When the bishops pressed the issue, attempting to either increase the estates to four (inclusive of the clergy) or exclude the king as an estate, the upper house backed Lord Saye in a showdown vote.[96] In rejecting the Laudian position and accepting the principles of Lord Saye the House of Lords unwittingly confirmed the doctrines propounded seventy years earlier by John Hooker. Subsequently, in the early years of the Long Parliament, these views were reaffirmed by the House of Commons and proclaimed by many propagandists who sided with parliament during the Civil War.[97] Ultimately, as Weston has shown, they were reformulated into a theory of mixed monarchy.[98] Thus did the political tenets of the Elizabethan antiquary remain a living part of the English constitution long after he was laid to rest in his beloved Exeter.

96. For a good discussion of this incident see M. J. Mendle, "Politics and Political Thought, 1640–1642," in Conrad Russell, *The Origins of the English Civil War* (New York, 1973), p. 227.

97. Ibid., p. 228. As Mendle points out, Sir John Strangeways, Edward Bagshaw, and Henry Parker subscribed to the Hookerian view of the three estates.

98. See her *English Constitutional Theory and the House of Lords, 1556–1832* (New York, 1865), especially pp. 23–86. Although she touched upon Ponet, Aylmer, and Cartwright, Weston said nothing of Hooker.

Text of the Exeter Edition of the *Order and Usage*

The
Order and
Usage of the Keeping
of a Parlement
in England,
and the Description
of the Olde and Ancient
Cittie of Excester.

Collected by John Vowel
Alias Hooker Gentleman.

[1b]TO THE RIGHT VVORSHIPFUL;
Grave and prudent, the Maior and Senators of the moste ancient and honorable Cittie of Excester,[1] John Vowel alias Hooker gentleman and Chamberlain of the same, wisheth a happy successe in government with the long continuance therof to the benefit of the publique welth and increace of vvorships.

WHEN I DO THINK and consider (rightworshipful) of the noble state and great majestie of the high Courts of Parlements of this Realme which for the exellẽcie and worthines therof, is of all true English men to be honored and imbraced: I doo foorthwith fall in great dislike as wel with my self as with others, which beeing in learning ignoraunt, in wisdome weke, in experiẽce unskilful, and in every respect very unfit for such an honorable assembly, should be chosen and admitted to the same.

1. Specifically, the mayor of Exeter in 1572 was John Periam, the elder. An affluent merchant involved in French trade, he had been active in civic affairs for several years, serving as mayor in 1563 and as a burgess to parliament in 1566 (see MacCaffrey, *Exeter,* pp. 150, 214, 223). In 1584 Hooker gave him copies of his pamphlets as a New Year's gift (see EXRO, book 57). From the context it would appear that the "Senators" to whom Hooker dedicated his booklet were the two MPs representing Exeter in the 1572 parliament, Geoffrey Tothill and Simon Knight, both of whom were native Exonians and active in local politics (see Alexander, "Exeter Members," and MacCaffrey, *Exeter,* pp. 224–27). It is interesting to note that in 1563, when he also sat for Exeter in parliament, Tothill had written letters to Hooker about certain bills in the House of Commons (see HMC Exeter, pp. 51–52).

For by the ancient orders and prescribed lawes of this land: onely such are to be elected and to have place there as for gravitie, wisdome, knowledge and experience, are reputed and knowen to be the moste chosen and principall personages [2a] of the whole land and Realme.[2] And this court beeing in authoritie highest, and in power cheefest: none should to be thorderers, Judges and councellers therof, but such as in vertues and good conditions are answerable to the same.

The order (therfore) among the Romains was that none should be receiued or allowed to be of their Senate house: unlesse he were grave in yeeres, and wel experienced in common affaires of the publique welth. The Lacademonians admitted none to be an Ephorus amõgst them: but that he were a tryed man for knowledge and experience. The Athenians would be assured that he should be wise and lerned, that should be of their counsail.[3]

The like order also was and is within this Realm, the same being derived and taken cheefly from emong the Romains, emong and under whome: divers of tholde and ancient Kings of this Realm, have ben bred and brought up.

And by meanes of the wisdome, learning and knowledge, learned emong them, have not onely attained to the Septer of this realme: but also some of them have been the monarches and [2b] Emperours of the whole world.[4]

These good Kings and Princes (I say) finding this land by disordered life, lawles libertie, and lose behavior to be brought to an utter ruin, decay and desolation, no reason longer ruling, nor good order allowed, then as privat affections and self wil

2. Here Hooker seems to refer to the various statutes dating from the Lancastrian era which regulated elections, specifically: 7 H.4.c.15; 13 H.4.c.1; 1 H.5.c.1; 6 H.6.c.4; and 8 H.6.c.7.

3. Sir John Fortescue incorporates similar allusions to Athens and Sparta in his *Governance of England*, ed. C. Plummer (Oxford, 1926), pp. 149–50, 190–92.

4. In all likelihood Hooker is referring here to those Roman occupational governors of Britain who eventually became emperors of the Roman Empire.

would allow and like of: after many devises, consultations and attempts for redresse, no way could be found so good, no remedie so present, nor help so speedy: as to erect and establish a Senate of the moste grave, wise and expert personages of the whole Realme, called by the name of a Parlement. For as Patricius in his third Book, *De institutione Reipub,* saith. The best order of governmet of the common welth: procedeth alwais frō tholde and ancient Senators, which are reputed and taken to be the fathers of the common welth. For as fathers for their Children: so these for the cōmon welth are moste careful and tender.[5]

And albeit the King or prince be never so wise, learned and expert: yet is it impossible for any one to be exact and perfit in all things, but a Senate of wise, grave, learned and expert [3a] men, beeing assembled in councel togither: they are as it were one body, having many eyes to se, many feet to go, and many hands to labour withall, and so sircumspect they are for the government of the commōwelth: that they se all thĩgs, nothing is hid or secret, nothing is straunge or new, nothing is to great or weightie to them, but whether it be in causes of war, or of peace: they wilbe wel advised, and measure all things, with good reason, circumspection and policie.

Moyses therfore, although (having talked with God face to face, he were above all others most wise, discreet and learned, yet not trusting all togither to his owne wittes: made choice of all thelders of Israel, and by their councel did order and direct the publique state & cōmon welth of his people, and likewise beeing councelled by his father in law Jethro, to provide emong all his people, strong, couragiouse and valeat men, (and suche as feared God, dealed truely, and hated covetousnes) to be rulers over the people, to govern and judge

---

5. Francesco Patrizi, *De institutione reipublicae.* Hooker probably used either the 1559 edition printed in Paris, which was an epitome, or the 1567 edition edited by John Charron also printed in Paris. It is possible that most of the classical authors cited in both dedicatory epistles came from Patrizi for all of them appear in *De institutione.*

them, he did so, onely the greatest and weightiest matters whiche touched God: were brought before him alone.[6]

[3b] Wherfore according to the good profitable and ancient orders of the Romans and Israelits: these good Kings doo erect a Senate or Parlemet.[7] Lawes are prescribed how the same shuld be kept, orders made what manner of persons shalbe elected and chosen for the same, and constitutions set foorth how and in what sort lawes and ordinaunces shalbe made for the benefit of the common welth. And surely these good and wholsome orders being put in use and execution: the benefit therof grew so much in short time, that there was as it were a Metamorphoses of the state of the publique weale in those daies, for what Sedition and contention had disordred: good order and concord recovered. What loosenes and dissolutnes of life had marred: honest behaviour restored. What disobedience had decayed: loiable obedience amended. And finally what soever by any disorder was amisse: was by these means reformed and redressed: and the evils which were crept and brought in by ambition, covetousnes, debate, malice or envy: were so reformed as that the people beeing better governed and instructed: would not be caryed with [4a] every affection, neither yet prefer private profit and wilful lusts, before the common and publique welth.

Lo, suche are the frutes which grew of the Parlements, and thus doth it fare in all estates where good men doo rule, wholsome lawes are made, and good order kept and observed, and so long doo common welths florish: as when princes do rule and governe by law, and people loyally obeying doo live under law.

Erasmus in his Book *De institutione principis Christiani*, saith, that good lawes under a good Prince: doo make a happy

6. Exodus 18:13–26.

7. Hooker speaks of "good kings" in both dedicatory epistles without specifying individual sovereigns or dynasties. From the context it would appear that he means Anglo-Saxon kings, probably Ethelred or Edward the Confessor, both of whom are singled out below.

Realme and fortunate governmet. *Cuius tum felicissimus est status, cum principi paretur ab omnibus atque ipse Princeps paret legibus leges autem, and architypum aequi et honesti respondet nec alio spectant, quam ad Rem commune in melius prouchendam.* [8] Whose state is then moste fortunate when the people doo obey the Prince, and the Prince obeyeth the lawes, and when lawes bee made just and right, and for the better aduauncement of the common welth. And surely these are so inseperable that in a good common welth they cannot be disseuered, but a good Prince [4b] and good lawes must be concurrant, for although it be a rule that *Quod principi placet legis habet vigorē*, & that Princes heasts ar lawes:[9] yet the Ethnicks them selues doo holde thoppinion and affirme, that vnlesse the lawes be iust and made according to the rule of wisdome, and for the comonwelth: it is no law, for that is a law, *Quod sapienti bonoque principi placet cui nil placet, nisi quod honestu, ac quod seniorū, iuditio atque setentia probatum est fore Republica.* [10]

And surely in my oppinion, if it behoueth Princes to be valeant in armes, and expert in martiall affaires, wherby to withstand the enemye, and to represse the rebel; much more ought he to be wise and learned, that he knowing the lawes and keeping the same, may the better gouerne his people in peace and keep them in dutiful obedience.

Wherfore Iustinian the Emperour in the proheme to the instituts, hath this sentence. *Imperatoriam maiestatem, non solū armis decoratam sed et legibus armatam esse oportet, vt vtrumque tem-*

8. See *Opera Omnia Desiderii Erasmi Rotterdami Recognita et annotatione critica instructa notisque illustrata,* 5 vols. (Amsterdam, 1974), vol. 4, part I, p. 194. Hooker's translation is quite accurate. Numerous editions were available to sixteenth-century readers.

9. "What pleases the prince has the force of law." This is a Roman legal maxim found in Justinian's *Institutes,* 1.2.6., and the *Digest,* 1.4.1. Very likely the word *heasts* meant hasty actions.

10. "What is pleasing to the wise and good prince to whom nothing is pleasing but that which is approved by the judgement and decision of the nobler and more honorable for the Republic." This is a paraphrased version from Patrizi, *De institutione;* see *Opera Omnia,* vol. 4, part I, p. 194.

pus, et bellorum, et pacis, recte possit gubernari. an Emperour or a
king ought not onely to be skilful in feates of armes: but also
to be wel learned and instructed in the [5a] lawes: that he may
prevail against his enemye, as also peaceably governe his Subjects.[11] It is also an olde sentence, and for the worthines therof
graven in Golde among the professors of the common lawes
of this Realme, *Arma Regum Lex.*[12]

And therfore the Egiptians did think it more honorable and
commendable that Kings should be rather learned in good
studyes, then addicted to martiall feates, and therfore their
kings did with great diligence apply the[m] selves to the studyes
of wisdo[m]e and knowledge, neither did any King emong them
think that he did or could governe wel: unlesse (as in authoritie, so also in wisdome, vertue and learning) he did excell all
the rest of his Subjects and people.[13] Then if it be so necessary
and expedient for the commonwelth that the same be governed by learned and wise rulers, and guyded by just and good
lawes: how happy, blessed & fortunate is this realme of Eng-
la[n]d, which hath fou[n]d both thone & thother?

For neither Athens with their Solon, and his lawes. Sparto
with their Licurgus and his lawes: Egipt with Mercurius and his
lawes. Rome with their Romulus and his lawes. The [5b] Itali-
ans with their Pithagoras and his lawes, and finally a number

11. This quotation comes from the proem of Justinian, *Institutes*. In his
rendition Hooker transposed the words *armatam* and *oportet*. It is interesting
to note that Sir John Fortescue used the same quotation in his *De Laudibus:*
see p. 4 of the Chrimes edition.

12. Literally, "Law is the armor of kings."

13. For the influence of Egypt on Renaissance humanists and Protestants
see Frances A. Yates, *Giordano Bruno and the Hermetic Tradition* (Chicago, 1964).
Hooker could have been influenced by the writings of Cicero and Italian
humanists like Patrizi and Ficino, or by those of Erasmus, Peter Martyr, and
Thomas Elyot. In the next paragraph Hooker claims that the Egyptians received their laws from the Egyptian sun god Mercurius—a claim put forward
by Cicero, one of the transmitters of the hermetic tradition, in his *De natura
deorum.* Yates discusses this in pp. 4–43. That Hooker held Cicero in high
esteem is evident in his life of Sir Peter Carew; see Philips's edition in *Archa-
elogia* 27 (1840): 151–52.

of other famose contries and worthy governors, of whome great advaunt is made:[14] are not to be compared to this little ile and Realm, which in bothe respects hath passed and excelled them all. For the Kings and rulers therof (not for a short time: but in the course of many hundrethes of yeeres) have not been so valeant as wise, not so couragious as prudent, not so puissant as learned, and not so politique in the feeldes: as grave in the Senates. Likewise the lawes, in equitie most upright, in judgemēts most true, and in conscience moste resonable. The observation and keeping of which lawes: hath heertofore preserved this Realme from forain enemyes, defended it from civil seditions, and kept the people in safetie, so that is vrified whiche Melanchthon writeth of Solon. *Denique vita hominum, tranquilla et honesta manebit: seruandi leges, dum pia cura manet.*[15]

It resteth now that if we doo minde to be the naturall Children of so wise fore Fathers, the obedient Subjects of moste worthy Rulers, the observers of moste godly and wholsome lawes: [6a] that like to our ancestors we doo carefully and obedyently in all dutifulnes live after their race and dispose our selves after their examples: for if we doo once yeeld to the breach therof, then be assured, the destruction of our selves, the decay of our posteritie, and utter ruin of our common welth wil shortly and immediatly folow.

For no longer shall our life be in safetie: then we doo

14. Nowhere does Hooker reveal the sources of these historical allusions, many of which also appear in his other writings, but no doubt his humanistic education exposed him to Cicero, Plutarch, Polybius, Augustine, Patrizi, Erasmus, and others who made use of these allusions. Whether Hooker had these sources in his own library or used the libraries of Richard Stanihurst, Sir Peter Carew, or the Exeter Cathedral is not clear.

15. "Then will the life of men be quiet and virtuous when the conservation of laws remains a pious duty"; see Philippi Melanchthonis, *Opera Quae supersunt omnia,* 28 vols. (Halle, 1834–60), vol. 17, col. 876. This quote is from Melanchthon's interpretation of Demosthenes' elegy on Solon. It would have been available to Hooker in numerous editions published between 1541 and 1562 in Wittenberg, Basle, and Antwerp.

dutifully obey the Prince and obediently observe the lawes.

The olde and ancient Fathers in the former ages, were so straight in this poynt, that they would in no wise commit the least breach of any law. For Chilo[16] the Lacedomonian, was of the oppinion, that the commonwelth could no longer endure then whē the lawes were firmely observed.

Heraclitus of Ephesus saith, that Citizēs are more bounden to fight for defence of their lawes: then for keeping of their walles, for with out walles the Cittie might stand, but without lawes it could not continew, and yet bothe are to be defended.[17]

Archidamus saith, that in all wel governed commõwelths: all degrees and estates of [6b] people are like obedient to the order of the lawes as wel the magistrat: as the inferior, & the King: as the Subject.[18] Saint Paule saith, that he is not the just man, which onely knoweth the lawes: *Sed qui factis legem exprimit* which living under the law dooth obey and keep the same.[19] And surely if we English men would doo the like, and folow the steps of such common welths, as whose states continued so long as they kept their lawes, and also consider how this Realme hetherto, by that meanes hath been and is preserved: we shall not need to feare of our estate, dout of our fall, or mistrust of our decay. No forain invations shall prevail against us, nor yet intestine seditions be able to anoy us, for such is the nature of the parlements, that all mischeefs, inconveni-

16. Probably a reference to Chilon, a Spartan king mentioned in Polybius, *Histories* (4:81).

17. I have not located the source of this quotation, but Polybius refers to Heraclitus in *Histories* (4:40 and 12:27).

18. The source of the quotation has not been located, but Plutarch makes several references to Archidamus as a Spartan king who ruled during the time of Pericles; see the *Lives* (Everyman's edition), 1:233, 257; 2:196, 351, 372, 378, 380. There were numerous editions in Latin and French before Thomas North published his English translation in 1579.

19. This quotation seems to be a garbled transliteration of Romans 2:13, which reads "Truly, not those who hear the law, but those who execute the law will be justified."

ences and evels are foreseen: and all good orders devised as befor the common and publique weale, no man of what estate so ever he be: can go awry or transgresse his commission, but is under the order of that assembly, and of such ordinaunces as by the same are to be devised. For the King himself although he be the cheefest ruler, yet by the laws of this realme, he cannot establish order or make [7a] any law: but onely in Parlement, and with advise and $\overset{n}{conset}$ of all the estates and sages of the same, which law being kept, how can he with tiranny oppresse his people, or with exactions ransack and spoile his $\overset{n}{commos}$? If the noble man can be no farther allowed, then to do and speak that which shalbe liking to the King and his whole Parlement: what $\overset{n}{wrogs}$ or injuries can he offer or minister? If no $\overset{n}{ma}$ ought to be a knight of the Parlement, unlesse he be *Cinctus gladio:*[20] that is to say, wise, prudent, expert and politick in martiall affaires: what warres can advisedly or rashly be taken in hand? if no man can be a Citizen or a Burgessether, unlesse he be ancient, wise, grave and resiant in the place for whiche he is chosen: what evil lawes can passe and be concluded? yea what things amisse in any parte of the Realme, shall not upon diclosing, foorthwith and spedely be redressed?

If $\overset{n}{Salomos}$ wise and $\overset{n}{anciet}$ senators ought to have place in Parlement: what shall the rash and yung $\overset{n}{coucellers}$ of Roho$\overset{m}{boha}$ do ther?[21] If Moises by the advise of such ancient elders of Israel as were wise, $\overset{n}{valeat}$, dealed truely, feared God, [7b] and hated covetousnes, did direct the people in judgement and govern $\overset{m}{the}$ in justice: what shall children, yungmen, and such as neither fear god nor hate iniquitie, which are of no

20. This phrase, literally "girt with a sword," appeared in the writs sent to the sheriffs of each county; see Hakewill, *Ancient Customs,* and D'Ewes, *ACJ,* p. 39.

21. See 1 Kings 12:6 for the historical allusion to Solomon and Rehoboam. For a discussion of the rhetorical questions in this paragraph—really criticisms of MPs and electoral practices—see above pp. 43–45. On the presence of minors in parliament see Gilkes, *TTP,* pp. 65–66.

experience or knowledge: sit in Senate of the wise, and give judgemet emong the grave and learned? Finally if the olde Senators and wise Fathers, ought there to sit in ancient order and in grave maner: what place is there for punies, rash heddes and yung men, who having no learning, and lesse experience, are caried away (as a fether with the winde) with every light toy, making no account nor having any regarde at all to the publique weale?

And surely that our Parlements should be kept in such order: the good ancient Kings of this realme with great advise did so ordain, and great penalties are prescribed, and punishments appointed against such as shalbe remisse in observing, or guiltie in the breach therof. If we therfore, for whose safetie and preservation so good and wholsome lawes, which have been made and heertofore observed, should degenerate from our forefathers, and be remisse or carelesse [8a] in the keeping of the same: let us be assured that as we shall right worthely, so shall we assuredly feel the smart therof to the utter destruction of our selves, the subvertion of the common welth, and decay of our posteritie, for so hath it happened and be fallen to all the estates, kingdomes Realmes, Citties and commonwelths, of all the world, whose destruction and decay began with the contempt and decay of their lawes and orders.

Where is the wel governed estate of the Atheniences? What is become of the noble estate of the Romains? What is become of the prudent government of the Ephoros in Sparta? Nay what is become of the Israelits the chosen people of God? are not they driven out of their owne land, and become vagabods through the whole world? are not they so lothesome that all sorts of people doo in a manner shun and abhorre them? It is an olde saying: *Felix quem faciunt aliena pericula cautum,* happy is he that can beware by an other mannes harme.[22] Wel, if their

22. This quotation is from Erasmus, *Adages;* see *Operum Omnium,* 10 vols. (Leiden, 1703), vol. 2, col. 496e. If Hooker did not use one of the Latin editions of the *Adages* which were available to him, he could have used Richard Tavener's editions of 1539 and 1552. He could also have obtained it from the

be any feare of God in us, if any zeale to our cõmon weale, any
care of our posteritie, or account of our owne safetie: let us
[8b] have an ernest regarde to the preservation of that which
is the preservation of us. Let us keep that which keepeth us,
maintain that which maintaineth us, and defend that whiche
defendeth us. Let us prevent and beware that in choice of the
Knights, Citizens and Burgesses: none be chosen which are
straungers to the commonwelth, yung of yeeres, weke of dis-
cretion, and timerose to speak: but such as are grave, wise, and
anciẽt, and expert, fearing God, dealing truely, according to
the auncient orders, lawdable customes and prescribed lawes
of this Realme.

And for as much as the orders, usages and customs of the
Parlements of this Realme, are for the most part, and to most
men hidden and unknowen, and yet moste expedient and necessary, that none should be ignoraunt of them: I have thought
good upon considerations to make a collection of them, and
finding some alteration and varietie of the Parlements in these
dayes, from them which were used in the elder dayes: I have
made the discription bothe of the one and thother.

The first and ancientest orders I have tran- [9a] slated out
of an olde, and an ancient Lattin Record, which I have of the
Parlemẽts kept in the time of King Edward the Sonne of King
Etheldred, named Edward the confessor, about the yeer of our
Lord, 1046, which were duely for many yeers before and after
his dayes kept and observed.

The others are of mine owne devise and collection, according to that which I saw and learned at the Parlement holden
at Westminster, in the xiii. yeer of the reign of Queene Elizabeth, Anno. 1571, at which I was present, being one (though
unworthy) of the said house and assembly. I have bee the more
willing to set the same foorth: because I knowe it moste necessary and needful to be knowen, and that it toucheth the whole

---

published sermons of Hugh Latimer or Thomas Norton's *Goroduc,* published
in 1570, both of which used the quote. Hooker's English rendition of the
adage leaves something to be desired.

estate and common wealth of this Realme very neer. For if the Rulers and governours of Cities and townes, doo not more carefully look to the choice of their Citizens and Burgesses: their states may paradventure be in danger to be shaken, and their governments be in peril to perish.

And as for zeale and good wil to the whole [9b] common welth, and my native Contrey, I have taken this little travail: so of bounden deutie, I have thought good to offer and preseñt the same unto you, partly that a Legiar & memoriall of so worthy and necessary a matter: might remain and be emong your Records, for the better instruction of your selves, and all others which shal repair unto you for the same. But cheefly to yeeld myself unto you moste humble and thankful, for your good wil and tender affection towards me, for albeit you had the choice of sundry wise men, which (for their gravitie, experience and knowledge farre exceeding me) were more fit to have supplyed a place in that honorable assembly: yet you of a good wil conceiving the best, made choice of me preferring me before the wise, and joyning me with the discreet, and although by meanes of sicknes, the use of my speech not serving, I could not speak my minde in that pluce, as of duety and consciēce I ought and would have doon: yet in such credit of that assembly I was, that by a whole and a generall concent of the Parlemēt: I was eftsoones chosen to be a Comitte in sundry matters of charge and [10a] importaunce, and they with whome I was joyned, although they were personages of much honor,[23] and great experience: yet such credit they gave to my words and so allowed of my sayings: that with good allowance

---

23. According to the *CJ* (1:84), on 12 April 1571 a bill concerned with Bristol trade was committed to "Mr. Comptroller, Sir Nicholas Poynts, Sir Nicholas Arnold, Sir John White, Mr. Newton, Mr. John Younge, Mr Popham, Mr. Fleetwood, Mr. Norton, Mr. Alforde, Mr. Hall of Yorke, and Mr. Hooker." The members were directed to hear both parties of the bill and report back to Commons. In his "Diary" Hooker also notes that he was a member of the committee. Subsequently, the bill was engrossed on 23 April and sent to the upper house five days later.

they relyed unto the same. Whatsoever credit or c$\overset{m}{o}$mendation, groweth to me heerby, I doo, must and wil, wholly impute it unto you. And therfore as one bounden unto you, and altogither dedicated to your service and commaundement: I doo offer this my simple and rude collection unto your worships, praying and beseeching you not to have respect to the simplicitie, rudenes and sclendernes of the matter offred: but to the good wil of the offerer.

I have before this attempted and begun to to draw and make a discourse, of the antiquitie, estate and government of this Cittie, thinking when I began: I should long ere this have absolved the same, and have offred it unto you.[24] But in the middle of my travails, beeing by your consets, called to folow the weightie affaires of the right worshipful, Sir Peeter Carew knight, in Ireland: I was cut of and dissapointed, sithens [10b] beeing returned, I have for the moste part been so over charged with sicknes, and mine affections have been and are so distempered: as that oportunitie and power have not yet served to folow the absolving of that, whiche my good wil and ernest desire wissheth.

Neverthelesse, having perused the discription of this Cittie, which was of mine owne collection: I have upon the sight of more matter enlarged, augm$\overset{n}{e}$ted and brought the same to such a perfection, as for the time and matter sufficient. The imperfections (if any be) I wil beer after as occasion shall serve: supply and amend, in the meane time, having joyned the same unto this, and thinking it moste meet to be offred unto you: I doo moste humbly pray you, accept the same in good parte.

The Lord God from whome commeth what so ever is good, and who directeth the councels of the Just, and prospereth the divices of the godly: send his holy spirit upon you, that you living in the feare of him, may hate iniquitie, abhorre covetousnes, and without affection give [11a] just Judgements, and

24. This refers to Hooker's description of Exeter—a project started in the 1560s and completed between June 1571 and October 1572—which was appended to the Exeter edition of his *Order and Usage*.

in all trueth, equitie and justice: governe, rule and direct the people, over whome he hath made you the governers and Rulers, whereby his name may be glorified, the common welth prospered: and you at length sitting with the xxiiii Elders,[25] may be crowned with them, and injoy that peace and blessing whiche is prepared for such as execute justice and give true Judgements.

25. This reference to the twenty-four members of the chamber makes it clear that the "Senators" referred to on page 1 were MPs and not members of the chamber.

[12b] The olde and auncient order of keeping of the Parlement in England used in the time of King Edward the confessor.[1]

First the monicion or summons of the Parlement ought to be made or doon forty dayes before the beginning of the Parlement.[2]

The Summons of the Spiritualtie.

All Bishops,[3] Abbots, Priors and all other great Clarks that holde by countie or barony, by reason of their holding, ought to be monished, and also to come to the Parlement, and none other inferiours of the Clergie, unlesse their presence were profitable and necessary for the Parlement. And to those the King is bound to give their cost comming & abiding at the

1. Nowhere in his twin publications did Hooker employ the Latin title *Modus Tenendi Parliamentum,* the title used by Lambarde, Coke, Hakewill, and others to describe the medieval tractate. The proem of most extant versions (excluding the Irish) contains a phrase attributing the *Modus* to the time of Edward the Confessor. See Clarke, *Medieval Representation,* pp. 7, 249, 374.

2. As pointed out in the introduction, the Exeter and Fitzwilliam editions of the *Modus* contained minor variations, mainly typographical. Rather than reproduce both editions, I have decided to reprint the Exeter edition and then annotate the nontypographical variants in footnotes. The compositor for the Fitzwilliam edition freely changed punctuation, spelling, abbreviations, and capitalizations from the Exeter edition, from which he set his type; the following collation, while ignoring these, singles out differences in organization and substance.

3. While most manuscript versions of the *Modus* included the rank of archbishop in this list of greater clergy, it is omitted in both of Hooker's editions. It is included in the second paragraph, however. See Clarke, *Medieval Representation,* p. 374.

Parlemēt, and such inferiour Clarks not to be monished to come to the Parlement. But the king was accustomed to send his writs unto such discrete men, desiring them to come and be at the Parlement.[4]

Also the king was accustomed to send his monicions or summons to the Archbishops, Bishops and other exempt persons, that is to say, Abbots, Priors, Deanes and other ecclesiastical persons that have jurisdiction by such exemption and distinct priviledges, that they for every Deanry and Archdeconry through England should elect and choose or cause to be elected & chosen, two discrete and wise proctors of their owne Archdeconry whiche should come and be at the parlement, there to sustain and alow, and to doo that thing that every man of their Deanry or Archdeaconry might doo if they weer there in proper persons, & those[5] Proctors so sent, for the Clergie: should bring with them their double proxies sealed with double seales of their superiours. The one of the proxies to remain with the Clarks of the Parlement: and thother to remain [13a] with the said proctors, and under this maner the Clergie ought to be called to the Parlement.

The Summons of the Temporaltie.

Also all and every Earle, Baron and their peeres, that is to say, that have lands and rents to the value of an Earldome or of a whole Barony, that is to say, xx. knights fees, every fee contayning .xx. pound land, which amounteth to iiii. hundred pound in the whole, or to the value of an whole Barony, that is to say xiii. fees: and the third parte of a knights fee, every fee accounted at xx. pound. which amounteth in the whole to iiii. hundred Marks. And no inferior persons of ẙ Temporaltie shall come to the Parlement by reason of his holde unlesse his presence be necessary and profitable, and they to be ordred

---

4. The Fitzwilliam edition does not have a paragraph break at this point.
5. The Fitzwilliam edition reads *these*.

for their charges at the kings costs, as is spoken of before of the inferior Clerks.

The Summons of the Barons of the Five Portes.

Also the King ought to send his writs to ẙ warden of the five portes that he should cause to be elected or chosen for every of ẙ said portes: two discrete & wise Barons that should come and be present at the Parlement, there to answere, sustain, aledge and doo all things concerning the said parlement, as wel as if all and every of the Barons were there personally.[6] And these Barons so elect and chosen: shall bring with them their double proxies, double sealed with the common seal of the port. The one therof to be delivered to the Clarkes of the Parlement: and the other to remain with the said Barons so chosen and elected. And when it shall chaunce the said Barons (licence obteyned) to departe [13b]: they were accustomed to have a writ sealed with the great seal to the warden of the five portes for their reasonable expences doon from the first of their comming [to the Parlement, until the time of their departing and comming][7] home, to be levied of ẙ comminaltie of every party having expresse mention made in the writ from the said first day of their comming: until the time of their licence obteyned, and it was accustomed that mention should be made in the said writ what every Baron should take of the cõmons for a day, that is to say, some more, some lesse, a consideration and respect had to the honestest, for their tarying, labours & expences, and it was not accustomed that any certain sum was limitted by the said Court.

Of the knights of the Parlement.

Also the king was accustomed to send his writs to all the Shirifs within the Realme, that they should cause to be chosen

---

6. The Fitzwilliam edition has a paragraph break at this point.

7. The compositor for the Fitzwilliam edition dropped this bracketed phrase. No doubt his eye skipped from the first *comming* to the second.

two honest, wise and discrete knights for every Sheere to come
to the Parlement with such proxies,[8] as is before spoken of the
Barons of the five portes. But for the expences of the said two
knights for every sheere was not accustomed to be graunted
aboove .xiii. shillings .iiij. pence for a day.

Of the Citizens of the Parlement.

IN the like the Maior of London and the Shiriffes. The Maior
and Baliffes, or the Maior and Citizens of York, and all other
Cittyes were wunt to be warned that they for the comminaltie
of their cittyes should elect & choose two discrete honest &
wise Citizens[9] to come and be at ẏ Parlement under the fourme
as is spoken of before of the Barons and of the knights of the
sheere.[10] And the said Citizens were accustomed to be like and
equall in their expences for comming, [14a] abiding and returning to and from the Parlement as are the knights.

Of the Burgesses of the Parlement.

IN like manner the Bayliffes and wise men of the Boroughes
were accustomed, and ought to be warned that they should
choose two discrete, honest, and wise Burgesses of them
selves, and by thē to come and be at the Parlement, in like
maner as is spoken of the Citizens.[11] But it was not accustomed
that two Burgesses should have for their charges aboove x.
shillings, & sometime not aboove vj. shillings. vii. pence, and
that should be taxed by the Court, after the habilitie of the
borough, and the honestie of the Burgesses.

---

8. Hooker has a bad copy or renders an erroneous translation at this juncture. Most versions of the *Modus* contain the word *warrantis* and say nothing
of proxies.

9. Repeatedly Hooker changes the order as he translates. Instead of following the order in the *Modus* inherent in the Latin phrase "idoneos, honestos
et peritos," he invariably changes the order. See Clarke, *Medieval Representation,* chapters I, IV, VI, and VII, and pp. 374-77.

10. In the Fitzwilliam edition a new paragraph begins after *sheere.*

11. The compositor of the Fitzwilliam edition began a new paragraph here.

Of the two principall Clarkes of the Parlement.

ALso two principall Clarkes of the Parlement shall sit in the midst of the Justices which shall inrolle all plaintes, and matters of the Parlement. And it is to be knowen that these twoo Clarkes be not subject to any of the Justices of England, nor that any Justice hath any aucthoritie in the Parlement except[12] he be assigned to any thing by the King, and Peeres of the Parlement.

And when they be assigned with other Suetors of the Parlement to hear and determin divers pleaes and peticions to be finished by Parlement, yet the twoo Clarks to be immediat subjects to the King and Parlement in common, unlesse one of ye Judges or two be assigned to examin and amend their inrolling. And if the peeres of ye Parlemet be assigned to hear & examin any speciall petition, after they have broken their matter: they shall give their sentence and Judgement in the ful Perlement,[13] and the two [14b] Clarks inrolle the same, and all other plaints and judgements of the Parlement in the principall of the Parlemet, and there to deliver those rolles to the Treasurer before the Parlement be finished.

Provided that the said Clarks shall have a transumpt or Copy of it, if they list, and these two Clarks shall have for their exp eces xiii. shillings and iiii. pence, unlesse they have any fees or offices by the king, and be dayly waitors having meat and drink of the Kings cost: and then they to have .vj. shillings and viii. pence every day during the Parlement.

Of the five Clarks.

ALso the King shall assigne five Clarks, wise and approbate, of whom, the first shall atted the Bishops. The second the proctors of the Clergie. The third the Earles and Barons. The fourth the knights of the Sheeres, and the fifth: the Citizens and Burgesses.

---

12. The Fitzwilliam edition substitutes the word *unlesse* for *except.*

13. This typographical misspelling was corrected in the Fitzwilliam edition to read *Parlement.*

And every of them shall have ii. shillings a day: unlesse they be the Kings servants, and have sufficient living of the King, & then they to have but xij. pence the day, which Clarks shall write all doutes between the King and the Parlement, and they to be at their coūcels[14] where so ever they be commaūded. And in cace they shalbe vacant: they shall help ẙ two principall clarks to inrolle their busines.

Of the causes and douts of the Parlement.

WHen any breach, difficultie of dout, or defuse[15] cause of warre or peace dooth appeer within the Realme or without, that cace ought to be declared in writing in the ful Parlement, there to be treated and disputed among the Peeres of the Parlement, and if it be necessary: the King shall commaund or [15a] in the Kings name it shalbe commaunded that every degree, and the persons of every degree of the Parlement shalbe present in the parlement, and to the Clark of every degree in the Parlement, the cause, breach and dout shall be delivered, and by him at a certain place to be to them delivered and declared.[16]

And therupon they to study, imagine and consider how this dout or breach may be provided for, as they in time com-ming shall make answere for the prservation[17] of the King, them selves, and the commons whose persons they doo rep-resent,[18] and so in this behalfe they shall make their answere or councel to be written, so that every degrees answere and advisement heard: the whole Parlement to admit and alowe the best and wisest councel and therafter to doo, and wheras been divers opinions: then to incline to the more parte of the Parlement.

---

14. Meaning "counsels" or, as in the Fitzwilliam edition, *councels.*
15. The Fitzwilliam edition reads *diffuse.*
16. This paragraph break was omitted in the Fitzwilliam edition.
17. An *e* was added in the Fitzwilliam edition to correct the misspelling.
18. The Fitzwilliam edition has a paragraph break here.

And in cace there be any discorde between the king and any of the estates, or between estates, wherby the peace of the Realme, or the people of the countrie might be disturbed: in this cace if the King think it expedient, it ought to be commoned[19] of, and reformed by the advise of all the Peeres of the Realme. Or in cace the King and Realme been troubled with warres, or a doutful cace be depending before the Chaūceller of England, or a defuse[20] judgement be depending before the Justices, and if in those the Peeres of the degrees of the Parlement cannot agree: then the Earle Steward, the Earle Constable, and the Earle Marshall, or twoo of them: shall elect .xxv. persons of every degree of the peeres of the Realme, $\overset{e}{y}$ is to say: twoo Bishops, three proctors for the Clergie, two Earles, three Barons, five knights of the Sheeres, five Citizens, and five Burgesses, and these .xxv. may condiscend into xij. of them selves, and these xij. into .vi. of them selves, and these six may condiscend into three, but these three cannot condiscend into a lesse number without the Kings concent, and then those three may condiscend into two, and the two into one, and after his opinion and determination: [15b] the matter shalbe ordered unlesse the King wil discent as he may, and then may he and his councel examin and amend the ordination, so it be unwritten and doon out of the Parlement house without their concents.

Of matters of the Parlement.

THe matters whereof the Parlement is holden or kept: ought to be delivered into the Parlement, and to be called upon in manner of a kalender, according to every mannes petition, and no respect to be had to any mannes person: but that he who layeth first his bil in: shalbe first heard.

19. The word *communed* in the Fitzwilliam edition is probably a more accurate: see Clarke, *Medieval Representation*, p. 380.
20. *Diffuse* in the Fitzwilliam edition. In the *Modus* the Latin word is "difficile"; see ibid.

In the Kalender of the Parlement every matter ought to be had in[21] memory under this manner and forme.

First: of warres if their be any, of matters concerning the King and Queenes person, and of their Children.

Secondly: of matters concerning the common weale, and to ordain new lawes debarring th'olde lawes made in times past, whose execution have been prejudiciall.

Thirdly: the matters concerning the privat weale, and these to be examined according to the file and Kalender as is before writen.

The dayes and houres of the Parlement.

THe Parlement shalbe holden every day, Sundaies, Allhallon day, all soules day & the nativitie of Saint John the Baptist excepted. And every seriall day it should begin at mid prime time, and that houre: the king is bound to be in the Parlement and all y peeres of the Realme. On the holy daies the parlement shall begin at the prime, because of the divine service should be first heard.

[16a]   The degrees of the Parlement.

THe King is head and cheef at the beginning and at th'end of the parlement, and to him no comparison is to be made, and so the King is one degree by him self.

The second is of Archebishops, Abbots and Priors, holding by Baronyes.

The third is of the Proctors of the Clergie. The fourth of Earles Barons and other estates and gentles holding to the value of an Earledome or Baronye as is before written. The fift of Knights of the Sheeres.

The sixt[22] of Citizens and Burgesses, and so the Parlement is of six degrees. And it is to be noted that if any of the said

---

21. The Fitzwilliam edition at this point repeats the word *in*, obviously as typographical mistake.

22. Corrected in the Fitzwilliam edition to read *fifth* and *sixth*.

degrees be absent after their first lawful[23] monicions or summons: the Parlement is not of sufficient effect.

The forme of the Parlement.

SIth it is showed under what forme every man ought to be
monished, and how long time the monitions should be, and
what they be that [should come unto it: it is to be knowen who
they be that][24] ought to be monished to come to the Parlement
by reason of their offices. And also it is to be noted that the
two principall Clarks of the Parlement for the King and his
Councel, and other secondary Clarks, of whom and of whose
office mencion shalbe hereafter made.[25]

The cheef Cryer of England with his deputies, and the cheef
Porter of England, howbeit these two offices were accustomed
to be occupyed by one person, these ought to be there the first
day of the Parlement.[26]

The Lord Chaunceler of England, the Treasurer, the Chamberlain, the Barons of the Eschequer, the Justices, all the kings
Clarks and knights, with Sergeants at the [16b] Law of the
kings retinew or fee: ought to be there the second day, unlesse
they have a resonable impediment or let.[27]

Of the beginning of the Parlement.

THe King ought to be in the Parlement the first day and
should sit in the midst of the high bench. The sixt day: the
Chaunceller, the Treasurer, the Barons of the Eschequer and

23. The compositor dropped this word in the Fitzwilliam edition.
24. This bracketed phrase was dropped by the compositor of the Fitzwilliam
edition whose eye, undoubtedly, skipped from the first *that* to the second and
missed the phrase between them.
25. As pointed out by Hodnet and White, this is a crucial identifying paragraph characteristic of the B versions of the *Modus*. Since the clerks have
already been covered, the whole chapter has been transposed from the beginning to the middle of the tractate.
26. The Fitzwilliam edition omits the paragraph break at this point.
27. Meaning "permission" or "license."

the Justices were accustomed to recorde the defaults doon in the Parlemēt in forme folowing. The first day they must call all the Citizens and Burgesses of all England, and for lack of their apparaunce: a Citty shalbe amerced in a C. pound, and a borough a C. marks.

The second day: they shall call knights of Sheeres, and in default of their apparance: the sheere shalbe amerced a C. poūd.

The third day: the Barons of the five portes, & after them th'other Barons, and then the Earles, and for lack of apparance of every Baron: they shalbe amerced a C. marks, and of an Erle: a C. pound, the like shalbe doon to them that be Earles and Barons Peeres, that is to say, as have Lands and rents to ẙ yeerly value of an Earledome or of a barony as is before expressed. The fourth day: the Proctors of the Clergie shalbe called, and for lack of their apparance: their Bishops shalbe amerced a C. marks for every Archdeaconry that maketh default.

The fifth day: Deanes, Priors, Abbots, Bishops and Archbishops, and for lack of apparaunce of an Archbishop: he shalbe amerced a C. pound, a Bishop, an Abbot and a Prior, whiche holde an whole barony: a C. marks.

Of the Proclamations.

THe first day of the Parlement proclamation shalbe made first in the Hall or in the Monastery or some other open place where the Parlement shalbe holden or kept, and after in the Citty or Town opēly that every man having Bil or Peticion to be examined or determined in ẙ Parlement that it should be laid in within five dayes of the beginning of [17a] the parlement.

Of the preaching of the Parlement.

AN Archbishop or some famose discrete and eloquent Clark to be assigned by the Archbishop in whose province the Parlement shalbe kept and holden, shall preach on the

first of y̆ five dayes in the ful Parlement & in the Kings presence, and he shall begin when all the Parlement or the moste
parte shalbe there assembled, & in his orison or prayer he shall
require all the whole Parlement that they humbly beseech
almightie God for the peace and tranquilitie of the King and
Realme.

Of the Speaker of the Parlement.

AFter the Sermon doon: the L. Chaunceller of England or
the cheef Justice elect, shall stand declaring in the parlement
house, first generally and then specially the causes of the
Parlement, and wherfore the same is holden.[28]
And it is to be noted that every man (the King excepted)
shall stand while the said Speaker dooth declare his matter, to
th'entent that every man may hear him: & in cace he doo speak
obscurely or darkly or so lowe that he cannot be heard: he
must begin again, or els an other speak in his place.

What the King shall say after the Speaker hath doon.

THe King [after the speaker hath declared the causes of the
Parlement:][29] shall desire the Spiritualtie and the Temporaltie
naming every degree, that is to say, Archbishops, Bishops,
Abbots, Priors, Archdeacons, proctors and others of the Clergie, Earles, Barons, knights, Citizens and Burgesses, and others of the Temporaltie, that they doo diligently studiously and
loovingly indever them selves to examin pertract[30] and handle
the causes [17b] of the Parlement, to the honor of God princi-
pally: secondarely to the Kings honor, and lastly to the welth
of the Realme.

28. This paragraph break is omitted in the Fitzwilliam edition.
29. The compositor of the Fitzwilliam edition placed parentheses around
the bracketed phrase.
30. A synonym for *handle* or *treat*.

Of the Kings absence.

THe King ought dayly to be present in the Parlement, unlesse he be sick or diseased: and then he may keep his chamber, so that he lodge not out of the manor or town, where the Parlement is holden, and then he ought to send for xij.[31] persons of the great estates that be monished or summoned to the Parlement, wherof two to be Bishops, two Earles, two Barons, two Knights, two Citizens and two Burgesses, to see his person & to certifie of his estate, & in their presence he ought to commit power to the Archbishop of the Province, to the Lord Steward and to the cheef Justices, that they joyntly and severally shall begin and continew the Parlement in the Kings name, making expresse mention in his commission of his disease to th'other estates, and that the persons aboove named can expresse the same, for it is a perilous cace and dangerous for the communaltie and Realme that the king should be absent from the Parlement: but onely for bodely sicknes.

Of places and seates in the Parlement.

FIrst as it is before said, the King shall sit in the midst of the bench, upon the right hand the Archbishop of Canterbury, at his left hand the Archbishop of Canterbury, at his left hand the Archbishop of Yorke, and then Bishops, Abbots, and Priors in order, and then every man in his degree, and amongst his peeres, and that this order be kept: the Lord Steward of England is bound to look unto, unlesse the King assigne some other.

At the Kings righ[32] foot, the Chaunceller of England, the cheef Justice of England with his felowes, and their Clarks, that be of the Parlemet. And at his left foot shall sit the Treasurer,

31. The compositor of the Fitzwilliam edition misread this number, confusing an *x* with an *i*, and printed *iii persons*.

32. The missing *t*, a typographical error, was picked up and added by the compositor of the Fitzwilliam edition.

the Chamberlain, the Barons of the Eschequer, the Judge of the [18a] common place with their Clarks that been of the Parlement.

Of the porters of the Parlement.

THe cheef Porter of the Parlement shall stand within the great gate [or Monastery,][33] hall or place, wher the Parlement is holden and shall attend that no man enter into the Parlement except he be called for matters that he sheweth in the Parlement. And it is expedient that the said Porter have knowledge of every mannes name that shall enter into the Parlement, and if need require to have many porters under him.

Of Cryers of the Parlement

THe Cryer shall stand without the Parlement door, and the Porter shall shew him when and what he shall call. The king was accustomed to appoint his Sergeants at armes to keep the Parlement door, that no thrust, presse, or noyse, were made there, by meanes wherof the Parlement might be letted, and that such thrust, preace[34] or noyse might be avoyded, and proclamation should be made that no person enterprise such things there, under pain of imprisonment, for by Law: the Parlement door should not be shut, but be kept by the Porter or Sergeaunt at Armes.

Of the help for the King.

THe King was not accustomed to demaund, help of his Realme but onely for war that was instant, or for the creation of his Sonnes to bee made knights: or his Daughters[35] to be maryed, and these helps ought to be demaunded in the ful

33. The compositor of the Fitzwilliam edition picked up this error and corrected it to read *of the Monastery.*

34. Meaning "press," as in the previous clause.

35. In the Fitzwilliam edition this word is singular.

Parlement, and in writing to be delivered unto every degree, and they in writing to make an- [18b] swere. And if this help ought to be graunted: then every degree of the Parlemet should cõcent therto. And it is to be knowen, that two Knights or two Citizens, or two Burgesses whiche come to the Parlement, in graunting or denying any thing demaunded in the Parlement: have more aucthoritie then the greatest Earle in England. And in like cace, two proctors for the Clergie in one diocesse: have more aucthoritie then their Bishops in things to be graunted or denyed in Parlement, and ỹ reason is this. The King may holde his parlemẽt for the communaltie of his Realme without Bishops, Earles or Barons, so that they have lawful sumons and come not, for some time there was no Bishop, Earle nor Baron, and yet ỹ King did keep his Parlemẽt, but of the contrary, if the communaltie of the Clergie and of the Temporaltie be monished to the parlement as they ought to be by the Law, and for certain causes they doo not or wilnot come, as if they pretend that the King hath not ruled or governed them accordingly, and doo therin expresse wherin he hath not ruled them accordingly: in this cace the Parlement whiche the King holdeth with the Bishops, Earles and Barons is of no effect, and therefore in all things that are to be graunted, ordayned, established or broken by parlement: the communaltie of ỹ parlement of necessitie must concent therunto. For in the cõmunaltie are conteyned iiii. degrees of Parlement, that is to say, proctors of the Clergie, Knights of Sheers, Citizens of Cittyes and Burgesses of Townes, & these persons doo represent the whole cõmunaltie of England wheras th'other estates doo represent but their owne persons.

For billes and peticions of the Parlement.

THe Parlement ought not to bee ended whiles any peticion dependeth undiscussed or at least to whome a determinate aunswere is not made, and if the King permit the contrary: hee is perjured, also no Peere of the Parlement shall departe from the same without licence obtayned of the King [19a] and of his peeres, which licence is to be obteyned in open parlement, and to be recorded in rolle of Parlement.[36] And if it happen any of the Peeres to be sick, during the Parlement so that he cannot come to it: then for three dayes he shall send his excuse to the Parlement, but if after three dayes passed he come not: then two of his peeres shalbe sent to him to see his person, and therof to advertise the Parlement, and if any suspition be had: these two Peeres shalbe sworne to testifie the very trueth, and if it appeer he have fained him self sick: he then to be amerced as a fault for his not appeeraunce at the beginning of y Perlement[37], and if he be sick then before: then he shall make a sufficient[38] to appeer in Parlement for him.

No person of the Parlement can be excused having his helth and memory.

The ending of the Parlement.

THe finishing of the Parlement must be assigned, appointed and openly proclamed bothe in the Parlement, and within the palace of the Parlement. And if there be any wil say, that he hath no answere of his bil delivered into the Parlement: then the Parlement to continue, but if no man so say: it is to be supposed that every man hath remedye or assigned how to have remedy by the Lawes, and at the proclamation made, if there be no Billes to be laid in: the King may licence[39] his Parlement.

Of the Coppyes[40] of the Records of the Parlement.

THe Clark of the Parlement shall deny to no man the coppy of his processe, but shall deliver unto every man that de-

---

36. The Fitzwilliam edition has a paragraph break at this point.

37. This spelling error was corrected in the Fitzwilliam edition to read *Parlement.*

38. A noun such as *proctor* or *attorney* is missing in both editions.

39. Hooker's literal translation of *licentiabimus.* Obviously, the context implies dismissal or permission to leave.

40. The compositor of the Fitzwilliam edition dropped one of the *p*s in this heading.

maundeth it, taking for every ten lines a peny. And if the party
be poore and therupon maketh his othe to have nothing: the
rolle of the Parlement shalbe tenne inches [19b] brode. The
Parlement shalbe kept whersoever it shall pleas the King.[41]

THese orders in processe of time did surcesse, and were out
of all use, few or no Parlements beeing kept, from the time of
William the Conqueror, until the reign of King Edward the
first, who by th'advise of his wise & learned counsailers prescribed a forme & order how the Parlements within this
Realme should be observed and kept, which orders also in the
course of certain yeeres grew out of use in many points, and
the order heer ensuing: is that which is in our dayes received
and used.

41. The *Modus* ends at this point. The following transitional paragraph,
present in both editions, represents Hooker's own views on the evolution of
parliament.

[20b]   The Order and U-
Sage how to keep a Parlement in England in these dayes, colected by John Vowel alias Hooker gentleman, one of the Citizens for the Cittie of Exeter at the Parlement holden at Westminster Anno domine Elizabethae Reginae decimo Tertio. 1571.[1]

By whome and for what cause a Parlement ought to be summoned and called.[2]

THe King who is Gods anoynted beeing the hed and cheef of the whole Realme and upon whome the government and estates therof doo wholy and onely depend: hath the power and authoritie to call and assemble his Parlement, and therin to seek & aske the advise, councel and assistace of his whole Realme, and without this his authoritie: no parlement can properly be summoned or assembled. And $\tilde{y}$ King having this authoritie, ought not to summô his Parlement: but for weightie

1. The 1571 parliament was convened on 2 April and dissolved on 29 May. According to his own diary of that parliament, Hooker attended every daily session, at least he submitted an expense bill for £13 8s to cover fifty-nine days in London and eight days travel (see Davidson, "Hoker's *Journal*" pp. 468–69). For a complete description of the deliberations see Neale, *EP*, 1:177–240.

2. Compared to Sir Thomas Smith (*De Republica Anglorum*, pp. 48–49), Hooker's causes are more general and abstract. Whereas Smith singles out such specific matters as regulation of weights and measures and the definition of rights, Hooker speaks of "suppression of Traitors" and "subduing of Rebelles," two matters of great concern in the wake of the 1569 rebellion. Both men allude to war, peace, succession, religion, subsidies, and the updating of former statutes.

& great causes, and in which he of necessitie ought to have the advise and counsel of all the estates of his Realme, whiche be these and suche like as foloweth.

First for Religion, for, for asmuche as by the Lawes of God and this Realme, the King next and immediatly under God is his deputye and Vicar in Earth, and the cheefest ruler within his Realmes and dominons: his office, function and duty is, aboove all things to seek and see that God be honored in true Religion and Vertue, and that he and his people doo bothe in profession and life live according to the same.

Also that all Idolatries, false Religions, heresies, scismes, errors, supersticions, and what so ever is contrary to true Religion, all disorders and abuses, either among the Clergie or the Laietie, be reformed, ordred and redressed.[3]

[21a] Also the assuraunce of the King and Queenes persons, and of their Children their advauncement & preferment in mariages, the establishing of succession,[4] the suppression of Traitors, the advoyding or eschewing of warres, the attempting or mooving of warres, the subduing of Rebelles, and pacifying of civil warres and commotions, the levying or having any aide or Subsidye for the preservation of the King and publique estate.

Also the making and establishing of good and wholsome Lawes, or the repealing and debarring of former Lawes, as whose execution may be hurtful or prejudiciall to the estates of the Prince or common welth. For these and such like causes, beeing of great weight, charge and importaunce: the King (by $\overset{e}{y}$ advise of his councel) may call & summon his high Court of Parlement, and by the authoritie therof establish and order

3. Whereas parliament also met to "establisheth formes of religion," according to Smith (ibid.), Hooker stressed parliament's authority to reform religion. Again, this seems to reflect the puritan efforts to reform the established church in 1571 and Hooker's rather tacit approval of those efforts.

4. Again, while Smith claims parliament "giveth formes of succession to the crowne" (ibid.), a rather innocuous claim smacking of the Henrician measures, Hooker goes further in this paragraph.

such good Lawes and orders as then shalbe thought moste
expedient and necessary.

The order and manner how to Summon the Parlement

THe King ought to send out his writs of summons to all the
estates of his Realme, at least forty dayes before the beginning
of the Parlement. First to all his Lords and Barons, that is to
wit, Archbishops, Bishops, Dukes, Marquesses, Earles, Vi-
countes and Barons, and every of these must have a speciall
writ, then to the Clergie, and the writ of their summons must
be addressed to every perticuler Bishop, for the Clergie of his
diocesse, & all these writs which are for the Clergie: the King
alwaies sendeth to y̌ Archbishops of Canterbury and York, &
by them they are sent and dispersed abrode to every perticuler
Bishop win[5] their severall provinces, and so the Bishops give
summons to the Clergie.

Lastly, for the summoning of the Commons: hee sendeth his
writ to the Lord warden of the five portes,[6] for the election
[21b] of the Barons therof, and to every severall Shiriffe, for
the choice and election of Knights, Citizens, and Burgesses
within his countie.

How and what persons ought to be chosen for the Clergie, and of their allowaunces.[7]

THe Bishop ought upon the receipt of the writ sent unto
him for the sūmoning of his Clergie: forthwith to summõ and

---

5. A contraction used by Hooker meaning *within.*

6. This practice of sending writs to the Cinque Ports dated from 1322 when
Edward II summoned representatives to the Parliament of York; see Clarke,
Medieval Representation, p. 172. In Elizabethan times the writ was directed to
the lord warden, who in turn called for nominees from each of the seven
towns. This practice continued until 1689. *Baron* was a courtesy title granted
the representative, but it carried no privilege.

7. All of the clergy covered in this chapter sat in Convocation, which Hooker
considered part of parliament. Hooker's knowledge of these procedures probably came from his personal knowledge of the Exeter diocesan administration

warne all deanes and Archdeacons within his diocesse to appeer in proper person at the Parlement, unlesse they have
some sufficient and resonable cause of absence, in whiche cace
he may appeer by his Proctor having a warrant or proxie for
the same.

Then must he also send the like summons to the Deane and
Chapter of his Cathedrall Churche, who shall forthwith assemble their Chapter and make choice of some one of them selves
to appeer in their behalf, and this man thus chosen: must have
thrir commission or proxie.

He must also send out his summons to every Archdeaconry
and peculier, requiring that the whole Clergie doo appeer
before him, his Chaũceller or Officer at a certain day, time, and
place, who beeing so assembled: shall make choice and election of two men of the said Clergie to appeer for them, and
these shall have their commission or proxie for the same.

These Proctors thus to be chosen ought to be grave, wise,
and learned men, beeing professors either of Divinitie or of
the ecclesiasticall Lawes, and that can, wil, and be able to
dispute in cause of controversie, convincing of heresies, ap-
peasing of Scismes, and devising of good and godly constitutions concerning true Religion, and orders of the Church.

These Proctors (thus elected) ought to have resonable allowances for their charges, according to the state, qualitie, or
condition of the person, as also a respect had to the time, the
proctors of the Dean and Chapter are to be paid out of the
Esche-[22a] quer of the Cathedrall Churche. The Proctors of
the Clergie are to be paid of the Clergie, among whome a
collection is to be levied for the same, according to an olde
order used among them.[8]

---

and contacts with several ecclesiastics in that diocese. It is entirely possible
that he witnessed the electoral processes described in this chapter. We know
that he worked for Bishop Coverdale and knew Chancellor Robert Weston.

8. Perhaps Hooker had the second chapter of the *Modus* in mind; see above
p. 129.

How and what maner of Knights, Citizens, and Burgesses
ought to be chosen, and of their alowances.[9]

THe Sheriffe of every Countie having received his writs:
ought foorthwith to send his precepts & summons to the Mai-
ors, Bayliffes, and hed Officers of every Citty, Town corporate,
Borough, and such places as have been accustomed to send
Burgesses, within his Countie, that they doo choose and elect
among themselves two Citizens for every Citty, & two Burgesses
for every Borough, according to their olde custome and usage.
And these hed Officers ought then to assemble them selves
and the Aldermen and commen councel of every Citty or
Town, & to make choice among them selves of two able and
sufficient men of every Citty or Town, to serve for and in the
said Parlement.

Likewise at the next Countie day to be holden in the said
Countie after the receipt of this writ, the Sheriffe ought openly
in the Court of his Sheer or Countie, between the houres of
viii. and ix. of the fore noon: make Proclamation that every free
holder shall come into the Court, and choose two sufficient
men to be Knights for the Parlement, & then he must cause the
writ to be openly and distinctly read, wherupon the said free
holders then and there present: ought to choose two Knights
accordingly, but he him self cannot give any voice, neither be
chosen.[10]

These elections aforsaid so past and doon: there ought to

9. Within the general framework of the electoral mechanics outlined by
Hooker in this chapter there was considerable diversity. For discussions of the
diverse practices see Neale, *EHC*, pp. 19–288; Edward Porritt, *The unreformed
House of Commons*, 2 vols. (Cambridge, 1903), especially 1:29–84; Cedric Ward,
"Disputed Elections in the House of Commons," Ph.d. dissertation, University of Nebraska, 1974, especially pp. 1–76; and Derek Hirst, *The Representative
of the People?* (Cambridge, 1975), particularly pp. 29–64.

10. The number of electoral disputes involving sheriffs increased during the
late sixteenth and early seventeenth centuries. Despite prohibitory laws and
customs, sheriffs gave their voices, used their influence, chose themselves, and
violated the letter and the spirit of the law. For a discussion of the county
elections and disputes see Ward, "Disputed Elections," pp. 191–245.

be severall Indentures made between the Sheriffe & the free holders of the choise of the knights, and between the Maior and the hed. Officers of every perticuler Cittie & Town of the choice of their Citizens and Burgesses, and of their names & of their [22b] mainperners and Sureties. Of these Inde^{n}tures, the one parte beeing sealed by the Sheriffe: ought to be returned to the Clark of the Parlement, and th'other parte of the Indentures, sealed by such as made choice of the Knights, and such as made choice of Citizens and Burgesses under the severall common seales of their Citties and Townes: ought to remain with the Sheriffe, or rather with the partyes so elected and chosen.[11]

The charges of every knight and Citizen was wunt to be alike, which was xiii. shillings. iiii. p^{n}ce by the day, but now by the Statute it is but viii. shillings, that is, to every Knight, & every Citizen iiii. shillings, & to every Burgesse the olde usage to have v. shillings, but now it is but iii. shillings & iiii. pence limitted by the Statute, which alowaunces is to be given from the first day of their jorney towards the Parlement, until last day of their return from the^{n}ce. Provided that every such person shalbe alowed for so many daies as by jorneying xxvii. miles every day in the Winter, and xxx. miles in the Summer, hee may come and return to and from the Parlement.[12]

11. Very likely Hooker had some firsthand acquaintance with the electoral mechanics described in this paragraph. But, whether he did or not, the indenture process was open to considerable abuse, for the indentures could be forged, rigged, and falsified. The abuses, when detected and protested, evoked an increasing number of electoral disputes (ibid.).

12. The accuracy of this paragraph is open to question and the source of Hooker's information is not clear. The writs *de expensis,* analyzed by Pollard, *EOP* (pp. 317–9, 387–429), reveal that local customs varied considerably in medieval parliaments, that is some boroughs paid as little as 12d per diem while others paid up to 14s 4d a day. Custom rather than statute seems to have prevailed throughout the fourteenth century. But in the fifteenth century the daily wages allowed appear to have been lower and uniformly set at 4s a day for knights of the shire and citizens and 2s for borough members. The older and higher per diem scale would appear to be that paid by Exeter in medieval times—a rate Hooker would have been aware of as chamberlain—while the

In choice of these Knights, Citizens and Burgesses: good regarde is to be had that the Lawes & customs of the Realme be heerin kept and observed,[13] for none ought to be chosen: unlesse he be resiant and dwelling with in the Sheer, Citty or Towne, for which he is chosen. And he ought to be a grave, wise, learned, skilful, and of great experience in causes of policies, and of such audacitie as bothe canne and will boldely utter and speak his minde according to duety, and as occation shall serve, for no man ought to bee silent or dum in that house, but according to his talent hee must and ought to speak in the furtheraunce of the King and common welth.[14]

And the Knights also ought to be skilful in martiall affaires, and therfore the woords of the writs are that such should be chosen for Knights as be *Cincti gladio,*[15] not because they shall come into the Parlement house in armoure, or with their Swoordes: but because they should be suche as have good experience, and knowledge in feates of Warre, and of martiall affayres, whereby they may in suche caces give the [23a] King

---

lower and recent scale appears to come from the Henrician statues which extended the English scale to the Welsh constituencies and Chester in 1536 and 1543 respectively. For discussions of the wages see Neale, *EHC,* pp. 308–18, and Gilkes, *TTP,* p. 49.

13. There were several statutes pertaining to the election of commoners, most dating to the Lancastrian era. Although Hooker does not cite these statutes, he is fully cognizant of their contents. Sir Thomas Smith says nothing about the qualifications of commoners and the electoral procedures, although some of the Elizabethan legal treastises cover these matters. Very likely the deliberations on a nonresidency bill which took place in 1571 also sparked Hooker's interest in this subject and his staunch defense of the status quo.

14. Hooker emerges in all the records as a forthright proponent of freedom of speech and debate in parliament. For other statements similar to this see below pp. 166, 184.

15. Literally, armour-clad. The writs addressed to the sheriffs, as Hooker states, still included the medieval dress requirement, although the practice of appearing in military garb had long since passed into desuetude. Likewise, a law passed during the fourteenth century (7 Edward II) forbade weapons in parliament. Yet, it should be noted that in early Stuart times some lords in the upper house occasionally sported their swords; see Foster, "Procedure in the House of Lords," p. 63.

and Realme good advise and councel, likewise they ought to be Lay men and of good fame, honestie, and credit, beeing not utlawed, excõmunicated, or perjured, or otherwise infamose, for such persons: ought not to have place or to be admitted into the Parlement house.[16]

The degrees of the Parlement.

IN times past there were six degrees or estates of the Parlement,[17] whiche every of them had their severall officers and ministers of attendaunce, but now the same are reduced into foure degrees. The first is the King, who in his personage is a ful and whole degree of him self, and without whome nothing can be doon.

The second degree is of the Lords of the Clergie and of the Temporaltie, and are all called by the names of Barons.

The third is of knights, Citizens, and Burgesses, and these be called by the names of the communaltie.

The fourth: is of the Clergie which are called by the name of convocacion, and these persons have no voice in the Parlement, nether can they doo any thing other then to intreat in causes of Religion, which from them is to be commended to other estates.[18]

16. It is not clear where Hooker secured his information about disqualifying conditions for membership in the House of Commons. Some came from his own experience in the 1571 parliament, for an excommunicant by the name of Garnons was disqualified; a bill concerned with perjury was considered; and one Thomas Long, who bribed his way into the Commons, was expelled midway in the session. Also, later in the session Peter Wentworth launched a verbal attack upon Gilbert, as "infamose." Thus, it would appear that Hooker's knowledge stemmed from cases occurring within his own experience. For information on Garnons see J. E. Neale, "More Elizabethan Elections," *EHR* 61 (1946):18–27; for Long and Wentworth see D'Ewes, *ACJ*, pp. 164, 175. For the precedent-making outlaw case in 1593 also see ibid., p. 480.

17. This refers to the *Modus*, of course. It should be noted here that in this chapter he delineated four estates, the fourth being the lower clergy in Convocation, but that subsequently (see below pp. 181–82) he eliminated that estate.

18. Hooker omits another important function of Convocation: namely, the voting of the clerical subsidies.

Of the places and houses of the Parlement.

AS it lyeth in the King to assigne and appoint the time when the Parlement shall begin, so that he give at the least forty dayes summons: so likewise he may name and appoint the place where it shalbe kept, but wheresoever it bee kept, th'olde usage and maner was that all the whole degrees of the parlement, sat togither in one house, and every man that had there to speak: did it op_ely before the king and his whole Parlement, but heerof did growe many incon- [23b] veniences, and therfore to avoid the great confusions which are in such great assemblies: as also to cut of th'occasions of displeasures which eftsoones did happen, when a mean man speaking his conscience freely, either could not be heard, or fel into the displeasure of his betters, and for sundrye other great greefs, did devide this one house into three houses, that is to wit, the higher house, the lower house and the convocation house.[19]

In the first: sitteth the King, and his Lords spirituall and Temporall called by the name of Barons, and this house is called the higher house.

The second is: where the Knights, Citizens and Burgesses doo sit, and they be called by the name of Commons, and this house is called the lower house.

The third is: where the prelats and Proctors of the Clergie sit beeing called by the name of the Clergie, and this house is called the convocation house, of every of these houses: their orders and officers, we wil breefly subject and declare perticulerly in order as foloweth.

19. Hooker is the first commentator to discuss the evolution of parliament from a unicameral body to a multicameral assembly. His source for this information is not evident, but it could well have been the *Modus* or other records he uncovered in his researches. Most legal antiquarians followed Hooker's interpretation. In fact, Sir Edward Coke seems to paraphrase the *Order and Usage* in a speech delivered in 1593; see D'Ewes, *ACJ*, p. 515. For a modern view see Pollard, *EOP*, pp. 72–76.

Of the higher house.

THe higher house (as is said)[20] is where the King and his Barons doo sit in Parlement, where the King sitteth highest, and the Lords and Barons beneath him eche man in his degree, the order is this.[21] The house is much more in length then in breadth, and the higher end therof in the middle is the Kings seat or Throne hanged richly with cloth of estate, and there the king sitteth all waies alone. On his right hãd: there is a long bench next to the wall of the house whiche reacheth not so farre up as the Kings seat, and upon this sit the Archbishops and Bishops every one in his degree. On his left hand: there are two like bẽches, upon the inner: sit the Dukes, Marquesses, Erles and Vicounts. On the other which is the hindermoste & next to the wall: sit all the Barons every man in his degree. In the middle of the house between the Archbishops seat and the Dukes seat: sitteth the [24a] Speaker, who commonly is the Lord Chaunceller, or keeper of the great Seale of England, or the L. cheef Justice of England as pleaseth the King,[22] who dooth appoint him, and he hath before him: his two Clarks sitting at a Table before them upon which they doo

20. In this chapter and in the one entitled "The Lower House" Hooker incorporates this parenthetical phrase to obviate any adverse criticism of his nomenclature. Sir Thomas Smith used similar adjectives when he wrote of the "higher house," "the Upper House," and the "neather house" (*De Republica Anglorum*, pp. 50–56). At this time the lords met in a large, upper-level chamber in Westminster Palace, while the commoners met in St. Stephen's Chapel, smaller and in the lower reaches of the palace, hence the elevational adjectives.

21. Hooker's description appears to be based upon personal observations; we can assume that in 1571 he was in the upper house for the preliminary and/or concluding ceremonies. For another contemporary description see ibid., pp. 52–54. For more recent and critical discussions see Pollard, "The Clerk of the Crown," p. 313, and *EOP*, pp. 380–86.

22. In 1571, because of Sir Nicholas Bacon's disability, the lord chief justice presided as Speaker of the House of Lords during the last days of the session; see *LJ*, 1:716 ff. Bacon, the lord keeper, had the same duties and powers of the lord chancellor without having the actual title. See John Lord Campbell, *Lives of the Lord Chancellors*, 10 vols. (London, 1868), 2:213–36.

write and lay their Bookes. In the middle Rowme[23] beneath them: sit the cheef Justices and Judges of the Realme, the Barons of ẙ Eschequer, the Queenes Sergeants and all such as be of the Kings learned Councel, either in the common Lawes of the Realme: or of the Ecclesiasticall lawes, and all these sit upon great Wool sacks, covered with red cloth.[24]

At the lower end of all these seates is a bar or a Rail, between which and the lower end of the house: is a void rowme serving for the lower house, and for all Sutors, that shall have cause and occasion to repair to the King or to the Lords. This house[25] as it is distinct from the others: so there bee distinct Officers to the same belonging and appertaining, whiche all be assigned and appointed by the King, and all have allowances for their charges at the Kings hands, of which Officers what they are, what is every of their offices, and what allowances they have: shalbe written in order heerafter.

Of the Officers of the higher house and first of the Speaker, and of his office.

The cheefest Officer of the higher house: is the Speaker, who is appointed by the King, and commonly he is the Lord Chaunceller or keeper of the great Seale, or Lord cheef Justice of England, his office consisteth in divers points.[26]

23. Meaning "space," as in the following paragraph, not a separate room.

24. These specially summoned "assistants" are discussed in a separate chapter (see below p. 176). It is interesting to note that in this sentence Hooker used both *Queenes* and *Kings* to denote the crown's legal advisors. He also employs *ecclesiastical* rather than *civil* to describe the masters of chancery, and doctors of civil law, who carried out a variety of functions; on this see Pollard, "Receivers of Petitions," pp. 214–26.

25. Meaning the House of Lords. This entire sentence is in fact a transitional prelude to the next four chapters.

26. "The Office and Jurisdiction of this man, is manifold," wrote Lambarde in *Archeion* (p. 32), "For usually he is a great Personage, a Counsellor of the Estate, and Proluctor or Mouth of the higher House of Parliament: He is also Keeper of the Great Seale of the King, and was wont to be elected hereunto by authoritie of Parliament." Similarly, seven pages later, Lambarde called the

First: he must on the first day of the Parlement, make his oration in the higher house, before the king, his Lords and commons & then & there declare the causes why the King hath summoned that parlement, exhorting and advising every man to do his office and duty, in such sorte as may be to the glory of God, honor of the King, and benefit of the common welth.

Also he must make one other oration, but in way of answere to the Speakers Oration, when he is presented to the King.

[24b] Likewise he must make the like, on the last day of the Parlement, and you shall understand that upon these three dayes: he standeth on the right hand of the King neer to his seat, at a bar there appointed for him, but at all other times: he sitteth in the middle of the house as is before said.[27]

When he hath ended his oration upon the first day: he must give order unto the lower house in the Kings behalf, willing them to repair unto their house, and there (according to their ancient order and customes) make choice of their Speaker,

All Billes preseted unto the higher house: he must receive, which he hath foorthwith to deliver to the Clarkes to be safely kept.

All Billes he must cause to be red twise before they be ingroced, and beeing red three times: he must put the same to question.[28]

If any Bil put to question doo passe with their conset: then

Chancellor "the Mouth, as it were, of the Prince, as appeares by his imployment in the Session of Parliament."

27. A woodcut illustration used as the frontispiece to D'Ewes, *ACJ*, depicts the bar and the Speaker behind it; during the plenary meetings he sat on the empty woolsack shown in the same illustration.

28. Smith's comments are similar: "After it hath bin once or twise read, and doth appeare that it is somewhat liked as reasonable, with such amendment in wordes and peradventure some sentences as by disputation seemeth to be amended: In the upper house the Chauncelor asketh if they will have it engrossed, that is to say put into parchment: which doone, and read the third time, and that eftsoones if any be disposed to object disputed againe among them, the Chauncelor asketh if they will go to the question" (*De Republica Anglorum*, p. 53).

the same must be sent to the lower house, unlesse it came first from thence, and in that cace: it must be kept until the end of the Parlement.

If any Bil be denyed, impugned, and cleere overthrowne:[29] the same is no more to be thencefoorth received.

If any Bil be put to question, and it be doutful whether side is the greater and giveth moste voices: then he must cause the house to be devided, and then judge of the Bil according to the greater number.[30]

If any Bill be imperfect or requireth to be amended: hee must choose a certain number of that house, as he shall think good, and to them commit that Bil to be reformed and amended.[31]

If any Bil or message be to be sent to $\overset{e}{y}$ lower house: it is his office to make choice of two of the Kings learned councel there beeing to be the messengers therof.[32]

---

29. Smith used the term *dashed* (ibid.), but the result was the same; once rejected, the measure could not be reintroduced during the session.

30. Hooker and Smith appear to be at variance on voting procedures in the upper house. The former claims that the lords voted by means of a division while the latter (see ibid., p. 56) contends they indicated approval or disapproval individually and verbally by a "Content" or "Not Content," first for themselves and then for the proxies they held. Possibly Hooker, a member of the lower house, is in error. For a complete discussion of the complexity of voting and proxy-voting see my article "A Rejoinder to Mr. Graves' Reassessment of Proctorial Representation," *JBS* 10 (1971): 41–46.

31. Hooker makes few comments about committees in parliament, fewer than either Smith or Lambarde, and they concern commitment in the upper house. In 1571, although most bills were committed after their second reading, some were approved and engrossed without being committed. By the turn of the century, however, all bills were committed. Whereas the Speaker of the House of Lords in 1571 determined the size and membership of committees, apparently, in early Stuart times the members rather than the Speaker appointed the chairman and determined the size, members, place and time; see Foster, "Procedure in the House of Lords," p. 66.

32. Specifically, the judges, sergeants, or masters of chancery, all were regarded as assistants. Invariably two were used in intercameral communications. As Pollard noted, they were not messengers as such but *nuncios;* see "Receivers of Petitions," p. 218 ff.

If any Bil or message be sent from the lower house: hee must come from his place to the bar & there receive the same, and beeing returned to his place and every Straunger or messenger departed: he must disclose the same to the Lords.

[25a] Item if any disorder be committed or doon in the house by any Lord or other person: he ought with the advise of the Lords to reforme the same, but if it be emong the Lords, and they wil not be reformed: then he must foorth with advertise the King.[33]

Item he ought at the beginning of the Parlement: to call by name all the Lords of the Parlement, and likewise at other times as he seeth occasion, whose defaults ought to be recorded, and they to pay their fines unlesse they be dispenced with all by speciall licence from the King, or have some just and resonable cause or absence.[34]

Item he must see and cause the Clarks to make true entries and true recordes of all things doon there, and to see that the Clarks doo give and deliver the copyes of all such Billes there red to such as demaund for the same.[35]

Item he shall keep the secrets and cause and commaund every man of eche degree in that house to doo the like.[36]

---

33. Presumably Hooker is referring to indecorous behavior within the confines of the upper house (e.g., defamatory remarks or unruly actions) which violated the unwritten code of that body. It is interesting to note that the queen was supposed to be informed of violations of that code—a fact which helps explain her actions and those of her privy councillors in several cases.

34. Although the Speaker was responsible for the roll calls and for the enforcement of the rules pertaining to absenteeism, the clerk of the parliament or his assistant actually called the roll and kept the records. For a more complete discussion of abstention see my "Proctorial Representation in the House of Lords during the reign of Edward VI," *JBS* 8 (1969): 4–7.

35. Eventually this supervisory role of the Speaker over the records was superseded by a committee appointed to inspect the journal and verify its accuracy; see Maurice F. Bond, "The Formation of the Archives of Parliament, 1497–1691," *Journal of the Society of Archivists* 1 (1957): 154.

36. Secrecy, the order of the day in both houses, was difficult to maintain and enforce. As indicated above, the Speaker himself was expected to divulge disorderly behavior to the sovereign. We also know that the queen learned of

Also he ought not to go any where, but the gentleman Sergeant ought to attend upon him, going before him with his Mace, unless he be Lord Chaunceller for then he hath a Sergeant of his owne.

His alowance that he hath is at the Kings charges.

Also for every private Bil that passeth and is enacted: his hath x. pound for his parte.[37]

Of the CHaunceller of the higher house.

THe Chaunceller is the principall Clark of the higher house, and his charge is safely to keep the recordes of the Parlement and the Acts whiche be past.[38]

All suche Statutes as be enacted: hee must send to the Kings severall Courts of recordes to be enrolled, as namely the Chauncery, the kings Bench, the common place, and the Eschequer.[39]

[25b] All suche Acts as are to be imprinted: he must send to the Printer.

All such private Acts as are not imprinted, if any man wil

---

certain speeches and parliamentary maneuvers from members of both houses; in fact, Privy Council members in both houses were more or less expected to inform the queen of words and actions vital to crown interests.

37. Although proponents of private bills incurred several charges in each house, the fee paid to the Speaker of the House of Lords was the largest. For other fees see below pp. 160–61.

38. The special responsibilities of the lord chancellor or lord keeper included the promulgation and publication of statutes (that is, public acts of parliament) and the preservation of the official records of parliament. With these clerical functions in mind, Hooker used the terms "Chauncellor of the Higher House" and "principall Clark of the higher house," both of which lacked technical accuracy. Hooker details the duties of the chancellor or lord keeper *qua* court of chancery not as Speaker of the House of Lords in this chapter and all of them were performed after the session. It is interesting to note that Smith also uses the term *Chancellor* (*De Republica Anglorum*, pp. 51–57). In his *Archeion* (p. 36) Lambarde discusses the record-keeping responsibilities of the chancellor. For a complete discussion of the court of chancery see W. J. Jones, *The Elizabethan Court of Chancery* (Oxford, 1967), especially pp. 27–30, which pertain to Sir Nicholas Bacon.

39. Meaning common pleas and exchequer.

have the same exemplified: he must transmit the same to the Lord Chaunceller to be ingrossed and sealed, and for the same, he to take the fees appointed and accustomed.

He hath for his alowance an ordinary fee for terme of life of the King.

Of the Clarks of the Parlement.

THere be two Clarks, the one named the Clark of the Parlement: and the other named the Clark of the Crown.[40] The Clark of the Parlement his office is to sit before the Lord Speaker, and to read such Billes presented as hee shalbe commaunded.

He must keep true records and true entries of all things there doon and to be entred.[41]

If any require a coppy of any bil there: he ought to give the same receiving the ordinary fees.[42]

40. In *De Republica Anglorum* (p. 52) Smith referred to the "Clarke of the parliament, who readeth the bills" and ignored the Clerk of the Crown. For full discussions of these officials see Maurice F. Bond, "Clerks of the Parliaments, 1509–1953," *EHR* 73 (1958): 78–85, and A. F. Pollard's three articles: "The Clerical Organization of Parliament," "The receivers of Petitions and Clerks of Parliament," "The Clerk of the Crown" in *EHR* 57 (1942): 31–58, 202–26, 312–33. Regarding nomenclature, both Hooker and Smith use the term *Clerk of the Parliament* while John Taylor in the early sixteenth century and John Browne in the late seventeenth century use *Parliaments*, the preferred term today.

41. Hooker seems to refer to the journals which by 1571 were the official record of parliament; however, the quality and quantity of that record varied considerably in the sixteenth century. In 1597, after a heated controversy over the accuracy of the record, the House of Lords appointed a special committee to read and authenticate the *LJ* at the end of each week. See D'Ewes, *ACJ*, p. 528; Foster, "Procedure in the House of Lords," p. 64. After 1607 the Commons entrusted the committee for privileges with similar authority.

42. The fees from copying both public and private bills constituted a most welcome supplement to the £40 annuity which the clerk of the parliament received from chancery to perform his normal duties. In 1571, when Hooker sat in the House of Commons, Francis Spelman was the clerk of the parliament; see Bond, "Clerks of the Parliaments," pp. 82–83.

If any Bil after his ordinary readings, be to be ingrossed he must doo it.

The councel of the house he may not disclose.

At the end of the Parlement: he must deliver up unto the Chaunceller, all the Acts and records of that house, saving he may keep a transumpt and a coppy therof to him self.[43]

He hath his alowance of the King.

Also for every private Bil whiche is enacted: he hath three pound.[44]

Also for every Bil wherof he giveth a coppy: he hath for every ten lines a peny according to the custome,[45]

The Clark of the Crown:[46] his office is to supply the place

43. The practice of surrendering the official records to the lord chancellor continued, but gradually parliament acquired its own official archive and clerical bureaucracy which superseded chancery in importance. Until parliament acquired its own permanent office for records the individual clerks retained the transcripts in their own possession—a practice which has produced much confusion regarding the nature of the records themselves. For excellent discussions of this see Bond, "Formation of the Archives of Parliament," pp. 151–58; and G. R. Elton "The early Journals of the house of Lords," *EHR* 89 (1974): 481–512.

44. The role of the clerk of the parliament as a promoter of private bills has never been adequately described. The fees required to secure the passage of a private bill were considerable: presumably the clerks along with the Speaker actually sponsored and guided these bills through the upper house.

45. See above footnote 42. For an excellent discussion of these fees in early Stuart times see Foster "The Painful Labour of Mr. Elsyng," especially p. 10. In 1626 Elsyng received 2 shillings per sheet for copying. The "custome" mentioned by Hooker in this sentence was the *Modus* (see above pp. 143–44); if Hooker is correct, the rate in 1571 was the same as in the fourteenth century.

46. The 1583 edition of Smith's *De Republica Anglorum* speaks only of the clerk of the parliament, while the 1589 edition alludes to "two Clarkes, the one for the Higher House, the other for the Lower" (p. 154). However, in the latter, in that section concerned with chancery, Smith's continuator notes that "the Clarke of the Crowne is the chief Guardian of all the matters of the Crowne" (p. 155), but nothing is said of his place and duties in the House of Lords. According to Hooker, he assisted the clerk of the parliament, filled in for the clerk when called upon, exemplified those statutes not in print, and

and the rowme of the Clark of the Parlement in his ab-[26a] sence, and hath in all things the like charges and profits, as the Clark ought to have.

He must give his attendaunce to the higher house from time to time and doo what shalbe injoyned him.

All suche Acts as be not imprinted, if any man wil have them exemplified under the brode Seale: he must exemplifie them, and have for the same his ordinary fees.

These two Clarks at the end of the Parlement: ought to be present in the house, and within the lower bar at a boord before them, their faces towards the King, and there the one must read the billes which are past bothe houses; and the other must read the concent or disagreement of the King.[47]

Of the Sergeants or porters of the higher house.

There is but one Sergeant whiche hath the charge of keeping of the doores, for though there be divers doores: yet the keepers therof are at his assignement.

He ought to see the house be cleene and kept sweet.

He ought not to suffer any manner of person to be within the house, so long as the Lords be there sitting, other then such as be of the learned councel, and of that house, and except also such as come in message from the lower house with Billes or otherwise, and except also such as be sent for, and be admitted to have any thing there to doo.

Also he must attend and go alwaies with his Mace before the

---

participated in the closing ceremonies. For a fuller discussion see Pollard, "Clerk of the Crown," especially pp. 328–33. In 1571 Thomas Powle succeeded Thomas Martyn as "clericum corone."

47. For a description of the material in this paragraph see A. F. Pollard, "Hayward Townshend's Journals," *BIHR* 12 (1934): 24. In 1597/8, as Townshend records, the clerk of the crown (still Powle) received the subsidy bill from the Speaker of the House of Commons and laid it on the table before the Speaker of the House of Lords. Then, after the lord keeper's speech he read the titles of the bills, while the clerk of the parliaments (Mr. Thomas Smith) gave the royal responses.

Speaker, unlesse he be Lord Chaunceller, or keeper of the great Seale, for then he hath a Sergeant of his owne.[48]

He ought to keep safely such prisoners as be commaunded to his warde, and to fetch or sẽd for such as he shalbe commaunded to fetch.[49]

This Porter or Sergeant hath besides his ordinary fee: a standing allowance for every day of the Parlement.

[26b] Also he hath for every private Bil which is enacted: xl. s.

Also he hath for every prisoner committed to his warde: a certain alowance for his fees.

Also he hath of every Baron or Lord of that house, a certain rewarde.

Of the lower house.

THe lower house (as is said)[50] is a place distinct from the others, it is more of length then of breadth, it is made like a Theater, having foure rowes of seates one aboove an other ro ũd about the same.[51] At the higher end in the midle of ỹ lower

48. In 1571 Sir Nicholas Bacon, lord keeper, was Speaker for the first few days of the session; but, upon becoming ill on April 9, his place as Speaker was filled by the lord chief justice, Robert Catlin. In this situation, presumably, the lord keeper's aide remained with him while the upper house's sergeant at arms attended the substitute Speaker and carried the mace. See *LJ*, I:671.

49. This responsibility was exercised most frequently in freedom from arrest cases. Most prisoners under the upper house's custody were confined to the Tower of London (see below p. 185).

50. In *De Republica Anglorum* (p. 54) Smith uses the same term, *the lower house* interchangeably with *neather house* and *Commons*. As before Hooker includes a parenthetical phrase to indicate that the term, which could be construed as a derogative, was not his own making.

51. This verbal description of the House of Commons corresponds closely to the pictorial views that have survived; see Pollard, *EOP*, pp. 380–85. The sitting arrangement—no doubt a matter of custom—reflects the elevated roles assumed by royal officials and Londoners in the deliberations, committees, and conferences. In fact, the arrangement may well help explain the makeup of the committees, for most of the important committees were chaired by and filled with front-benchers. The special place for MPs representing London

rowe: is a seat made for $\overset{e}{y}$ Speaker, in which he alwaies sitteth, before it: is a table boord, at which sitteth the Clark of the house and there upon layeth his Books, and writeth his recordes. Upon the lower rowe on bothe sides the Speaker: sit such personages as be of the kings privy councel, or of his cheef Officers, but as for any other: none claimeth nor can claime any place, but sitteth as he $\overset{m}{co}$meth, saving that on the right hand of the Speaker, next beneath the said Councelles: the Londoners and the Citizens of York doo sit, and so in order should sit all the Citizens accordingly. Without this house: is one other in which the under Clarks doo sit, as also such as be Suters and attend$\overset{n}{a}$t to that house, and when so ever the house is devided upon any Bil: then the rowme is voided, and the one parte of the house commeth down into this to be numbred.

The office of the Speaker of the lower house.

[27a] THe cheef or principall Officer of this house: is the Speaker, and is chosen by the whole house or the more parte of them, he himself beeing one of the same number, and a man for gravitie, wisdome, experience, and learning: chosen to supplye that Office during the time of the Parlement, and is to be presented to the King the third day folowing.[52]

---

and York is well known; however, the deference to citizens vis-à-vis burgesses and knights may well be wishful thinking on Hooker's part, for he uses the subjunctive form.

52. In *De Republica Anglorum* (p. 51) Smith uses similar phraseology to describe the Speaker. The commoners, he notes, "are willed to choose an able and discreete man to be as it were the mouth of them all, and to speake for and in the name of them, and to present him so chosen by them, to the prince." Most scholars agree that the selection of a Speaker in Elizabeth's reign generally involved a prearranged agreement between the crown and the leaders of the lower house, especially those who had official posts. The best general survey of this office, namely A. I. Dasent, *The Speakers of the House of Commons* (New York, 1911), has been superseded by several specialized studies. For the Elizabethan period see Neale, *EHC*, pp. 343–46; for the pre-Tudor period see J. S. Roskell, *The Commons and their Speakers in English Parliaments*

His Office is to direct and guide that house in good order, and to see the ordinances, usages, and customs of the same to be firmly kept and observed.

When he is presented unto the King sitting in his estate royall in the Parlement house, for the purpose: he must then and there make his oration in commendation of the Lawes and of the Parlement,[53] whiche doon: then he hath in the name of the house of the commons: to make to the King three requests.[54]

(Manchester, 1964); for the post-Tudor era see C. G. Sims, "The Speaker of the House of Commons," *AHR* 45 (1939): 90–95, and D. H. Willson, *The Privy Councillors in the House of Commons* (Minneapolis, 1940), especially pp. 9–12, 217–25, 295–98.

53. Although very much aware of the disabling procedures, as evidenced in his diary, Hooker omits them from this analysis; see Davidson, "Hoker's *Journal,*" pp. 473–74, for his account of the disabling ritual and the Speaker's oration in the 1571 parliament. For other contemporary accounts see Smith, *De Republica Anglorum,* p. 51, and D'Ewes, *ACJ,* pp. 140–41; for an extended discussion see Neale, *EHC,* pp. 342–46.

54. There seems to be a contradiction here, for Hooker indicates "three requests" in this line but then goes on to list four. In his diary (p. 474) Hooker makes a general statement about parliamentary "privileges, customs and liberties yn times past" and then singles out: (1) freedom of access; (2) freedom of speech; and (3) freedom from misinterpretation and punishment. At first glance he seems to omit freedom from arrest; yet he construes freedom of access to include it, for he notes that no MP "might be molested vexed or sorried." In this section of the *Order and Usage* he borrows from his diary and then resorts to paraphrase and elaboration. It is interesting to note that Sir Christopher Wray (according to D'Ewes, *ACJ,* p. 141) petitioned for four freedoms and that Smith listed four in *De Republica Anglorum* (p. 52). While the D'Ewes account parallels Hooker fairly closely, Smith is somewhat different: "Then the speaker maketh certaine requests to the prince in the name of the commons, first that his majestie would be content that they may use and enjoy all their liberties and priviledges that the common house was wont to enjoy. Secondly that they might franckely and freely saye their mindes in disputing of such matters as may come in question, and that without offence to his Majestie. Thirdly that if any should chaunce of that lower house to offend or not to do or say as should become him, or if any should offend any of them being called to that his highnes court: That they themselves might (according to the ancient custome) have the punishment of them. And fourthly, that if there came any doubt, whereupon they shal desire to have thadvise or confer-

First: that it may please his majestie to graunt that the commons assembled in the Parlement may have and injoy the ancient priviledges, customes and liberties as in times past have appertayned and been used in that house.[55]

Then that every one of $\stackrel{e}{y}$ house may have libertie of speech, and freely to utter, speake and declare his minde and oppinion to any Bil or question to be proponed.[56]

---

ence with his Majestie or with any of the Lordes, that they might doe it: All which he promiseth in the commons names that they shall not abuse, but have such regarde as most faithfull, true and loving subjects ought to have to their prince." It should be noted that Smith omits freedom from arrest and substitutes the freedom of Commons to confer with the House of Lords and the sovereign. He also claims for Commons the right to punish delinquents—a right claimed by Hooker in a subsequent chapter but not included in the "three requests"—which subsequently became a major theme in Lambarde's *Orders, Proceedings, Punishments, and Privileges of the Commons-House of Parliament in England,* a study which remained in manuscript until 1641. For a more complete discussion see Neale, *EHC,* p. 34, and *EP,* 1:188–90.

55. This paragraph is almost identical to an entry in his diary (see Davidson, "Hoker's *Journal,*" p. 474). However, in that entry Hooker explained "nam[ely] first that everie of that howse might h[ave fre]e access for selff & his men to the saide plament and that none of they [m] might be molested vesed or sorried." It would appear that Hooker transcribed the first portion of the entry and then dropped the concluding portion; he does not include some of the terms below in his statement covering freedom from arrest. Note also the similarity to Smith's statement quoted in the preceding footnote.

56. Sir Christopher Wray, according to the D'Ewes, requested four freedoms in the following order: (1) freedom from arrest; (2) freedom of access to and conference with Her Majesty; (3) freedom to be heard in cases of verbal misunderstandings; and (4) freedom of speech. Hooker changed the order and terminology in both his diary and the *Order and Usage;* whereas Wray considers freedom of speech last, Hooker places it second, as did Smith (*De Republica Anglorum,* p. 52). It should be noted also that Lord Keeper Bacon, in response to Wray's petition, circumscribed freedom of speech to matters "propounded unto them," excluding all "matters of State." Hooker took notice of that limitation in his diary when he noted "her highnes thinketh it not meet that any sholde have further lybertie to speke or talke yn that howse any matter other then that w^h is there to be propounded and that they sholde leave to talk *rhetorice* and speke *logice* to leave longe tales w^h is rather an ostentacon of wytt then to any effecte & to deall wth these things as there were to be proponed" (Davidson, "Hoker's *Journal,*" p. 474). It would appear that

Also that every Knight, Citizen and Burgesse, and their servants, may have free comming and going to and from the said Parlement, as also during the time of Parlement, and that they, nor any of their Servants nor retinewe: to be arested, molested, sued, imprisoned, or troubled by any person or persons.[57]

And lastly, that if he or any other of that company, beeing sent or come to him of any message, and doo mistake him self in dooing thereof: that his Majestie wil not take the advantage thereof but gratiously pardon the same.[58]

He must have good regarde and see that the Clark doo enter and make true records, and safely to keep the same, and all such Billes as be delivered into that house.

[27b] He must on the first and third day, and whensoever he els wil, call the house by name, and recorde their defaults.[59]

All billes to be brought and to be presented into that house: he must receive and deliver to the Clark.

Hooker incorporated the essence of this limitation in the last half of this statement. Smith's definition is even more limited in nature; see above, note 54. For a survey of this topic see John Neale, "The Commons' Privilege of free speech in parliament," in *Tudor Studies*, ed. R. W. Setton-Watson (London, 1924), pp. 257–86.

57. It should be noted that this freedom customarily included the twenty-day periods before and after the convention and dissolution dates. Again, Lord Keeper Bacon warned that "no man should under their shadows, untruly protect any others," a precaution precipitated by instances in which MPs sold their protection. Most of the cases concerned debtor and creditor relationships. For a more complete discussion of this freedom see G. W. Prothero, "The Parliamentary Privilege of Freedom from Arrest and Sir Thomas Shirley's Case, 1604," *EHR* 8 (1893): 733–40, and A. S. Turberville, "The Protection of the Servants of Members of Parliament," *EHR* 42 (1927): 590–600.

58. "If any sent should not truly report," D'Ewes quotes the anonymous diarist in his *ACJ*, (p. 141), "or in any part mistake the meaning of the House, that the same should be by her Highness favourably heard." In response to this petition the lord keeper noted, to continue D'Ewes, "she could not imagine that among so many wise men it could happen; but if it should, her Grace would be content to remit it." Smith does not comment on this privilege.

59. For the calling of the house and recording of abstentions and excuses see Neale, *EHC*, pp. 399–401.

He ought to cause and command the Clark to read the Billes brought in, plainly and sensibly, which doon: he must breefly resite and repete th'effect and meaning thereof.[60]

Of the Billes brought in he hath choice, which and when they shalbe red: unlesse order by the whole house be taken in that behalf.[61]

Every Bil must have three readings, and after the second reading: he must cause the Clark to ingrose the same, unlesse the same be rejected and dashed.[62]

If any Bil or message be sent from the Lords, he ought to cause the messengers to bring the same unto him, and he to receive the same openly, and they beeing departed and gone: he ought to disclose and open the same to the house.[63]

If when a Bil is red, divers doo rise at one instant to speak to the same, and it cannot be discerned who rose first: then shall he appoint who shall speak, neverthelesse every one shall have his course to speak if he list.[64]

---

60. The Speaker received all bills—those originating in the lower house and those received from the House of Lords—and then gave them to the clerk for the first reading. "But when any bill is read," noted Smith in *De Republica Anglorum* (p. 55), "the speakers office is as brieflie and as plainly as he may to declare the effect there of to the house." The similarity of phraseology here between Smith and Hooker raises the obvious questions: was Hooker aware of Smith or vice versa?

61. The prerogative of the Speaker in determining the order of bills gave him an informal power which, if used discreetly so as not to offend too many MPs, could influence the flow and final outcome of legislation. Only an order of the house could overrule him. See Sims, "The Speaker," especially p. 91.

62. As Neale has pointed out in *EHC*, pp. 356–59, there were exceptions to these general procedures spelled out by Hooker.

63. Substantially like Smith, who wrote of the messengers: "They being gone and the doore againe shut the speaker rehearseth to the house what they sayde" (*De Republica Anglorum*, p. 53). Generally the messengers were sergeants, masters in chancery, or judges.

64. Smith's comments on the order of deliberations (ibid., p. 54) are more complete: "All bils be thrise in three diverse dayes read and disputed upon, before they come to the question. In the disputing is a mervelous good order used in the lower house. He that standeth uppe bareheadded is understanded that he will speake to the bill. If moe stande uppe, who that first is judged to arise, is first harde, though the one doe prayse the law, the other diswade it,

If any speak to a Bil and be out of the matter: he shall put him in remembrance and wil him to come to the matter.

If any Bil be red three times, and every man have spoken his minde: then shall he aske the house whether the Bil shall passe or not, saying thus, as many as wil have this Bil passe in maner and forme as hath been red: say yea, then the affirmative parte say yea, as many as wil not have this Bil passe in maner and forme as have been red: say no. If upon this question the whole house or the more parte, doo affirme and alowe the Bil: then the same is to be sent to the higher house to the Lords.[65] But if the whole house or the more parte doo denye the Bil: then the same is dashed out and to be rejected, but if it be doutful upon giving of voices, whether side is the greater: thē must a devision be made of the house, and the affirmative parte must arise, & departe into the utter rowme, which (by [28a] the Sergeant) is voided before hand of all persons that were there, and then the Speaker must assigne two or foure to number them first which sit within, & then the other which be without, as they doo come in, one by one, and as upon the triall the Bil shalbe alowed or disalowed by the greater number: so to be accepted as is before said.[66]

---

yet there is no altercation. For everie man speaketh as to the speaker, not as one to an other, for that is against the order of the house. It is also taken against the order, to name him whom ye doe confute, but by circumlocution, as he that speaketh with the bill, or he that spake against the bill, and gave this and this reason. And so with perpetuall Oration not with altercation, he goeth through till he do make an end." Yet, it should be noted that Smith says nothing of the Speaker's discretionary authority in determining the order of debate when several speakers rose at the same time and in confining debate to germane matters.

65. Hooker omits one step in the legislative procedure, a step which Smith includes (ibid., p. 56): "After the bill hath beene twise reade, and then engrossed and eftsoones reade and disputed on ynough as is thought: *the speaker asketh if they will goe to the question.* And if they agree be holdeth the bill up in his hande and sayeth, as many as will have this bill goe forwarde, which is concerning such a matter, say yea."

66. Hooker's description of the division is more complete than Smith's, in that he alludes to the tellers, the role of the sergeant, and the tabulative process (cf. ibid.).

If upon this triall the number of either side be like: then the Speaker shall give his voice and that onely in this point, for other wise he hath no voice.[67]

Also if any of the house doo misbehave him self, and breke the order of the house: he hath to reforme, correct, and punish him, but yet with the advise of the house.[68]

If any forain person doo enter into that house, the assembly thereof beeing sitting, or doo by arresting any one pers$\overset{n}{o}$ there of, or by any other meanes breke the liberties and priveledges of that house: he ought to see him to be be punished.[69]

---

67. Smith says nothing about this tie-breaking role of the Speaker, although he does write (ibid., p. 55): "The Speaker hath no voice in the house, nor they will suffer him to speak in any bill to moove or diswade it." Regarding the latter point, it should be noted that in 1593 Sir Edward Coke spoke on matters of substance. However, he prefaced his speech with an apologetic explanation of his unorthodox behavior: "I desire that I may be heard a word, not that I have any Voice or assent to give, though I am of the House, but because I am a Servant to the House and have somewhat to speak. It appertaineth to my duty and place, which I desire to have leave to utter, for my Speech shall not tend to meddle to decide the Question, but only to inform the House of my knowledge" (D'Ewes, *ACJ*, p. 482). He then proceeded to discuss several precedents bearing upon the Fitzherbert election case. One month later, after making a similar request, he lectured the house on the *Modus* and the pristine composition of parliament (see above p. 89).

68. In early parliaments, according to Hooker in the dedicatory epistle of the Exeter edition (p. 7a), the English kings exercised the disciplinary functions detailed in this paragraph, and Queen Elizabeth I's actions in numerous cases reflect the residuary authority of the sovereign in this matter; see Neale, "Free Speech in Parliament," pp. 258–59. Nevertheless, it is also clear that in Hooker's time both houses were becoming more assertive and jealous of their own disciplinary authority.

69. On 5 April 1571 two "strangers" (really gentlemen from Inner Temple) were discovered and taken into custody by the sergeant. Hooker witnessed the search and arrest, as is evident in his diary entry for that day (Davidson, "Hoker's *Journal*," p. 475). For other cases in 1575, 1580, and 1594 see D'Ewes, *ACJ*, pp. 248, 283–88, 334, 487, 511. In most cases the "stranger" was committed to the Sergeant's Ward, examined, and punished by the whole house. In 1593 one John Legg, a servant of the earl of Northumberland, was discovered and committed; however, upon a plea of innocence to the violation, he was freed after an admonition by Sir Edward Coke, the Speaker.

Also during the time of the Parlement: he ought to sequester him self, from dealing or intermedling in any publique or private affaires, and dedicate and bĕd him self wholly to serve his office and function.[70]

Also he ought not to resorte to any noble man, counceller or other person to deal in any of the Parlement matters: but must and ought to have with him a compitent number of some of that house, who may be witnesses of his dooings.

Also during the time of Parlement: he ought to have the Sergeant of Armes with his mace to go before him.[71]

Also he hath the libertie to send any offender, either to Sergeants warde, or to the Tower, or to any other prison at his choice, according to the qualitie and quantitie of the offence.[72]

He hath allowance for his diet, one hundred pounds of the King for every Sessions of Parlement.

Also he hath for every private Bil passed bothe houses and enacted: five pounds.[73]

At th'end, and on the last day of the Parlement: he maketh his oration before the King, in moste humble maner declaring the dutiful service, and obedience of the Commons then assem- [28b] bled to his Majestie: as also moste humblye praying his patron if any thing have been doon amisse.[74]

---

70. It is not clear where Hooker secured this information about the restrictions and prohibitions imposed upon the Speaker while parliament was in session; none of the other commentators allude to these ethical standards. It is possible that he had discussed the matter earlier with Thomas Williams, the Exeter MP who had served as Speaker in 1563; see Neale, *EP*, 1:97.

71. In contrast to the upper house, where the sergeant served the lord keeper rather than the house, the Commons' sergeant at arms served the house not the Speaker.

72. The Speaker's authority to commit was contingent upon the will of the House of Commons; see Smith, who notes that the house sent irreverent and seditious speakers to the Tower (*De Republica Anglorum*, p. 55). Also see below p. 185 for the authority of the "residue of the house" in punishing offenders.

73. For a discussion of fees with the passage of private bills see above pp. 160–61.

74. For a brief account of the Speaker's oration and the royal pardon in 1571 see Davidson, "Hoker's *Journal*," pp. 488–89.

Of the Clark of the lower house.

THere is onely one Clark belonging to this house, his office is to sit next before the Speaker, at a Table upon which he writeth and layeth his books.[75]

He must make true entrie of the recordes and Billes of the house, as also of all the orders thereof.

The Billes appointed unto him by the Speaker to be red: hee must read openly, plainly and sensibly.

The Billes which are to be ingrossed, he must doo it.

If any of the house aske the sight of any Bil there, or of the book of the orders of the house: he hath to deliver the same unto him.[76]

If any desire to have the copy of any Bil; he ought to give it him, receiving for his paines after ten lines a peny.[77]

He may not be absent at any time of sitting, without speciall licence.

He ought to have for every private Bil passed and enacted: forty shillings.[78]

He hath allowed unto him for his charges (of the King) for every Sessions: ten pound.

75. For a fuller discussion of the responsibilities of the clerk of the House of Commons see Neale, *EHC,* pp. 320–21. His official title was under-clerk of the parliaments and his fee of £10 contrasted to the £40 of the clerk of the parliament. For the early Stuart period see Shelia Lambert, "The Clerks and Records of the House of Commons, 1600–40," *BIHR* 43 (1970): 215–31.

76. Presumably Hooker refers here to the original bill and the journal, which included orders and actions taken by the lower house, or possibly a Book of Orders.

77. For similar duties of the clerks in the House of Lords see above p. 160. The rate here was identical to that in the *Modus;* see above p. 144.

78. See above p. 161 for my comments on the fees connected with private bills. Whereas the clerk of the parliament received £3 for each private bill passed, the clerk of the lower house received only £2 upon passage. Yet, it should be noted that in 1571 the clerk of Commons received more remuneration from private legislation fees (£24—e.g., 12 bills at £2 each) than from his allowance (£10) mentioned in the next paragraph.

Of the Sergeant or porter of the lower house.

THe Sergeant of this house is commonly one of the Kings Sergeants at Armes, and is appointed to this office by the King. His office is to keep the doores of the house, and for the same: he hath others under him, for he him self keepeth the door of the inner house,[79] wher the commons sit, and seeth the same to be clene.

Also he may not suffer any to enter into this house during the time of the sitting there, unlesse he be one of the house, or [29a] be sent from the King or the Lords, or otherwise licenced to come in.[80]

If any such person doo come: he ought to bring him in, going before him with his Mace upon his shoulder.

If any be commited to his warde: he ought to take charge of him, and to keep him in safetie until he be required for him.

If he be sent for any person or to go in any message: hee must leave a substitute behinde him, to doo his Office in his absence.

He must alwaies attend the Speaker, and go before him, carying his mace upon his shoulder.

His allowance (during the time of the Parlement) is xii. S. the day of the Kings charges.

Also he hath of every Knight and Citizen: ii. shillings and vi. pence, and of every Burgesse, ii. shillings.[81]

If any be commaunded to his warde: he hath of every such Prisoner, by the day. vi. shillings and viii. pence.

---

79. This refers to the inner chamber not the outer room, where the subordinate clerical personnel and petitioners remained during the deliberations. For a discussion of the sergeant's duties and fees see Neale, *EHC*, pp. 328–29.

80. That the sergeants found it difficult to enforce this rule with well over 400 persons is evident in the trespass cases mentioned above in note 69. The rule served the interests of secrecy as well as order.

81. Considering the number of MPs, this could amount to upwards of £50, if all of them paid their fees.

If any private Bil doo passe and be enacted: he hath for every such Bil. xx. shillings.[82]

Of the Convocation House.

THe convocation house, is the assemblie of the whole Clergie at and in some peculier place appointed for the purpose.[83] But as the Barons and Lords of the Parlement have their house severall[84] and distinct from the Commons: even so the Archbishops and Bishops doo sequester them selves and have a house severall from the residue of the Clergie. And this their house is called the higher Convocation house, the other beeing named the lower Convocation house. Bothe these houses have their severall Officers, orders and usages, & eche Officer hath his peculier charge and function, as also certain allowances, even as [29b] is used in the Parlement houses of the Lords and commons.[85]

82. The sergeant serving the House of Lords received twice that figure, namely 40 s for each private bill enacted into law.

83. In all likelihood Hooker obtained his information from either his friend Robert Weston, onetime chancellor of the Exeter diocese, who assisted Archbishop Parker in the 1562 Convocation, or one of the bishops of Exeter, probably William Alley or William Bradbridge. Most of his information is accurate and seemingly derived from someone who had participated in the deliberations of Convocation. It should be noted that Robert Weston presided over the Irish House of Lords as lord chancellor of Ireland when Hooker took it upon himself to write the *Order and Usage.* In the absence of official journals, which were burned in 1666, the incomplete history of Convocation must be pieced together from the provincial registers and those extracts from the journals made before the fire of London. John Strype has done this and incorporated it in his *Annals of the Reformation*, 4 vols. (Oxford, 1820–40), 1:470 ff. The best description of procedures is Edmund Gibson's polemical but useful *Synodus Anglicana* (London, 1702), especially pp. 1–183. These sources reveal that Convocation usually met at St. Paul's, Blackfriars, or Westminster, generally in the chapter house, for the joint sessions of both houses. For an excellent discussion of the 1562 session see William P. Haugaard, *Elizabeth and the English Reformation* (Cambridge, 1968).

84. The word meant "separated" or "severed from." Like parliament, the two houses of Convocation met together for the opening and closing ceremonies and separately for the daily deliberations.

85. From Gibson, who reproduces most of the surviving records in *Synodus,*

The Archbishops and Bishops doo sit all at a Table and doo discourse all such causes and matters as are brought in question before the^{m}, either of their owne motions: or from the higher Court of Parlement, or from the lower house of Convocation, or from any private person. Every Archbishop and Bishop sitteth and taketh place according to his estate and degree,[86] which degrees are knowen by such degrees and offices in the Church: as to every of them is assigned, for one hath the personage of a Preest, another of a Deacon, this is a Subdeac^{n}o, he is a Sexten and so foorth, as such officers were wunt to be in $\overset{e}{y}$ Church.

The Bishops doo not sit at the fore noon, but onely at the after noon, because they beeing Barons of the higher house of parlement: doo resorte and assemble them selves there at the forenoones with the Temporall Lords.

The Convocaion house of the rest of the Clergie: doo observe in a maner the like orders as the lower house of the commons doo use, for beeing assembled togither on the first day with the Bishops: are by them willed to make choice of a Speaker for them, whome they call the *Proloquutor,* when they have chosen him: they doo present him unto the Bishops, and he thus presented: maketh his oration, and dooth all things as the Speaker of the lower house for the Commons dooth, as wel for the ordering of the Clergie and of the house, for his order in sitting, the order in speaking, the order of recording the things doon among them, and all other such like things.[87]

---

we learn that the archbishop of Canterbury presided over the whole Convocation, representing the sovereign, and acted as Speaker in the upper house. His title was "president." He had several assistants, including a registrar and commissary, who tended to clerical matters relating to summons, proxies, attendance records, and the daily journal. I have not been able to discover the amount of allowances and fee rates to which Hooker alludes.

86. Probably the same system that prevailed in parliament. Heading that precedence list were: the archbishop of Canterbury, the archbishop of York, the bishop of London, the Bishop of Durham, and the bishop of Winchester. The remaining bishops took places according to the seniority of consecration (also see Edelen, *Harrison's Description,* p. 123).

87. The lower house elected a moderator or speaker entitled a Prolocutor,

And this is to be understanded, that the whole Clergie can deale and intreate but onely of matters of Religion, and orders of the Church, whiche their dooings & conclusions cannot binde the whole Realme: unlesse they be confirmed by Act of Parlement, but yet sufficient to binde the whole Clergie to the keeping therof, so that the King (who is the supreme governour of bothe estates) doo consent and confirme the same. And forasmuch as by knowing the orders of the Parlement house: you may also knowe the orders of bothe the Convocation houses, which are like and correspondent to y̆ others.[88] These shal suffise [30a] for this matter.

Of extraordinary persons which ought to be Summoned to the Parlement.

BEsides the personages of the former degrees which ought to be summoned to the parlement: the King also must warne and summon all his councellers bothe of th'one Law and of th'other and those have their places onely in

---

although the archbishop seems to have had a voice in the selection plus the power to confirm or reject. The procedure of presentation was similar to that prevailing in the House of Commons. The lower house was composed of deans, archdeacons, and procurators elected by the diocesan and chapter clergy. There was also a clerk responsible for the journal, roll calls, and proxies. Most procedures were similar to those in the Commons, that is there were debates, committees, conferences, petitions, and votes. However, the whole procedure relating to the passage of articles, canons, and constitutions differed from Commons. Communications between the houses was through the Prolocutor alone. Voting on matters of substance was by subscription and proxies were allowable. Voting on procedural matters was by *viva voce*. On these matters see Gibson, *Synodus*, pp. 1–183.

88. Hooker has oversimplified the similarities here, for there were some rather significant differences in the procedures of Convocation and parliament. In Convocation the archbishops and bishops possessed the initiative while the lower clergy tended to be a debating and approving body with little or no initiative—a feature resulting from the hierarchical nature of the church, no doubt. This fundamental difference resulted in different procedures, particularly in the passage of measures and voting.

the higher house, namely the two cheef Justices and their associates, of the Kings bench, and the common places, the Barons of the Eschequer, the Sergeants, the Attorney, the Soliciter, the Maister of the Rolles, and his fellowes of the Chauncerye.[89]

The offices of these personages are to give councel to the King and Parlement in every doubtful cause according to the Lawes.

Also if any Bil be conceived and made disorderly: they ought to amend and reforme the same, upon order and commaundemet to them given.[90]

Also they must attend to come and go at the commaundement of the King and Parlement.

Also they may not speak nor give advise: but when they be asked and put to question.

Also they have no voice in Parlement: because they are commonly councellers to the same.

They are all retained at the Kings charges.[91]

Likewise all officers of the Parlement are to be summoned, as namely the Chaunceller of the Parlement, the Clarks, the

89. Presumably by "his fellowes" Hooker means the six masters in chancery. Hooker is the only commentator to discuss those summoned by writs of assistance to render advice at the behest of the House of Lords. Unfortunately their role in the lawmaking process has not been studied in depth, but the following are useful: Pollard, "Receivers of Petitions," pp. 202–26; McIlwain, *High Court of Parliament;* E. R. Adair and F. M. G. Evans, "Writs of Assistance," *EHR* 36 (1921): 356–72; and A. F. Pollard, "Queen Elizabeth's Under-Clerks and their *Commons' Journals,*" *BIHR* 17 (1939): 3–4.

90. These legal advisors possessed no initiative in legislative matters and no voting power; they could only react and respond to their superiors in the upper house. They frequently acted as messengers between the two houses, especially in matters requiring a conference between the houses, but oftimes they were appointed to committees as nonvoting members to render technical advice on a bill under consideration. In 1571, judges were assigned to several committees; see *LJ,* 2:669–708. In that same session, the queen's solicitor and attorney were also assigned to a committee (ibid., p. 670).

91. All of the assistants received compensation from the offices they held rather than from fees or per diem wages.

Sergeants, the Porters and such others, who likewise are retained at the Kings costs. Of their offices and charges, it is
alredy perticulerly declared.

Of the dayes and houres to sit in Parlement.

[30b] All dayes of the week are appointed saving and excepted the Sundayes and all principall feastes, as namely the
feasts of All hallown day, Christmas, Easter, Whitsontide, and
Saint John ẙ Baptists day, & also such other dayes as the Parlement by concent shall appoynt and assigne.

The beginning is at eight of the clock in the morning, and
dooth continew until xi. of the clock.[92]

They doo not sit at after noones, for those times are re-
served for Committies and the Convocation house.[93]

In the morning: they begin with the Common prayer, and
Letanye which are openly red in the house.

Of the King, his office and authoritie.

HAving declared of all the estates, degrees, and personages
of the Parlement: it resteth now to speak also of the King and
of his office, who is all in all, the beginning and the ending and
upon whome resteth and dependeth the effect and substaunce
of the whole Parlement, for without him and his authoritie:
nothing can be doon, and with it: all things take effect, neverthelesse when he calleth and assembleth his Parlement: there
are sundrye orders whiche of him are to be observed, and
which he ought to see to be kept and executed, or els the

92. In 1571 parliament extended the working day somewhat by beginning
with preaching at 7:00 A.M. and holding some afternoon sessions; see Neale,
EP, 1:212. Sometimes the upper house began at 9:00 A.M. rather than 8:00
A.M.

93. "At the afternoone they keepe no parliament," noted Smith in *De Republica Anglorum*, p. 55, but he indicates no reasons or specific hours for the
morning sitting, as does Hooker. In 1571, after Convocation completed its
deliberations—that is, late in the session—the House of Lords had several
afternoon meetings to consider pressing matters (see *LJ* 2:687 ff.).

Parlement surcesseth to be a Parlement and taketh not his effect, of whiche orders: these be the cheef which doo insue.[94]

First: the King ought to send out his summons to all the estates of his Realme, of a Parlemēt assigning & appointing the time, day and place.

Also his summons must be at the least forty dyaes before the beginning of his Parlement.

Also he must appoint and provide all such officers as ought [31a] to attend the Parlement, who must be found at his charges.

Also the King ought not to make any choice, or cause any choice to be made of any Knight, Cittzens, Burgesses, Proctors of the Clergie, Speaker of the common house, or *Proloquutor* of the Convocation house: but they must be elected and chosen by the lawes, orders and customs of the Realme, as they were wunt and ought to be, and the Kings good advise yet not to be contemned.[95]

Also the king ought to graunt, permit, and allow to all and every of the estates and to every perticuler man, lawfully elected and come to the Parlement all and every the auncient freedoms, priviledges, immunitie, and customes during the Parlement: as also during the times and dayes comming and going to and from the Parlement, but yet the same humbly to be requested of his highnes by the Speaker in his oratiō at the beginning of the Parlement.[96]

94. Again, Hooker is the only contemporary to comment fully on this subject, although Smith touches upon it in *De Republica Anglorum*, pp. 49, 57.

95. Hooker draws a very thin line of distinction here between the direct role of the sovereign as selector and the indirect role as nominator. We know that some favored circular letters and even suggested the names of MPs; we also know that the Speaker was more often than not nominated by the crown and then affirmed by the lower house. Perhaps Hooker drew a subtle distinction between the personal influence of the queen—which he disallowed—and that exercised by councillors, which is neither disallowed nor discussed. In any case, he allows "the Kings good advise" in the elective and selective processes.

96. Here Hooker reiterates the parliamentary privileges which every MP

Also the King in person ought to be present in the Parlement three daies at the least during the time of the Parlem^{n}et, that is to say, the first day when the whole estates according to the summons make their apparance, whiche is called the first day of the Parlement. On the second day when the Speaker of the common house is presented, which is counted the beginning of the Parlement. And the third day which is the last day when the Parlement is proroged or dissolved, for upon these dayes: he must be present, unlesse in cace of sicknes, or absence out of the Realme, for in these caces: the King may summon his Parlement by commission, and the same is of as good effect, as if he were present in person,[97] and as for any other dayes: he is at his choice and libertie to come, or not to come to the Parlement.

Also the King ought to propone unto the Parlement house in writing all such things and matters of charge, as for whiche he calleth the said Parlem^{n}et, and accordingly as the same shal then by the consent of all estates be advised, concluded and agreed, so the King either hath to allow or disalowe the same, for he can (of himself) neither adde nor deminish any Bil, but [31b] accept the same as it is presented unto him from the estates of the Parlement, or els altogither reject it.[98]

Also the King as he dooth prefixe and assigne the day, and time when the Parlement shall begin: so also he must assigne

---

could expect. This reiteration is somewhat extraordinary, for in so doing he implies that they are rights rather than graces; or, conversely, he implies that they are responsibilities incumbent upon the crown.

97. Convention by commission was common in the sixteenth century as was prorogation by commission. Hooker omits noting that the sovereign always appeared in the upper house and never in the lower house; in this context, however, the term *Parlement* could only mean the House of the Lords.

98. Hooker seems to say that the crown has an obligation to specify the primary purpose for summoning a parliament and submit those bills it needed and wanted. Presumably this was to be achieved through the initial speech at the beginning of each parliament, through royally-sponsored bills introduced by councillors in their respective houses, and through written directives presented during the session.

and appoint the time when the same shalbe proroged or dissolved, whiche ought not to be as long as any matters of
charge, weight or importaunce be in question, and the same
not decided nor determined.[99]

Of the dignitie, power and authoritie of the Parlement and of the orders of the same.

THe Parlement is the hiest, cheefest, and greatest Court
that is or can be within the Realme for it consisteth of the
whole Realme, whiche is devided into three estates, that is to
wit, the King, the Nobles, and the Commons, every of which
estates are subject to all suche orders as are concluded and
established in Parlement.

These three estates may joyntly and with one consent or
agreemet: establish and enact any Laws, orders, & Statutes for
the common welth, but beeing devided, and one swarving[100]
from the other: they can do no thing, for the King though hee
be the head,[101] yet alone: cannot make any Law, nor yet $\tilde{y}$ king
and his Lords onely, nor yet the King and his Commons alone,
neither yet can the Lords and the Commons, without the King
doo anything of avail. And yet neverthelesse if the King in due
order have summoned all his Lords and Barons, and they wil
not come, or if they come they wil not yet appeer, or if they
come and appeer, yet wil not doo or yeeld to any thing: then
the King with the concent of his Commons (who are repre-

99. Here Hooker perpetuates a medieval doctrine (found in the *Modus*)
which Tudor and Stuart sovereigns flouted or ignored. Frequently dissolution
or prorogation took place before all bills were determined. Many bills died in
committee and in 1614 no bills passed. In 1571 the bill to permit nonresident
MPs to represent boroughs died in committee.

100. Meaning to divide and move in different directions—as a river divides
because of a sand bar.

101. In using the word *head* to describe the king's role among the three
estates, Hooker borrows from the *Modus* (chapter xxvi) and subscribes to an
organic conception of society so characteristic of medieval political ideas. For
a discussion of this see Clarke, *Medieval Representation*, pp. 318–20.

sented by the Knights Citizens and Burgesses) may ordain & establish any Act or Law, which ar as good, sufficent and effectuall: as if they Lords had given their consents.

But of the contrary, if the Commons be summoned, and wil not come, or comming wil not appeer, or appeering wil not con- [32a] sent to doo anything, aledging some just weightie and great cause. The King (in these caces) cannot with his Lords devise, make, or establish any Law, the reasons are these, when Parlements were first begon and ordained: there were no Prelats or Barons of the Parlement, and the Temporall Lords were very few or none, and then the King and his Commons did make a ful Parlement, which authoritie was hetherto never abridged, again every Baron in Parlement dooth represent but his owne person, & speaketh in the behalf of him self alone.[102]

But in the Knights, Citizens, and Burgesses: are represeted the Commons of the whole Realme, and every of these giveth not consent onely for him self: but for all those also for whom he is sent.[103] And the King with the consent of his Commons: had ever a sufficient and ful authoritie to make, ordain, & establish good & wholesome Lawes for the commo welth of his Realme, wherfor the Lords beeing lawfully summoned & yet refusing to come, sit or cosent in Parlemet: cannot by their folly abridge the King and the Commons of their lawful proceding in Parlement.

102. Hooker's notion regarding the essentiality of Commons to the lawmaking process derives from the *Modus* and other sixteenth-century ideas regarding the original composition of parliament. See above pp. 65–67.

103. Whereas Hooker contends that whole realm is represented in the House of Commons, Sir Thomas Smith claims that whole realm is represented in parliament: "And to be short, all that ever the people of Rome might do either in *Centuriatis comitijs* or *tributis,* the same may be doone by the parliament of Englande, which representeth and hath the power of the whole realme both the head and the bodie. For everie Englishman is entended to bee there present, either in person or by procuration and attornies, of what preheminence, state, dignitie, or qualitie soever he be, from the Prince (be he King or Queene) to be lowest person of Englande. And the consent of the Parliament is taken to be everie mans consent" (*De Republica Anglorum,* p. 49).

The Lords and Commons (in times past) did sit all in one house, but for the advoiding of confusion: they be now devided into twoo severall houses,[104] and yet nevertheles they are of like and equall authoritie, every persõ of either of ẙ said houses beeing named, reputed, & coũted a peer of the Realme, for the time of the Parlement, ẙ is to say, equall, for Par, is equall.[105] And therfore the oppinion, censure and judgement of a mean Burgesse: is of as great avail: as is the best Lords, no regarde beeing had to the partie who speaketh: but the matter that is spoken.

They be also called Peeres as it were Fathers for *Pier,* is a Father, by which is ment that all such as be of the Parlement: should be auncient, grave, wise, learned and expert men of the land, for such were the Senators of Roome, and called *Patres conscripti* for the wisdome and care that was in them in governing of ẙ common welth.[106] They are also called Councellers, because they are assembled and called to the Parlement, for their advise and good councel in making and devising of suche [32b] orders and Lawes as may be for the common welth.

They, therfore which make choice of Knights, Citizens and Burgesses, ought to be wel advised that they doo elect and choose such as beeing to be of that assemblye, and therby equall with the great estates: should be grave, auncient, wise, learned, expert & careful men for their commonwelth, and who (as saith ful and trusty councellers) should doo that whiche should turn and be for the best commoditie of the common welth, otherwise they doo great injury to their Prince and common weale.

Also every person of the Parlement during the times of the Parlement, and at his comming and going from the same: is

104. For the significance of this paragraph, especially its impact on Coke and others, especially the Levellers, see my comments above pp. 109–10.

105. Needless to say, most contemporaries rejected Hooker's egalitarian doctrine and some of his etymological explanations of the terms *Parlement* and *Pier.*

106. Smith makes several allusions to Roman senatorial practices in his chapter on parliament (*De Republica Anglorum,* pp. 49–58).

free from all troubles, arrests and molestations, no action or
sute taking effect which during that time is begun, entred, or
commenced against him, in what Court so ever the same be,
except in causes of Treason, Murder and Fellony, and except
also executions in Law, awarded and graunted before the beginning of the Parlement.[107]

Also every person having voices in Parlement: hath free
libertie of speach to speak his minde, oppinion and judge-
mēt to any matter proponed, or of him self to propone any
matter for the commoditie of the Prince and of the common
welth, but having once spoken to any Bil: he may speak no
more for that time.[108]

Also every person once elected and chosen a knight, Citizen
or Burgesse & returned: cannot be dismissed out of that
house, but beeing admitted: shall have his place and voice
there, if he be a Layman. But if by errour a man of the Clergie
be chosen: then he ought and shalbe dismissed, also if he be
excomunicated, outlawed or infamose.[109]

Also every one of these houses ought to be incorrupt no
briber nor taker of any rewards, gifts, or money, either for
devising of any bil or for speaking of his minde: but to doo all
things uprightly, and in such forte, as best for the King and
common welth.[110]

107. In his earlier comments upon freedom from arrest Hooker did not
include these all-important exceptions to the privilege. It should be noted that
the parliamentary privileges discussed in this section apply to members of
both houses.

108. This is Hooker's third reference to freedom of debate. However, it is
well worth noting that he does not subscribe to an unlimited freedom of
speech. The speaker had to confine his remarks to the subject under consideration, in short "to any matter proponed," and his remarks had to be germane
to the subject. Moreover, once having said his piece on the matter, he could
not speak again "that time," meaning that day, on the same matter. On this
subject see Neale, "Freedom of Speech," pp. 272–86.

109. See above p. 44 and below note 110. For more details see Gilkes, *TTP*,
pp. 52–53.

110. Hooker's standards of conduct were violated in 1571 when one
Thomas Long of Westbury, Wiltshire, bribed his way into being nominated
and elected to the House of Commons. Once found out, as he was in mid-

Also every one ought to be of a quiet, honest, and gentle, behaviour, none taunting, checking or misusing an other in [33a] any unseemly woords or deeds, but all affections set a parte to doo and indever in wisdome, sobrietie & knowledge, that which that place requireth.[111]

Also if any one doo offend or misbehave himself: he is to be corrected and punished by the advise and order of the residue of the house.[112]

Also all the Prisons, wardes, gailes within the Realme and the keepers of the same: are at the commaundement of the Parlement for the custodie and safe keeping or punishment of all and every such Prisoners as shalbe sent to any of them by the said Palrement houses or any of them, how be it moste commonly the Tower of London is the prison which is moste used.[113]

---

session, he was disabled from sitting and the co-conspirators were apprehended. See *CJ*, 1:88 ff; and Neale, *EHC*, pp. 151–52.

111. In *De Republica Anglorum* (p. 55), Smith employs similar words: "No reviling or nipping words must be used. For then all the house will crie, it is against the order: and if any speake unreverently or seditiouslie against the Prince or the privie counsell, I have seene them not onlely interrupted, but it hath beene moved after to the house, and they have sent them to the Tower." In his *Aucient Customs of England,* published in 1641, William Hakewill borrows phraseology from both Smith and Hooker. Also see Elizabeth Read Foster, "Speaking in the House of Commons," *BIHR* 43 (1970): 35–55.

112. As above, Hooker lays claim to the authority of each house to judge and punish its own members. He was not alone in this matter, for both Smith and Lambarde comment on the authority of Commons to punish those violating the orders and customs of the House; see *De Republica Anglorum* (p. 52) and *Orders* (pp. 263–65). During the reign of Elizabeth this would appear to be a concurrent power or at least a contested power claimed by both crown and Commons, for on several occasions the queen ordered the seizure and commitment of MPs. In 1571, for example, William Strickland was detained by the crown for introducing a bill which the queen considered inimical to her prerogative. However, he was released after members of Commons protested; on this see the "Anonymous Diary," TCLD, MS 535, ff. 34–35. The best evidence of Hooker's claim is the Arthur Hall case. Thomas Long, who bribed his way into the House of Commons, was unseated when the crime was discovered; see D'Ewes, *ACJ*, p. 182, and *CJ*, 1:88.

113. The authority for this rather sweeping jurisdictional claim would appear to be Hooker's experience in the 1571 parliament. It is true that by

Also if any one of the Parlement house be served, sued, arrested or attached by any writ, attachment or minister of the Kings bench, Common place, Chauncery, or what Court so ever within this Realme: the partie so troubled and making complaint therof to the Parlement house: then foorth with a Sergeant at Armes, is sent to the said Court, not onely advertising, that the partie so molested is one of the Parlemet house: but also inhibiting and commaunding the Officers of the said Court to call in the said processe, and not to deale any further against the said partie, for the Parlement beeing the hiest court, all other Courts yeeld and give place to the same.[114]

Also as every one of the Parlement house is free for his owne person, for all maner of sutes to be commenced against him: so are also his Servants free, and not to be troubled nor molested but beeing troubled: have the like remedie as the Maister hath or may have.[115]

Also no manner of person beeing not one of the Parlement house: ought to enter or come within the house, as long as the sitting is there: upon pain of imprisonment or suche other

custom parliament usually used the Tower or the Sergeant's Ward for confinement purposes, but on occasion the Gatehouse, Fleet, and Marshalsea were used. Perhaps Hooker generalized from these and other precedents; perhaps he secured additional information from experienced MPs in Westminster. In 1571, as Hooker notes in his "Journal" (p. 483), the mentally deranged Thomas Long was sent to Bridewell.

114. In his earlier chapters Hooker says nothing about the intermediative role of the sergeant at arms in jurisdictional disputes involving MPs. No doubt the relief was temporary and did not cover the exceptions listed by Hooker earlier in this chapter (see above p. 185). See D'Ewes, *ACJ*, pp. 123, 283, 347–48, 655–56.

115. This seems somewhat repetitious. In an earlier chapter he discussed freedom from arrest for commoners; earlier in this chapter he claims the freedom for all members of parliament (see above pp. 183–84). Here he reiterates the freedom and extends it to the servants of "every one" in attendance. In 1571, when Sir Henry Clynton's servant was arrested, Commons took up the case and freed him; see *CJ*, 1:87. For other cases see D'Ewes, *ACJ*, pp. 83, 85, 249, 254, 629.

punishment, as by the house shalbe ordered and adjudged.[116]

Also every person of the Parlement ought to keep secret and not to disclose the secrets and things spoke^n and doon in the Parlement house, to any manner of person unlesse he be one of [33b] the same house: upon pain to be sequestred out of the house, or otherwise punished, as by the order of the house shalbe appointed.[117]

Also none of the Parlement house ought to departe from the Parlement: without speciall leave obteyned of the Speaker of the house, and the same his licence be also recorded.

Also no person beeing not of the Parlement house: ought to come into the same, during the time of the sitting, so every one comming into the same: oweth a dutie and a reverence to be given when he entreth and commeth in.[118]

If a Baron or a Lord come and enter into $\overset{e}{y}$ higher house: he ought to doo his obeysaunce before the cloth of estate, and so to take his place.[119]

Also when he speaketh: he must stand bare headed, and

116. The exclusion of nonmembers or strangers, a point made earlier with reference to the House of Commons, is now extended to cover "the Parlement house," meaning the House of Lords, presumably, or both houses. In 1571 two "strangers" from Inner Temple were seized and imprisoned; see Davidson, "Hoker's *Journal*," p. 474, and *CJ*, 1:83. The two men, Thomas Clerk and Anthony Bull, were discovered in the course of a roll call.

117. The secrecy rule applied to both houses, it is interesting to note, but more important is the logical inference from Hooker's statement that members from one house could not disclose deliberations to members of the other house. For an extended discussion see Neale, *EHC*, pp. 400–02. In 1571 several MPs disapproved of Sir Humphrey Gilbert's disclosures to the queen of their deliberations. John Brown's rendition of the secrecy clause sworn by councillors, quoted by Neale (p. 401), bears a close resemblance to this paragraph.

118. All nonmembers without business were excluded, Hooker seems to say, but those having business (such as a presentation of a petition or a response to an order) were expected to follow the customs and protocol of parliament. By "Parlement house" Hooker means the House of Lords.

119. In 1621, this paragraph was incorporated in the Roll of Standing Orders, as were several other phrases in this section; see Bond, *Lords Manuscripts*, pp. 3–5.

speake his minde plainly, sensibly, and in decent order.

If any come in message or be sent for to the higher house: they must stay at the inner door until they be called in, & then beeing entred: must first make their obeysaᵘce, and gooing forwards must in the middle way make one other lower curtesie, and then beeing come foorth to the Barre: must make the third curtesie, the like must be doon at the departure.[120]

Also when any Knight, Citizen, or Burgesse dooth enter and come into the lower house, he must make his dutiful and humble obeysaunce at his entry in: and then take his place.[121] And you shal understᵃd that as every such person ought to be grave, wise and expert: so ought he to show him self in his Apparail, for in times past: none of the councellers of ỹ Parlement came otherwise then in his gown, and not armed nor girded with weapon, for the Parlement house is a place for wise, grave and good men, to consult, debate, and advise how to make Lawes, and orders for the common welth, and not to be armed as men redy to fight, or to trye matters by the Swoord: and albe it the writ for the election of the Knights, have expresse woords to [34a] choose such for Knights as be girded with the Swoord, yet it is not ment therby that they should come and sit armed: but bee such as be skilful in feates of Armes, and besides their good advies: can wel serve in martiall affaires.[122] And thus the Romain Senators used, who

120. Hooker alone among Elizabethan commentators provides this detailed information about protocol and ritual.

121. Having completed his discussion of procedure in the House of Lords, Hooker devotes the remainder of this chapter to the House of Commons, but he switches without any formal indication of doing so.

122. After 1340, the phrase *"gladiis cinctos"* was omitted, but the rest of the phraseology remained intact; see William Stubbs, *The Constitutional History of England*, 3 vols. (Oxford, 1903), 3:412–18. It is entirely possible that in earlier centuries the knights of the shire attended parliament in military garb and arms; however, by the reign of Elizabeth I the practice was obsolete and contrary to parliamentary protocol, as is evident in the few extant illustrations. As indicated above (see p. 77), in 1586 when Perrot imposed Hooker's *Order and Usage* in Ireland, the garb prescribed in this paragraph evoked derision from the native Irish.

beeing men of great knowledge and experience as wel in martiall affaires, as in politique causes, sat allwaies in the Senate house, and places of councel in their Gownes and long Robes. The like also was alwaies and hath been the order in the Parlements of this Realme, as long as the aucient Lawes, the olde customes, and good orders therof were kept and observed.[123]

Also if any other person or persons either in message or beeing sent for, doo come: he ought to be brought in by the Sergeant & at the first entring: must (following the Sergeant) make one lower obeysaunce, and beeing past in the middle way: must make one other, and when he is come before the Speaker: he must make the third, and then doo his message, the like order he must keep in his return.[124] But if he doo come alone or with his learned councel, to pleade any matter, or to answere to any objection: he shall enter and go no farther then to the Bar within the door, and there to doo his three obeysaunces.

Also when any Bil is committed, the Committes have not authoritie to conclude: but onely to order, reforme, examin, and amend the thing committed unto them, and of their dooings they must give reporte to the house again, by whome the Bill is to be considered.[125]

Also every Bil whiche is brought into the house: must bee red three severall times, and upon three severall dayes.[126]

123. It is not clear what laws, customs, and orders Hooker meant, for the *Modus* contained no reference to parliamentary garb or a code of dress. In all likelihood he is reading history backward and establishing unverifiable links of continuity between the Roman senate and the English parliament.

124. The protocol of the two houses seems to be identical (see above p. 187).

125. Hooker's discussion of bills and committees is less detailed than either Smith (*De Republica Anglorum*, pp. 54–57) or Lambarde (*Orders*, pp. 260–65). Writing fifteen years later than Hooker, during which time the committee system became more sophisticated, Lambarde devoted separate chapters to each reading and cited numerous precedents.

126. Smith makes the same point in *De Republica Anglorum* (p. 54): "All bils be thrise in three diverse days read and disputed upon, before they come to the question." Writing later, Lambarde notes in his *Orders* (p. 260): "One bill may be twice read in one day." As Neale points out, there were exceptions to

Also every Bil which upon any reading is committed and returned again: ought to have his three readings unlesse the Committes have not altred the bil in any substaunce or forme, but onely in certain woords.[127]

Also when any Bil upon any reading is altogither by one concent rejected, or by voices after ẙ third reading everthrown: it ought not to be brought any more to be red during ẙ Sessions of Parlement.[128]

[34b] Also if any man doo speak unto a Bill and be out of his matter: he ought to be put in remembraunce of the matter by the Speaker onely and by none other, and be willed to come to the matter.[129]

Also whensoever any person dooth speak to any Bill: hee ought to stand up, and to be bare headed, and then with all

---

the normal procedure of three readings, each on a different day; see *EHC,* pp. 357–59. In 1571, in fact, several bills in the House of Commons were read twice and three times the same day, especially toward the end of the session; see *CJ,* 1:87–92.

127. This is a most interesting technicality—one omitted by both Smith and Lambarde—which explains why many bills had more than three readings. In fact, in 1571 several bills which encountered opposition were redrafted and introduced as new bills.

128. As a general rule bills were not rejected on the first reading, although Commons could and did reject a few. Most bills were by "gentlemen's agreement" allowed to pass the first reading without opposition, a point which Lambarde suggests in chapter III of *Orders* (p. 260). After the second reading of a bill Commons could: (1) reject it; (2) ingross it—that is, have it transcribed on parchment, an action indicative of approval without any opposition or demand for amendment; or (3) commit it for emendation to those whom the majority selected (see Lambarde, ibid.). However, once dashed or rejected, a bill could not be reintroduced during the session; this rule was not discussed by either Smith or Lambarde.

129. As indicated above (p. 168), Smith comments upon the rules of debate, but he does not touch upon the principle of germaneness. However, in *Orders* (chapter V), Lambarde borrows heavily from both Smith and Hooker; in fact, he uses identical words and paraphrases both authors: "If any speak too long, and speak within the matter, he may not be cut off; but if he be long, and *out of the matter,* then may the Speaker gently admonish him" (p. 261, emphasis mine).

reverence, gravitte, and seemly speech, to declare his minde.[130] But when so ever any Bil shalbe tryed either for allowances, or to be rejected: then every one ought to sit, because he is then as a Judge.[131]

Also every Knight, Citizen, and Burgesse before he doo enter into the Parlement and take his place there: ought to bee sworne and to take his othe, acknowledging the King to be the supreme and onely governour of all the estates within his Realme as also to renounce all forrain Potentates.[132]

The order of the beginning and ending of the Parlement.[133]

ON the first day of the summons for the Parlement, the King in proper person (unlesse he bee sick or absent out of the Realme) beeing apparailled in his royall and Parlement Robes: ought to be conducted & brought by all his Barons of the

130. In *De Republica Anglorum* (p. 54), Smith makes a similar observation: "he that standeth uppe bareheaded is understanded that he will speake to the bill."

131. Hooker, referring here to the final vote, omits any reference to divisions, which of course involved leaving the room for tabulative purposes. Smith elaborates: "After the bill hath beene twise reade, and then engrossed and eftsoones reade and disputed on ynough as is thought: the speaker asketh if they will goe to the question. And if they agree he holdeth the bill up in his hande and sayeth, as many as will have this bill goe forwarde, which is concerning such a matter, say yea. Then they which allowe the bill crie yea, and as many as will not, say no: as the crie of yea or no is bigger, so the bill is allowed or dashed. If it be a doubt which crie is the bigger, they divide the house, the speaker saying, as many as doe alowe the bill goe downe with the bill, and as many as do not sitte still. So they divide themselves, and being so divided they are numbred who make the more part, and so the bill doeth speede." (ibid., p. 56).

132. This practice—obviously out of place—was relatively new in that it was first introduced in the 1571 parliament. See D'Ewes, *ACJ*, p. 155; Davidson, "Hoker's *Journal*," p. 473; and Gilkes, *TTP*, pp. 83–84.

133. Hooker borrows the title and theme of this chapter from two separate chapters in the *Modus* (see above pp. 137, 143) but he updates the contents of course.

Clergie and Laitie, and the Commons summoned to the Parlement, unto the Church, where ought a Sermon to be made by
some Archbishop, Bishop or some other famouse learned
man.[134] The Sermon ended: he must in like order be brought
to the higher house of Parlement, and there to take his seat
under the cloth of estate, likewise every Lord and Baron (in his
degree) ought to take his place.

This doon: the Lord Chaunceller or he whom the King
appointeth to be the speaker of that house, maketh his oration
to the whole assembly, declaring the causes why & wherfore
that Parlement is called and summoned, exhorting and per-
swading every man to doo his best indevor in all such matters
as [35a] shalbe in the said Parlement proponed as shalbe
moste expedient for the glory of God, the honor of the King,
and the common welth of the whole Realme.[135] Then he directeth his talke, unto the Knights, Citizens, and Burgesses,
advertising them that the Kings pleasure is, that they doo
repair to their house, and there according to the olde and
auncient custome: to choose and elect some one wise, grave,
and learned man emong them selves to be Speaker for them,
and giveth them a day when they shall present him to the
King.[136] And these things thus doon: the King ariseth, and
every man departeth. This is accounted for the first day of the
Parlement.

134. Smith says nothing about the opening process and divine service which
usually took place in St. Margaret's Westminster, although he does comment
upon the opening ceremonies in the House of Lords (*De Republica Anglorum*,
p. 50). For the most complete coverage see the opening ceremonies described
in the "Anonymous Diary," TCLD, MS 535, ff. 1–3.

135. This information comes from Hooker's personal observations which
were recorded in his diary (see Davidson, "Hoker's *Journal*," p. 473). In 1571,
as Hooker noted, Lord Keeper Bacon made a special plea for funds.

136. Ibid. "This oration ended the lower howse was willed to asemble thyme
selffs together & to chose unto theyme selffs a speker & to present him the
thurseday folowinge, but the Quene shortned the tyme & apoynted the wenes-
daye. Then the lower howse assembled theym selffe & emonge others made
choyse of Sgeunt wraye to be the speker."

THe second or third day after, when the Speaker is to be presented: the King with all his Nobles (in like order as before) doo assemble again in the higher house, and then come up all the commons of the lower house, and then and there doo present their Speaker unto the King. The Speaker foorthwith maketh his dutiful obeysaunces:[137] beginneth and maketh his oration before the King, and prosequuteth such matters as occasion serveth, and as is before resited in the office of the Speaker, and this doon: every man departeth. And this is accounted for the beginning of the Parlement, for before the Speaker be presented, and these things orderly doon: there can no Billes be put in, nor matters be entreated of.

Lastly when all matters of weight be discussed, ended and dermined:[138] the King commaundeth an end to be made.

And that day the King, his Nobles and Commons doo again assemble in the higher house, in their Robes, and in like order as is before recited, where the Speaker maketh his oration, and is answered by the Lord Chaunceller or Speaker of the higher house.[139] Then all the Billes concluded and past in bothe

137. Ibid. The phrase "his dutiful obeysaunces" comes directly from his diary, indicating that Hooker no doubt used it in preparing the *Order and Usage* for publication. Also see D'Ewes, *ACJ,* pp. 140–42.

138. Obviously Hooker means "determined" or "terminated."

139. Smith presents a similar but longer account of the final ceremony: "But the last day of that Parliament or session the Prince commeth in person in his Parliament robes, and sitteth in his state: all the upper house sitteth about the Prince in their states and order in their robes. The speaker with all the common house commeth to the barre, and there after thankes given first in the Lordes name by the Chaunceller &c. and in the commons name by the speaker to the Prince, for that hee hath so great care of the good governement of his people, and for calling them together to advise of such thinges as should be for the reformation, establishing and ornament of the common wealth: the Chaunceller in the Princes name giveth thanks to the Lords and commons for their paines and travailes taken, which he saith the Prince will remember and recompence when time and occasion shall serve, and that he for his part is ready to declare his pleasure concerning their proceedings, whereby the same may have perfect life and accomplishment by his princelie authoritie, and so have the whole consent of the Realme. Then one reades the title of everie act which hath passed at that session, but only in this fashion: An act concerning

houses, that is to say, in the higher house of the Lords, and in the lower house of the commons, are there red by the titles, and then the King giveth his concent or discent to every of them as he thinketh good. And when the titles of all the the[140] [35b] Billes are red: the Lord Chaunceller, or Lord Speaker by the Kings commaundement, pronounceth the Parlement to bee proroged or cleane dissolved. And this is called the last day or the end of the Parlement, and every man is at libertie to departe homewards.

<pre>
      * *   * *
         *   *

            * *
               *
</pre>

---

such a thing &c. It is marked there what the Prince doth allowe, and to such he sayth: *Le roy* or *la royne le veult*. And those be taken nowe as perfect lawes and ordinances of the Realme of Englande and none other, and as shortlie as may be put in print, except it be some private cause or law made for the benefit or prejudice of some private man, which the Romans were wont to call *privi-legia*. These be onelie exemplified under the seale of the Parliament, and for the most part not printed. To those which the Prince liketh not, he answereth, *Le roy* or *La Royne saduisera,* and those be accounted utterly dashed and of no effect." (*De Republica Anglorum,* p. 57).

140. A typographical error—one among several substantiating my deductions regarding the printing of the *Order and Usage.* See above p. 30.

[36a]   The names of all such personages as ought to appeer and be in the Parlement.

In the higher house.[141]

The King.
The Lord Speaker.[142]
Proctor for the kingdome of Fraunce.[143]
Proctor for Scotland.
Proctor for the Duchie of Aquitane.

Proctor for the Duchie of Guyen.
Proctor for the Duchie of Angewe.

The Archbishop of Canterbury.[144]

141. This appears to be a summons list, although it could be an attendance list used by the clerk of the parliament. In the 1572 edition of his *Abridgement*, Richard Grafton appended a list of the counties, boroughs, and cities receiving writs of summons to parliament—a list that Harrison included in Holinshed's *Chronicles*—but he did not incorporate a list of peers or summons list. However, in both the 1577 and the 1587 edition of Holinshed's *Chronicles* Harrison included a precedence list of English peers followed by a list of the bishops summoned to parliament in 1563; see Harrison, *Description of England*, pp. 122–23. It should be noted that Harrison incorporated these lists in chapter V, which elaborates the social structure, rather than chapter VIII, which described parliament. Hooker's list is different from Harrison's in that he includes the king, the Lord Speaker, and the proctors and places the spiritual lords first. Other differences are also evident: he includes the duke of Norfolk, who was executed shortly after Hooker wrote in 1572, and he elevates the seniority of the bishop of Exeter and has precedence order different from Harrison's.

142. Sir Nicholas Bacon, the lord keeper, presided as Speaker until he became ill, at which time Robert Catlin substituted for him.

143. The basis for this information, which seems to be erroneous, is not clear. The official journal refers to the receivers and triers of petitions "d' Angleterre, Irland, Galles et d' Escosse," but nothing is said about Aquitaine, Guisne, or Anjou. Obviously Hooker is confused or used an outdated list.

144. Hooker lists all twenty-six sees, although the source of the list is not

The Archbishop of York.
The Bishop of London.
The Bishop of Durham.
The Bishop of Winchester.
The Bishop of Chichester.
The Bishop of Exeter.
The Bishop of Elye.
The Bishop of Coventrie.
The Bishop of Rochester.
The Bishop of Sarisbury.
The Bishop of Welles.
The Bishop of Norwich.
The Bishop of Lincolne.
The Bishop of Worcester.
The Bishop of Herford.
The Bishop of Oxford.
The Bishop of Glocester.
The Bishop of Peterborough.
The Bishop of Bristowe.
The Bishop of Westchester.[145]
The Bishop of Carliel.
The Bishop of Saint David.
The Bishop of Saint Asse.[146]
The Bishop of Bangor.
The Bishop of Landaffe.

The Duke of Norfolke.[147]
The Marques of Northampton.
The Marques of Winchester.
The Earle of Arundel.
The Earle of Shrewsbury.
The Earle of Oxford.
The Earle of Darby.
The Earle of Rutland.
The Earle of Cumberland.
The Earle of Worcester.
The Earle of Bathe.
The Earle of Warwick.
The Earle of Lecester.
The Earle of Sussex.
The Earle of Huntington.
The Earle of Penbrook.[148]
The Earle of Harford.[149]
The Earle of Sowthampton.
The Earle of Bedford.
The Vicecount Montagew.
The Vicecount Hereford.

[36b]

The Vicecount Bindon.

---

evident. His source may have been the official journal, but his order is different and he has given English rather than Latin names to the dioceses. Moreover, his list differs from Harrison's as well. Several of those summoned were absent and sent proxies.

145. In some sixteenth-century documents *Chester* appears as *Westchester*.

146. *St. Asaph.* Possibly a compositor's prank; the Latin form was *St. Assaven.*

147. Although summoned to parliament, or appearing on a summons list, the duke of Norfolk was in the Tower accused of treason and did not attend. Nevertheless, his name appeared on the daily attendance lists kept by the clerk. The order of temporal peers is somewhat different from that appearing in the official journal. Moreover, Hooker renders the titles in English rather than Latin.

148. *Pembroke.*

149. *Hertford.*

The Lord Sowch.[150]
The Lord de la ware.
The Lord Aburgaueny.
The Lord Awdeley.
The Lord Barkley.
The Lord Morley.
The Lord Cobham.
The Lord Dakers of the South.[151]
The Lord Dakers of Gudesiond.[152]
The Lord Gray.
The Lord Scroope.
The Lord Latimer.
The Lord Sturton.
The Lord Clinton.
The Lord Dudley Baron of Dudley.
The Lord Lomeley.[153]
The Lord Mountjoy.
The Lord Conyes.[154]
The Lord Mountegle.

The Lord Winsor.
The Lord Wentworth.
The Lord Sandes.
The Lord Vaux.
The Lord Mordant.
The Lord Borough.
The Lord Bray.
The Lord Wharton.
The Lord Rich.
The Lord Crumwel.
The Lord Euere.
The Lord Stafford.
The Lord Darcy of Penel.[155]
the Lord Willoughby.
The Lord Paget.
The Lord Darcy of Chiche.
the Lord Chandoys.
The Lord of Loughborough.
the Lord S. John of Blastowe.[156]
The Lord Buckhurst.
the Lord Hunsdon.

150. *Zouch.*

151. *LJ,* 1:668 prints it "Dacres Sowth" and Harrison (*Description of England,* p. 122) writes "The Lord Dacre of the South," seemingly to distinguish him from another Lord Dacre. Specifically, Gregory Fiennes, tenth Lord Dacre, who died without issue in 1594.

152. George Dacre, sixth Lord Dacre of Gilsland or Lord Dacre of the North, died in infancy in 1569 and the title fell into abeyance. This seems to indicate that the list was a peerage list dating from a pre-1569 period or a summons list to the 1563 parliament, which included the summons to the fifth Lord Dacre, who died in 1566.

153. *Lumley.*

154. *Conyers.*

155. There were two Lord Darcys. The first in this list was John Darcy, second Lord Darcy of Darcy and Meinill, who died in 1602. Also known as Lord Darcy of Aston, he is not to be confused with Lord Darcy of Chicle, whose name appears below.

156. *St. John of Bletsoe.*

The Lord of Effingham.[157]
the two cheef Justices
The Barons of Th'eschequer.
the Kings Attorney.
The Kings Sergeants at Law.
the Kings Sollicitor.
The Kings learned Counsel.

Likewise every such person whome the King endoweth and honoreth with the degree and es-tate of a Baron ought to be su̅moned to the Parlement and to

have place there emong the Bar-ons according to his degree.

And yet neverthelesse the So̅ne of a Duke, of a Marquesse, or of an Earle, though he bee a Baron (his Father yet living) he shall not have a place in the Parlement: except he be other-wise honored either by the King or bee advaunced by meanes of some Mariage to the degree of a Baron.

[37a]   What they be that ought to be
                      In the lower house.[158]

The Countie of Bukingham.
ii. Knights.
The Countie of Midlesex.
ii. Knights.
the Countie of Bedford
ii. Knights.
The Countie of Cornewall.
ii. Knights.

the Countie of Cumberland
ii. Knights.
The countie of Cambridge
ii. Knights.
the Countie of Chester
ii. Knights.
The countie of Darby
ii. Knights.

157. Lord Howard of Effingham, lord chamberlain.

158. For another list see Harrison, *Description of England* (pp. 154–62), which appeared in the 1587 edition of Holinshed. While Hooker's list is based upon status (i.e., knights, citizens, and burgesses, English first and Welsh last) Harrison's list is roughly alphabetical by county with knights listed first in each English county followed by the boroughs and cities within the respective county. At the end of the list Harrison includes a numerical breakdown ac-cording to social rank:

Knights	90
Citizens	46
Burgesses	289
Barons	14
	439

Within each social category Hooker's list is roughly alphabetical on a county basis with English counties first and Welsh last.

the Countie of Devon
ii. Knights.
The countie of Dorset
ii. Knights.
the Countie of Essex
ii. knights.
the Countie of Hertford
ii. Knights.
The countie of Hereford
ii. Knights
the Countie of Kent
ii. knights.
The countie of York
ii. Knights.
the Countie of Glocester
ii. Knights
The countie of Huntington.
ii. Knights.
The countie of Lincolne
ii. knights.
the Countie of Lecester
ii. knights.
The Countie of Lancaster
ii. knights.
the Countie of Monmouth
ii. knights.
The Countie of
Northampton
ii. knights.
The Countie of Notingham
ii. knights.
The countie of Norfolke
ii. knights.
The Countie of
Northumberland
ii. knights.
The countie of Oxford
ii. knights.
the Countie of Rutland
ii. knights.

The countie of Berkshere
ii. knights.
the Countie of Surrey
ii. knights.
The Countie of Stafford
ii. knights.
the Countie of Shropsheer
ii. knights.
The countie of
Sowthampton
ii. knights.
the Countie of Suffolke
ii. knights.
The countie of Somerset
ii. knights.

[37b]

The countie of Sussex
ii. knights.
the Countie of
Westmerland
ii. knights.
The countie of Wiltsheer
ii. knights.
the Countie of Worcester
ii. knights.
The countie of Warwick
ii. knights.
the Countie of
Mongomerie
i. Knight.
The countie of Radnor
i. Knight.
the Countie of Dinghby
i. Knight.
The countie of Pembrook
i. Knight.
the Countie of Cardigan
i. Knight.

The countie of Mayoth[159]
i. Knight.
the countie of Carmarthan
i. Knight.
The countie of Carnarvan
i. Knight.
the Countie of Brecknock
i. Knight.
The countie of Glamorgan
i. Knight.
the Countie of Anglesey
i. Knight.
The countie of Merioneth
i. Knight.

The Cittie of Carlile[160]
ii. Citizens.
The Cittie of Chester.
ii. Citizens.
the Cittie Excester
ii. Citizens.
The Cittie of York. ii. Citizens
the Cittie of Glocester
ii. Citizens.
The Cittie of Hereford
ii. Citizens.

the Cittie of Canterbury
ii. citizens.
The Cittie of Rochester
ii. citizens.
the Cittie of Lincolne
ii. citizens.
The Cittie of Westminster
ii. citizens.
the Cittie of London
ii. Citizens.
The Cittie of Norwich
ii. citizens.
the Cittie of Oxford. ii. citizens.
The Cittie of Winchester
ii. citizens.
the Cittie of Bristow. ii. citizens
The Cittie of Bathe. ii. citizens.
the Cittie of Chichester
ii. Citizens.
The Cittie of Salisbury
ii. Citizens.
the Cittie of Worcester
ii. Citizens.
the Cittie of Coventrie
ii. Citizens.

159. This should be *Flint.*
160. The order is not at first evident. However, it appears that Hooker possessed a list similar to that printed by Harrison—essentially a list of counties with the county, city, and borough seats listed under each county and the counties arranged in alphabetical order—and that he extracted the cities from the list.

[38a]   The Barons of the five Portes.[161]

Hastings.	ii. Barons.
Winchelsey	ii. Barons.
Rye.	ii. Barons.
Runmey.	ii. Barons.
Hyeth.	ii. Barons.
Dover.	ii. Barons.
Sandwich.	ii. Barons.

Burgesses.[162]

Bedford town.	ii. Burgesses	Truro,	ii, burgesses.
Buckingham		Bodmin,	ii, burgesses.
town.	ii. burgesses	Helston.	ii. burgesses.
Wickham,	ii. burgesses.	Saltashe,	ii. burgesses.
Ailisbury,	ii, burgesses.	Camelford,	ii. burgesses
New Windsor,	ii, burgesses.	Portlowe,	ii, burgesses.
Reding,	ii, burgesses.	Grounpound,	ii, burgesses.
Wallingford,	ii, burgesses.	Perin, [Penryn]	ii, burgesses.
Abingdon,	ii, burgesses.	Tregonye,	ii, burgesses.
Launceston,		Tresenna,	
[alias Newport]	ii, burgesses.	[Trevenna]	ii, burgesses.
Leskerd,	ii, burgesses.	Saint Ayes, [Ives]	ii, burgesses.
Lestuthiel,		Saint Germins,	ii, burgesses.
[Lostwithiel]	ii, burgesses.	Saint Michael,	ii, burgesses.
Dunheuet, [alias		Foy, [Fowey]	ii, burgesses.
Launceston]	ii, burgesses.	Saint Mawes,	ii, burgesses.

161. Harrison also treats the Cinque Portes separately; but, more significant, his order is identical to Hooker's.

162. Hooker's master list, like that of Harrison, comprised alphabetically arranged counties, English and then Welsh. Having extracted the county and city seats, Hooker then listed all the boroughs sending MPs to parliament, singling out the boroughs in the counties of Bedford, Buckingham, Berkshire, Cornwall, Cambridge, Derby, etc. The order in the resultant list is so strikingly parallel to Harrison's tabulation that one is bound to conclude that both utilized a common source or that Harrison borrowed from Hooker. The bracketed corrections are designed to eliminate confusion and insure the identity of the borough. The following boroughs were summoned in 1571 for the first time: East Loo, Foy, Cirencester, East Stratford, Queenborough, Woodstock, Christ Church, Aldborough, and Eye.

East Loo,	ii, burgesses.	Lempster,	
Cambridge,	ii, burgesses.	[Leominster]	ii, burgesses.
Derby town,	ii, burgesses.	Maidstone,	ii, burgesses.
Totnes,	ii, burgesses.	Bosten,	ii, burgesses.
Plimmouth,	ii, burgesses.	Grimesby,	ii, burgesses.
Barstable,	ii, burgesses.	Stampford.	ii, burgesses.
Plimpton,	ii, burgesses.	Grantham,	ii, burgesses.
Tauistock,	ii, burgesses.	Lecester,	ii, burgesses.
Dartmouth,	ii, burgesses.	Lancaster,	ii, burgesses.
Poole,	ii, burgesses.	Preston in	
Dorchester,	ii, burgesses.	Aldernes.[163]	ii. burg.
Lime,	ii, burgesses.	Liverpool,	ii. burgesses.
Melcombe,	ii, burgesses.	Newton,	ii. burgesses.
Weymouth,	ii, burgesses.	Wigan,	ii. burgesses.
Birtport,		Clithero,	ii. burgesses.
[Bridport]	ii, burgesses.	Monmouth,	ii, burgesses.
Shaftisbury,	ii, burgesses.	Northampton,	ii, burgesses.
Warham,	ii, burgesses.	Peterborough,	ii, burgesses.
Colchester,	ii, burgesses.	Berkley,	
Maldon,	ii, burgesses.	[Brackley]	ii. burgesses.
Kingston upon		Higham ferry,	
Hul.	ii, burgesses.	[Ferrars]	ii. burgesses.
Knaresborough,	ii, burgesses.	Notingham,	ii. burgesses.
Scatborough,		East Stratford,	ii. burgesses.
[Scarborough]	ii, burgesses.	Lin.	ii. burgesses.
Ripton,	ii, burgesses.	Yermouth,	ii. burgesses.
Haydon,	ii, burgesses.	Thetford,	ii. burgesses.
Boroughbridge,	ii, burgesses.	Castle, [Castle	
Tuske, [Thirsk]	ii, burgesses.	Rising]	ii. burgesses.
Aldeborgh	ii, burgesses.	New Castel upon	
Beverley,	ii, burgesses.	tine.	ii. bur.
Cicester,		Morepeth.	ii. burgesses.
[Cirencester]	ii, burgesses.	Barwick.	ii. burgesses.
Huntington,	ii, burgesses.	Woodstock,	ii. burgesses.
Saint Albons,	ii, burgesses.	Banbury,	ii. burgesses.
		Sowthwark.	ii. burgesses.
[38b]		Blenchingly,	ii. burgesses.

163. It is interesting to note that Harrison follows Hooker exactly here in his spelling of *Amounderness*.

Rigat.	ii. burgesses.	Brember,	ii. burgesses.
Gattan.[164]	ii. burgesses.	Steyning,	ii. burgesses.
Lichfeeld.	ii. burgesses.	East Greensteed,	ii. burgesses.
Stafford,	ii. burgesses.	Arundel,	ii. burgesses.
New Castel		Apelby,	ii. burgesses.
under Line.	ii. bur.	Wilton,	ii. burgesses.
Tamworth,	ii. burgesses.	Hindon,	ii. burgesses.
Shrewisbury.	ii. burgesses.	Heytesbury,	ii. burgesses.
Bridgenorth,	ii. burgesses.	Westbury	ii. burgesses.
Ludlow,	ii. burgesses.	Calve,[166]	ii. burgesses.
Great wenlock,	ii. burgesses.	Devises,	ii. burgesses.
Sowthampton.	ii. burgesses.	Chipenham,	ii. burgesses.
Portesmouth.	ii. burgesses.	Malmesbury,[167]	ii. burgesses.
Peterfeeld.	ii. burgesses.		
Stockbridge,	ii. burgesses.	[39a]	
Christes Church,	ii. burgesses.	Bodwin	
Ipswich,	ii. burgesses.	[Bedwyn] the	
Dunwich,	ii. burgesses.	great	ii. burgesses.
Oteford,		Ludgarsail.	ii. burgesses.
[Orford]	ii. burgesses.	Olde Salisbury,	ii. burgesses.
Aldborough,	ii. burgesses.	Wotton basset,	ii. burgesses.
Sudbury,	ii. burgesses.	Marleborough,	ii. burgesses.
Ey.	ii. burgesses.	Wiche.	
Welles.[165]	ii. burgesses.	[Droitwich]	ii. burgesses.
Taunton.	ii. burgesses.	Warwick,	ii. burgesses.
Bridge water,	ii. burgesses.	Mongomery.	i, burgesse.
Minhed,	ii. burgesses.	Radnor,	i, burgesse.
Horsham.	ii. burgesses.	Dingby,	
Midhurst,	ii. burgesses.	[Denbigh]	i, burgesse.
Lewes,	ii. burgesses.	Pembrook,	i, burgesse.
Shereham,	ii. burgesses.		

164. Harrison's list includes Guildford as a Surrey borough between Reigate and Gatton.

165. Instead of listing Wells as a city, as does Harrison, Hooker includes it here as a Somerset borough.

166. The compositor here turned the *n* upside down, hence the resultant misspelling.

167. Harrison includes the borough of Cricklade between Malmesbury and Bedwyn.

Cardigan,	i, burgesse.	Brecknock,	i, burgesse.
Flint,	i, burgesse.	Cardiffe,	i, burgesse.
Carmarthan.	i, burgesse.	Bew moris,	i, burgesse.
Carnaruan,	i, burgesse.	Harford west,	i, burgesse.

As the king (by advancing any man to the honor of a Baron) dooth inlarge and augmẽt the number of the Lords of the higher house: so dooth he also increace the number of the lower house, when he dooth make and erect any new Countie, or incorporate any Borough, or Town, so that in his letters Pattents hee dooth nominate them by the name of a Burgesse.

And therefore when so ever the King dooth call his high Court of Parlement: the writs of summons must be sent out for choosing of Knights, in the new Counties, and Burgesses in the new incorporated Boroughs or Townes, aswel as to the other olde and auncient Citties, and Townes, and every of them shall (upon such summons) bee bound to appeer and have the ful priviledges belonging to a Knight or a Burgesse of the Parlement.[168]

* *
*

168. It is obvious from these two concluding paragraphs that Hooker viewed parliament as a developing institution with the monarch as the initiator of change. In 1571 nine new boroughs were added to the list of parliamentary boroughs (see note 162 for the list). No doubt Hooker was aware of these additions and the deliberations which followed. See D"Ewes, *ACJ*, p. 156.

Appendix A: The Dedicatory Epistle of the Fitzwilliam Edition

[A.ii.] To the right honorable his
Very good Lord, Sir William Fitzwilliams, Knight, L.
Deputye of Ireland,[1] John Vowel alias Hooker, with all
humblenes and due reverēce, wissheth a happy successe
and a prosperous governmēt to th'encrase of Gods honor
in true Religion, the Queenes majesties service in due
obedience, and the administration of the publique welth in
Justice, Equitie and Judgement.

* *
*

BEEING (RIGHT honorable) at the Parlement holden at
Westmister in the yeer of our Lord 1571. and the xiii yeer of
our most soverain Lady & maistres Queene Elizabeth, whose
life and long reign the Lord God prosper and continue, and
then there one of the burgesses of that honorable assembly,
for the City of Excester, in which I was borne and am resiant:
I called to remembraunce certain questions and doutes
mooved in the Parlement holden at Dublin, before the right
honorable Sir Henry Sidney, Knight of the honorable order,
and Lord deputye of this Realeme in the xi. yeere of the reign
of the Queens Majestie. In which assembly I [B.i.] (though
unworthy) was then and there a burgesse. Which douts concerning the orders, usages, rites and directions of a Parlament
(none then presēt having the certain knowledge therof) were
lefte in suspence and not resolved. Wherupon I made promise

---

1. See *DNB*, 7:232–35, and Mary E. Finch, *The Wealth of Five Northamptonshire
Families 1540–1640* (Oxford, 1956), especially pp. 105–11, for biographical
information on Fitzwilliam.

at my returne into England: to procure a perfect instruction of thorders of the Parlements there used, and to send them hether to remain for a perpetuall direction of such Parlemets as henceforth ar to be used in this $l\bar{a}d$.[2]

And beeing thus placed in that honorable assembly: I thought it then a moste fit time for the acquittall of my said promise, wherfore diligently I did observe, consider and mark all maner of orders, usages, rites, ceremonies and all other cicumstances, which either I sawe with eye, or found regestred among the records of that assembly.[3] And having written the same: I did then confer with the exemplars and presidents of tholde and auncient $Parlem\bar{e}ts$ used in tymes past, within the said Realme of England, wherof I found two, the one was that which king [B.i. (b)] Edgar (or as some say, king Edward the $c\bar{o}fessor$) used, thother, which was in use in the time of $k\bar{i}g$ Edward the first. The forme[r] as wel for antiquities sake, as also for a $presid\bar{e}t$ to the good $governm\bar{e}t$ in tholde yeers: I have annexed to these presents, thother in soe things agreeable, & in many things dissagreeable, bothe $fr\bar{o}$ the first and the last: I have omitted.[4] This which now is in use being it which is onely to be folowed and used:

And surely when I doo consider the great benefits which doo growe to all common welths, when the Prince by thadvise of the grave, auncient, wise & prudent elders, dooth direct his goverment, as the same is moste joyfully to be liked and imbraced: so certainly that state which disorderedly is governed, is to be $lam\bar{e}ted$ and pittied, for the one brigeth with it self, a prosperous state, a happy life and a perpetuall sosietie: the other the utter subervion of the publike weale and confusion of mannes sosietie, wherof who so lusteth to see into the

2. This would seem to indicate that the dedicatory epistle was written in Ireland.

3. Presumably the summons lists, which he seems to use, bills, and official journals, but Hooker does not indicate precisely what records he used.

4. It is not clear which alternative treatise Hooker found and rejected; conceivably it could have been a variant text of the *Modus*.

estates and tymes of thages past: shall finde many, in-[B.ii. (a)]
finit and innumerable examples, which with out great greef
and sorow a man cannot consider, but of no nation more: then
of the Realmes of England and Ireland, eche of them having
tasted the benefits of the one, and felt the smarts of thother,
for in times past, the one before the c$\overset{n}{o}$quest of the Normands,
and thother before the conquest of King Henry Fitz emprise:[5]
their states were very incertain, perilouse and dangerouse,
because for the most parte they were directed and governed
by the proude, ambitious, contentious, bloody and evil disposed men, by menes wherof, the lands s$\overset{m}{o}$etime were rent and
devided with intestin rebelli$\overset{n}{os}$ and civil sedici$\overset{n}{os}$ & many t$\overset{m}{i}$es
devoured & spoiled with op$\overset{n}{e}$ & cruel warres. Of thone sprong
the decay of mutual concord and civil societie, without which
no estate can endure. For as Patricius in his first Booke *De
Iustitutione Reip,* saith, *Sine concordia nec firma nec stabilis omnino
civilis scocietas esse cernitur. Nullae enim vires satis esse possint, Nullu
presidium, Nullae opes, Nulla rectigalia illi Reip: que intestino bello
laborat.*[6] Of thother came the confusion and utter [B.ii. (b)]
destruction of publike state. For as Erasmus saieth in his book
*De institucione principis Christiani. Ex bello omnium bonarum rerum
naufragiu simul oritur, omniumque malorum rerum pelagus exundat.*[7]
And by these meanes beeing the preyes of the devourer, and
the enheritaunce of the spoiler, were embrewed and be-
wrapped in such extreme miseries: that none was left, who in
the course of sundry yeares, either would or durst to go before
the people to defend them from the enimie or to deliver them
from the Tirant. But suche as remained and escaped the dent
of swoord, beeing as Sheep without a pastor, left to the devo-

---

5. Henry II, who in 1171 invaded Ireland.

6. "Civil society is seen to be neither strong nor stable without inner har-
mony. No troop, no fortifications no wealth will suffice for the Republic which
suffers from internal war."

7. "From war proceeds the shipwreck of all good things, and from it also
pours forth the ocean of all bad things"; see *Opera Omnia* (1974), vol. 4, part
I, p. 213.

cion of the Woulfe, and as the sily cony without a warrener, left
to the curtesie of the vermin: endured under cruel tirants and
bloody invasors[8] such plagues and miseries as in suche dis-
tresses are laid upon all estates and common weales.

Then the good Kings and Princes of these Realmes, having an ernest zele and an inward care how to deliver the
same rom these extreme plagues and miseries [B.iii. (a)]
and how to recover them to their former estate and suretie,
did emong many devices finde no way so ready, no menes
so good nor remedie so present: as to treade the steps of
other wise Princes and folow the course of other wel governed common weales. *Nam vt gratum via oribus esse solet,
corum vestigia terere qui recte Ambularunt et optimi Gubernatoris est
ea arte cursum dirigere, qua facile plurimi in portum dilati snnt: sic
princeps qui reip, sua bene velit consultum, maiorum exemplis. Ac
optimarum rerump, institutis eam exolere debet.*[9] Wherfore as
Moises had his elders, Licurgus his Ephoros, the Athenien-
sis the Councels, the Romains their Senates, by whose wis-
domes & policies those cõmon welths were directed: so did
these assemble all the wise, grave, expert & prudent men frõ
out of all partes of their Realmes, and of them made a Senate
or Parlemet, and by their advise, such good lawes were made,
such wholsome order devised, and such worthy governmẽt
established: as that within a short time the common welths
were delivered from the bri- [B.iii. (b)] ers, weedes and
thornes of miserie and oppression, and therwith also they
grew and increaced to good estates. And truely a more perfet
or better way of government neither hath been: or can be. For

---

8. Probably *"invaders."*

9. "Now it is the wise custom of travellers to follow the tracks of those who
had travelled along the right path, so by the same method it is the habit of
the best pilots to steer the course which had brought many safely to the port.
Thus the prince who wishes the best counsel for this republic should care
for it according to the examples of the greater and institutions of the greatest republics." Probably from Patrizi's *De Institutione Reipublica;* see above
p. 45–46.

albeit the King or Prince him self be never so valeant, wise, prudent or learned, yet he cannot be perfet and absolute in all things. *Vnsu enim princeps qui omnes virtutes complectatur vel nuncquam est inuentus: Nam licet quecunque velit circumspiciat, Non tamen potest omnia concilio et ratione metire.* [10] For Moyses who spake face to face with God. David whom God chose according to his owne hart. Salomo who excelled all the men that ever were or shalbe in wisdome, yea and S. Paule who was rapted up into the third Heaven, had every of them their imperfections. Saint Barnard whome the Devines with great veneracion did esteme for his godlines of life, soundes of doctrin and profoundnes in Judgement, yet finding in him many imperfeccions: have it in a common proverb. *Bernardus non videt omnia.* [11] But many wise, learned, grave, and ex-[B.iiii. (a)] pert men assembled togither (out of all places of the Realme) they become as it were one man having many wits, many eies, many hands and many feet. *Qui omnia cernunt, omnia que prouident, Nihil eis obscurum, Nihil inopinatum, Nihil nouum, Nihil inauditum, Nihil que magnum videri potest:* [12] and thus by the government of wise Princes and by thadvise of wise men: these Realmes were delivered from thralldome, restored to libertie, and recovered to a perfet & sure government, which for the course of these sudry hudreths of yeers have cotinued and persevered, to the great joy & cofort both of the kings & people, how beit the Realme of Ireland though it have been under the happy governmet of the kings of England and in like manner ordred and directed, yet it hath not had the like good successe and happines, for aswel

10. "In fact, one prince who embraces all the virtues has never been found. For although whatever he wishes he may consider, he cannot however judge all things without counsel and discussion." From either Patrizi or Erasmus in all likelihood.

11. "Bernard doesn't see everything." A reference to St. Bernard of Clairvaux. In Chaucer's "Legend of a Good Woman" the monk named Bernard says "ne say nat al pardee."

12. "To those who comprehend all things and forsee all things, nothing can seem dark to them, nothing unexpected, nothing new, nothing unusual, nothing overwhelming."

though ignorance in throdrig[13] of the senats or parlemets, as
also of the good and wholsoe lawes which though with great
wisdome and for the preservation of the comon welth were
devised: yet being laid up in a secret and private [B.iiii.(b)]
place,[14] and nother published nor put in execution: great disorders and continual rebellions have growen dayly therby,
which great evils and inormities growing by thone, the
Queenes majestie of her goodnes and by the advise of her
prudent governors in this land hath for redresse caused, commaunded and willed all tholde wholsome and good lawes, and
Statutes of this land to be imprinted, & to be dispersed
throughout all the whole land, that ignoraunce by knowledge,
and disobedience by loyaltie, being banished and chased out
of this land: each man dutifully doth yeeld him self loially to
her highnes and obedient to her lawes, these being the onely
meanes and remedies to make a prosperous government and
a happy common welth.

   *Optime enim leges sub optimo principe Beatum Reddunt Regnum
cuius cum felissimus est status cum vtrisque ab omnibus exequo paretur.* [15]
Thother all beit it may seem to tuch but a perticuler estate, yet
moste necessary to be also knowen, for if a Parlement which
directeth orders to others be disordered it self, how great is
[C.i. (a)] that disorder? if the light which should give light to
thothers become darknes: *Quante sunt tenebere?* [16] if the spring
or fountain it self be invenomed: what wholsones or sweetnes
can be derived into the streames therof? Wherfore aswel for
the good zeale I here to the common welth of this realme of

13. "The ordering."
14. Presumably this refers to Dublin Castle wherein Hooker himself uncovered the Irish statutes and published an edition of them in 1572.
15. "The best laws under the best prince render a kingdom blessed, the
condition of which is happiest when both are obeyed by all." This quotation
was borrowed by Erasmus from Plato's *Laws:* see *Opera Omnia* (1974), vol. 4,
part I, p. 194. Hooker obtained it from one of the many editions of Erasmus's
works available to Elizabethans.
16. "How great shall be the darkness." From Matthew 6:23, which reads "If
the light which is in you is darkness, how great shall this darkness be!"

Ireland and for the acquitail of my promise made in this behalf:
I have collected as perfet an order as I could of the orders of
the Parlements of England, which I thought it my bounden
dutie to offer and present unto your good Lordship, now inprint for the further comfort of all others. I knowe and doo
confesse the thing it self beeing but of a small availe not
sufficient or meet so boldely to be offred to one of your honors
estate, and calling, neverthelesse the same touchig some parte
of government, and proceding also from him who in good wil
and sincere affection yeeldeth him self your Lordships moste
assured: I hope you wil not mislike with me heerin, and that
not weying the slendernes of the thing offred: wil consider
[C.i. (b)] of the good wil of the offerer.

For if Xerxes the noble King of the Persias beeing presented
but with a dish of water of one of his Soldiers, and Lodowick
the French king the eleventh of that name, beeing offred a
Radish root of a poor mᵃ, did (in respect of the good wil of
the offerer) thakfully accept the same, yea if Christ him self
affirmeth that the poor Widow casting but a mite into the
Gazio philacium the same beeing by her doon of an inward
good wil, was asmuch allowed as they who had cast in moste
money and greatest treasures: this then putteth me in that
comfort that my boldens beeing pardoned, and my simple
offer beeing allowed:[17] I shall finde your Lordship so wel bent
towards me as to accept the same in good parte.

The Lord God blesse and prosper you and increase his
good gifts in you, that under your government, God in true
Religion be honored, the Queenes highnes in due obedience served: and the common welth and [C.(a)] publike
state of this Realme in Justice and judgement duely admin-
istred and directed.

And that your Lordship at the length for your so wel doings
may receive with the encreace of honor, thanks of her highnes,

17. In his life of "Artaxerxes" Plutarch refers to an obscure man who gave
Xerxes a bottle of water; see the Mark 12:42 for the story of the Widow's Mite.

good reporte with immortall fame of the commonwelth, and in thend everlasting blessing of the everlivig God, which he of his goodnes and mercy graunt unto you.

The third of October. 1572.[18]

Your honorable Lordships moste assured to commaund. John Vowel alias Hooker.

18. The date Hooker completed writing the dedicatory epistle, not the publication date. For a discussion of the whole matter see above p. 36–38.

Appendix B: A Note on the Holinshed Version

As noted above, John Hooker incorporated in the 1587 edition of the *Chronicles* an updated history of Ireland through the administration of Lord Deputy Perrot. In his narrative covering the administration of Lord Deputy Sidney he inserted the *Order and Usage* in the context of the 1569 session of the Irish parliament. This republication, though in an anachronistic context, was based on the Exeter edition; in fact, it would appear that the compositor who set this section of the *Chronicles* used a copy of the printed edition (rather than a manuscript copy) from which to set his type. The result is an accurate rendition of Hooker's depiction of English parliamentary procedures in 1571.

Nevertheless, the compositor reset the type and in so doing introduced superficial changes in the text. Thus the 1587 version, though modeled upon the 1572 Exeter version, is replete with variations. The compositor changed the spelling, capitalization, and punctuation rather consistently, according to his own preferences and/or typographical limitations. He invariably changed the *y* to *i* (dayes to daies and laymen to laimen) and many *c*'s to *s*'s (councel to counsel). More often than not he reduced the initial letters in proper nouns from capital to lowercase type. He added commas and periods as he saw fit. He made a few minor changes in the paragraphization. He also preferred *eight* to *viii* and *shillings* to *s*. Occasionally he added or subtracted parenthetical symbols. Most of the variations reflect a consistent and methodical typographical copiest.

The compositor also incorporated a few minor changes in the text. At the behest of Hooker no doubt he changed the title to read: "The order and usage how to keepe a parlement in England in these daies, collected by John Vowell alias Hooker gentleman, one of the citizens for the citie of Excester at the parlement holden at Westminster, Anno Domini 1571, & Elisabethe Reg. decimo tersia and *the like used in hir maiesties realme of Ireland"* (emphasis mine). As pointed out above these changes were added after Hooker's *Order and Usage* was adopted by Perrot in the 1586 Irish parliament. A few other variations should also be noted. The compositor invariably changed the phrase "for as much" to "for somuch." He also corrected several typographical mistakes which had crept into the Exeter edition: he eliminated the superfluous "for" in the second paragraph on page 20a and dropped the superfluous "be" in paragraph four, page 27b. Similarly, on page 23b he changed "queenes Sergeants" to "kings sergeants." He also preferred the verb "ceasseth" to "surcesseth" on page 30a and added the verb "is" on page 32a to make more sense out of the phrase "as best for." These textual variations, it should be emphasized, were few in number and minor in consequence. In short, the Holinshed republication of Hooker's *Order and Usage* is reasonably accurate and complete.

Index